There are few thanks sufficient to

Bob and Mike

for the opportunity to edit this anthology.

I will get even.

The Thing About Love Is...

Edited by
Mark Wukas

Polyphony Press™

The Thing About Love Is...

Copyright © 1999 Polyphony Press

All rights reserved. No portion of this book may be reproduced or transmitted in any form or by any means, electronic or mechanical, including photocopying, recording or by any information-retrieval system without written permission of Polyphony Press.

For information, contact:

Polyphony Press
PMB 317
207 E. Ohio St.
Chicago, IL 60611

Publisher's Note

The works that follow are fiction. Names, characters, places and incidents are either the product of the author's imagination or are used fictitiously. Any resemblance to actual persons, living or dead, events or locales is entirely coincidental.

ISBN 0-9673109-0-3

First Edition

Printed in Chicago by Fisheye Graphics.
The text was set in 12-point Garamond.

Cover design: Mark Wukas
Cover photo © Robert N. Georgalas, 1999. The cover shows *Adam,* by Auguste Rodin, (Art Institute of Chicago).

Acknowledgements

Anthologies are never the work of one individual no matter who's listed as the editor, and *The Thing About Love Is...* is no exception. Many, many people played midwife to this anthology, and they deserve a mention.

So, those to whom I say "Let's do lunch!" are—

First and foremost, Michael Burke and Bob Georgalas, my unindicted co-conspirators in this project. When they approached me to edit an anthology, I was in no mood for any literary exercises, especially on the subject of love, but their persistence and enthusiasm won me over.

Joanne Pepe, for her critical eye, her blue pencil and, most important, her unflinching moral support; Robert Creason, who added a generous dose of moral support as well; and Lucy Douglass, who sacrificed valuable time *ad maiorem gloriam huius operis*.

Ed Underhill, who provided ready counsel, advice and a steady hand on the tiller as we navigated uncharted legal waters.

Lee Nagan, of Fisheye Graphics, who sat patiently through phone calls as I tried to figure out just what the h-e-doublebamboo shoots I was trying to do preparing this manuscript.

To all these I say, thanks, and promise that it'll be easier next time. *Insha'allah*.

Mark Wukas

Contents

Foreword	ix
Introduction	xi
Want Deborah E. Ryel	1
Bizarro Ballad Cris Burks	2
Big Love Michael Burke	18
Lady Moon Freyda Libman	27
With these New Tunes Adria Bernardi	28
Last Word Edward J. Underhill	40
Forgotten Note Nikki Lynch	72
Free Fall David McGrath	73
Vecchio Richard V. Russo	89
Insurance Scott Mintzer	99
Family Album Freyda Libman	132
Finding Momma Jotham Burrello	134
The Barbecue Janice Tuck Lively	148
You Can Take This Shit to Your Mama Sean Leenaerts	155
Thought Delayed Jo-Ann Ledger	168
Taking Off My Clothes Robert N. Georgalas	169
Harold Cowley's Summer Laundry William Meiners	182
Gypsy Threads Deborah E. Ryel	191
Waltzing in the Garden of Forgiveness Susan Strong-Dowd	193
Taking Small Steps Deborah E. Ryel	240
The Value of Pain Tom Montgomery-Fate	242
In the Tackle Shop Deborah E. Ryel	252
The Dead Sleep Mark Wukas	255
Contributors' Notes	284

Foreword

A book should contain pure discoveries, glimpses of terra firma, though by shipwrecked mariners, and not the art of navigation by those who have never been out of sight of land.
Henry David Thoreau (1817–1862)

Imagine this—

An evening in late December. Outside the air is frigid, the ground hard, but there is no snow. Inside, a group of friends lounge about a living room trimmed with the paraphernalia of the season. Stomachs sated by a hearty meal, we begin to bewail the sameness of so much contemporary writing and to criticize its lack of heart.

An hour or so later, emboldened both by alcohol and passion, someone in the group challenges us to do more than just whine. At first, there is a period of extended silence. Then, perhaps hypnotized by the flicker of pine-scented candles, or reassured by the general camaraderie, we dismiss the gruesome specters of toil and finance conjured by our inquisitor and pick up the gauntlet.

Amazingly, throughout the sober winter that follows, no one opts to abandon the project. Instead, deaf to the caveats of grizzled pioneers once mauled by the same intentions, we settle on a name for the press and conceive a series of volumes to carry its imprint.

Under the banner *The Thing About [X] Is...*, Polyphony Press

The Thing About Love Is...

will showcase the talents of poets, dramatists and short-story writers whose work deserves the attention of readers with gourmet tastes.

What follows is our initial effort: *The Thing About Love Is....* We feel confident that the literary banquet served up in this anthology will prove both savory and satisfying.

Keep your eyes peeled for future titles in the series.

And enjoy the feast.

Introduction

F. Scott Fitzgerald, who made a career writing about love, concluded his story, "The Sensible Thing," with the line, "There are all kinds of love in the world, but never the same love twice."

I happen to agree, so it's in that spirit that I mined these stories, poems and plays from a mountain of worthy submissions because each one resonated uniquely with deep truth, hinted darkly at some knowledge gained sadly, or simply touched a raw nerve.

The contributions to *The Thing About Love Is...* prove Fitzgerald right — there *are* all kinds of love in the world.

These tales of the heart run the gamut from heart-rending loss and longing to the burden of past loves to dark obsession to debilitating pain for which there is no balm.

Not a pretty picture, to be sure.

However, if there's one thing I have learned from reading and rereading these meditations on love, it is the resilience of the human heart and its capacity, despite repeated failure, for hope.

Things can and do have a way of working themselves out. And I know — it happened to me.

Let that be the message of this book.

Mark Wukas
July 1999

Want

Deborah E. Ryel

is a barnacle of lust
      (my tongue sweeps through your waters
        smelling you before you come)
         my offer: crusty
       sharp doors opening
        and closing
this well of moisture, heat
the muscle of love I clamp shut
      (swirl of sand and darkness
        tongue   mouth)
slipping in and pulling out.

Bizarro Ballad

Cris Burks

"Get out! Just get the hell out!" Marie's voice stormed from the living room down the short hall into the small bedroom.

Eight-year-old Neecey, kneeling on her bed, watched the north-south el rattle along its tracks. The red neon lights of Stateway Liquors blinked off and on. The muted sound of late-night traffic and the heavy, hot stench from the Chicago stockyards drifted into the open window. On a normal night, the apartment would be quiet. On a normal night, the house would be quiet. On a normal night, Neecey would be curled in sleep like Cates with one-year-old Odessa in the bed across from her.

"When this baby's born I'm gonna kick your ho's natural ass," Marie shouted.

Neecey had never seen Jesse's ho, but she knew her name — Gwen. Gwen had sucked the happiness from the pores of the glossy, white concrete walls.

Neecey's family was one of the first families to move into the gleaming white Stateway Gardens housing project. Marriage and employment were two of the requirements for an apartment in the project. Here Jesse and Marie socialized with other couples on their floor. For one year the family had enjoyed the beauty of the showy red geraniums and luscious, velvet grass surrounding the project. For one year they had enjoyed the convenience of living a block from Thirty-fifth and State, where they could walk three

The Thing About Love Is...

blocks east, pay a quarter admittance to the Louis Theater, and watch a double feature and six cartoons Saturday afternoons, or walk three blocks west to Comiskey Park and watch the Chicago White Sox and the Boston Red Sox dance around the field. Neecey had wallowed in the luxury of her own room, and it didn't matter that she had to share it with Cates and Odessa; she had a real twin-size bed. Her home, her life, had been just as comfortable as Princess on the television show *Father Knows Best*.

Now after one year of happiness, Gwen had intruded into their lives; invisibly, she sat at the table at dinner, walked the halls at night, and dragged Jesse away for days at a time. "You tell her not to call my house," Marie screamed.

"I see the moon, and the moon sees me," Neecey recited, looking up at the hazy full moon. She stuck her fingers in her ears and clicked her teeth together. Still, Marie's thunderous words crashed against Neecey's door, clanged in Neecey's head like a steel hammer on an iron anvil.

Glass shattered against a wall! Neecey squeezed her back into the corner and wrapped her twiggy arms around her bony knees. The moonlight cascading through the window dimly illuminated the room. In the dark, her familiar things contorted into frightful images. She thought she saw Boris Karloff standing in her closet. She looked again and saw it was only her bathrobe on a hook.

"I'm gonna make her face look like a damn tic-tac-toe field," Marie screamed.

"You gonna wake the kids," Jesse said.

Neecey thought she saw a line of girls with missing legs. She looked again and saw only her dresses on hangers. She thought she saw the block head of Superman's alter ego, Bizarro. She looked again and saw only her stack of DC comic books.

"My ainty didn't raise no fool!" Marie shouted.

Cates stirred and mumbled. Neecey quickly left her bed and

kneeled before his. She rubbed his back gently. His breathing deepened. She wiped the sweat from his brow and his bushy eyebrows. A few drops of sweat on his thick curly lashes sparkled in the moonlight. From his heavy eyebrows to his small mouth, he resembled Jesse. On the other side of Cates, Odessa slept peacefully with her thumb in her mouth. Neecey longed to curl up and snore, to sleep beyond the fight.

Neecey wondered if Annette, Darlene, and Jimmy had received her letters. She had written to most of the Mouseketeers and told them how she could sing and dance and wanted to be the next Mouseketeer. She would fly to Disneyland and get her own special shirt with her name Denise across her chest. No more fights. M I C, see you real soon. K E Y, why because we love you. And all the Mouseketeers would love her. She would be the first Negro on *The Mickey Mouse Club.*

"Don't I take care of you and the kids?" Jesse's velvet voice drifted from the hallway. No matter how angry Jesse became, his voice remained calm. His footsteps broke the slant of light underneath her door as he walked to the bathroom. Neecey followed Jesse's movements in the bathroom by their accompanied sounds; water splashed into the face bowl, the medicine cabinet whined open, the bottles and jars clattered together. "Any aspirin?" Jesse called to Marie.

"I'm the one with the headache," Marie yelled, as she followed him into the bathroom.

"I'm the one stuck in this damn apartment while you're screwing yo damn ho!"

"Yo mouth is worse than some thuggish niggers," Jesse admonished her.

"At least I don't act like trash. You won't catch me running around with somebody else's whorish husband."

"You gonna wake the kids with this nonsense," he said quietly.

The Thing About Love Is...

"Nonsense!" Marie shrieked.

WHOMP! WHOMP! THUMP! came the sound of bodies colliding, bumping into the wall, tussling around the small bathroom.

"Nigger, I'll kill you!" Marie screamed.

That scream roused Odessa, who sat up in the bed and wailed. That wail woke Cates with a start. "Mama!" Cates cried, as the ruckus continued in the bathroom. Neecey jumped into bed with Cates and Odessa. Odessa scrambled into Neecey's right arm and buried her face in Neecey's neck. Neecey wrapped her left arm around Cates. He struggled against her.

"Mama! Mama!" he cried.

"No, Cates! Stay here!" Neecey tightened her grip around him.

"I want my mama!" Cates cried and collapsed against Neecey. They huddled on the bed, crying. Neecey knew that as long as they remained hooked together, as long as she, Cates, and Odessa did not see the battle, and as long as the bedroom door muffled the sounds, the fight would not get vicious. If she or Cates or Odessa got into the middle of the battle, Marie would rage and charge into Jesse. "How could you do this to us?" she would scream and try to claw his eyes out.

"Hush, hush," Neecey soothed the children. "Shirley Temple went to France," Neecey rocked gently, "to teach the girls the Watusi dance."

"You got the kids upset," Jesse said.

"First on the heel, then on the toe," Neecey recited. "Round and around and around she goes."

"When you turn me loose, I'm gonna slice you to kingdom come."

"Salute to the Captain. Bow to the queen," Neecey whispered. "Search the sky for a special dream."

"You're acting like one of those cows on the street," Jesse said.

The Thing About Love Is...

"Just get the hell out," Marie screamed. "I don't need you."

Cates' and Odessa's tears and mucous soaked Neecey's gown. Her own tears soaked her face. Suddenly, everything was still and quiet outside the bedroom door. Another el rattled across the tracks. In the distance, the wail of a fire truck surged toward the building. The curtains fluttered at the window, and the sweet stench from the stockyard whizzed around their heads. This peace, Neecey knew, was deceptive. In the bathroom, Jesse's arms were wrapped around Marie in a dance, in an embrace, in the lull before Marie got her second breath.

"Turn me loose," Marie's voice crackled.

"When you calm down and listen to reason," Jesse promised.

"You can't hold me forever," Marie said.

Except for Odessa's hiccuping sobs, the children were quiet, expectant. "Sh-sh-sh." Neecey stroked Odessa back. Soon Odessa stuck her thumb into her mouth and sucked. Cates burrowed his face into Neecey's lap. Soon, Neecey knew, part two of the fight would start, and it would be more vicious than the first part. Soon, in his attempt to placate Marie, Jesse would inadvertently say something to tick her off. A new surge of strength would come, and Marie would break from his hold.

"You need to stop this foolishness," Jesse said.

"Foolishness!" Marie shouted. *"Foolishness!"*

A loud thump against the bathroom door, a short scuffle in the hall, and then *Boom!* The bedroom door crashed open. Neecey jumped. Cates took advantage of the moment to escape Neecey's arm.

"Mama!" he cried, as he leaped from the bed. The doorway framed Jesse and Marie like a photograph. Marie, a short, golden brown woman, heavy in pregnancy, with her hair twisted around brown, kit curlers and her swollen feet stuffed into Jesse's old brown slippers, struggled to escape Jesse's bear hug. Jesse's t-shirt hung in shreds across his muscular chest and back. He strained to keep his arms around her.

Cates stood in the middle of the bedroom wailing, "Mama! Mama!" Neecey rocked Odessa in her lap. Odessa's diaper leaked through her plastic pants and soaked Neecey's gown. Marie pressed her shoulder against Jesse's chest, shoved until he stumbled back into the hall wall. She reached up and clawed his face.

"Damn!" Jesse yelled. He shoved Marie back. She stumbled into the room and plopped onto Neecey's bed. Marie bounced up from the bed and flew into him. She grabbed another hunk of flesh. Blood flowed down his face. *WHACK!* Jesse backhanded Marie across the face.

"I'll kill you," Marie yelled and rushed into him.

"Damn!" he said.

Jesse grabbed her arms and pinned them behind her back. Marie struggled to get loose. She tried to raise her knee to his groin. Jesse bumped his body back. He maneuvered his body around to her back and held her. Marie continued to twist and turn in his arms, but she could not break his grip.

"I want you out of here," she cried. "I want you out!"

"You know I love you," Jesse said.

"What you know 'bout love is less than the last line of a matchbook cover," she snarled.

"You wanna break up our family?" Jesse said.

"You already broke up our family! The first time you touched that bitch you broke up our family!"

"Think about the kids," he said.

"I don't need no cheating man," Marie hissed.

"You just upset."

"I want you out, Jesse," Marie cried, and there was no bitterness in her voice, only simple resignation. "I want you out."

The Thing About Love Is...

In the summer of 1958, the sweet stench from the stockyards was omnipresent, like skin on the body—always there. The stench would fly into every open window of the 36A State Street bus. Oh, how you wanted to hollow a notch into the green leather seat and stick your nose deep into the cotton tick as the bus rumbled underneath the Thirty-ninth Street viaduct and passed Bowman's Dairy Company. You endured, and soon the bus eased into the heavenly aroma of freshly baked bread drifting from Schultz Bakeries. The funk surrounding your brain and smothering your common sense would drift away.

The second Saturday of August was such a day. A hot odor from the stockyards rose like steam in the air. A brilliant, white-hot sun burned all the blue from the sky. Marie, pushing Odessa's stroller, led her brood to the bus stop. In the basket attached to the stroller sat Marie's pocketbook and a grey quart thermos. A damp washcloth that she used to mop the sweat from all their brows was slung upon the handle. Neecey trailed behind her, while Cates, jaunting ahead of them, aimed his cap gun at the passing cars and shouted, "Bang! Bang!"

Sun rays sparkled in Marie's tawny red hair. Her green-and-white striped maternity top billowed over her stomach. To Neecey she looked like a walking umbrella. The children, as always, were immaculate. Neecey's and Odessa's pink sundresses were stiff with Argo starch. Large pink bows adorned their thick braids. Cates' brown short pants and short-sleeved polo shirt were complemented by the cap guns in a holster slung around his waist. Marie, the children, and the bus made it to the corner simultaneously. They rode to Fifty-ninth Street, where they changed buses. At Fifty-ninth and Green, Della stepped from the shadows of a building and helped Marie with Odessa's stroller. Perspiration flowed passed her pencil-thin eyebrows and into the sunken hollows of her jaws. Her small eyes seemed to disappear

The Thing About Love Is...

in her tiny pinched face. *Ainty Della,* Neecey thought, *always looked as if she had sucked a bowl of lemons.*

"Girl, I thought you was coming over earlier than this," Della said, "I been driving round and round this block like a fool." She nervously glanced up and down the street. "I finally parked over on Halsted. I told Pete I was going to the Bud Biliken Parade with my cousin Ethel," Della spoke rapidly. "Feel like I'm gonna have a heat stroke."

"Where's Pete?" Marie asked as she pulled the kids around the corner. A small slant of shade protected them.

"Tee-Tee," Odessa tugged at Della's skirt.

"Overtime, he said." Della sniffed as she bent and gave Odessa a tight hug. "But I don't trust none of them Shades." She pulled a Mary Jane penny candy from her pocket, unwrapped it and popped it into Odessa's mouth.

"Ainty Della, I want some candy!" Cates cried as he tugged her sleeve.

"You got the extra keys and the lighter?" Marie asked.

"Girl, before I give you these keys, you promise me nobody will know my part in this mess," she said, digging in her pocket for more candy. "I don't want no trouble with Louise and her spoiled boys." She handed Neecey and Cates two Mary Janes each.

"My word, Della," Marie promised. "If you had'na told me what was going on, Louise would still be grinning up in my face and stabbing me in the back."

"I wanna Nut Chew!" Cates whined.

"Stop begging, Cates," Marie said.

"Girl, I know she ain't gonna treat me no better than she treats you," Della said as she rose. "She just let Pete and Jesse do whatever the hell they want."

"Raise damn mama's boys," Marie cussed, "that's all."

"You want me to keep the kids?" Della asked, putting her hand on top of Cates' head.

"Naw, girl," Marie shook her head. "They'll know for sure you had a hand in helping me."

"It might not be safe for them, caught up in the middle ... "

"Nobody gonna hurt my babies!" Marie hissed.

"You got guts, Marie."

On a normal visit to Louise, Marie would allow the kids to run ahead of her. Neecey would race along with Odessa squealing in her speeding stroller. Cates would fly down Peoria and up the steps to where Louise sat on the porch waiting for them.

"Peewee, Peewee." Louise would sing to Cates, "Mu'Dear just loves you." Cates would beam and snuggle into Louise's arms. When Neecey and Odessa finally made it up the steps, Louise would pull Odessa onto her lap and praise her beauty, "Li'l lovely, li'l doll." Finally, she would look at Neecey and smile, "Come here, you." Yet no matter how tightly Neecey hugged her, Louise's arms around Neecey would be loose, distant.

At Louise's the children would feast on hamburgers and French fries or Louise's special tuna-and-macaroni salad. Always, lunch would end with bowls of Neapolitan ice cream smothered with chocolate syrup. Always, Louise would pack an A&P shopping bag with goodies for them to take home.

This Saturday it was hot in the shade. The street was deserted. Most of the black residents of Englewood were lined along South Park Boulevard, watching the Bud Biliken Parade, or waiting in the park on Fifty-fifth Street for the picnic afterward.

Marie, in her no-nonsense, I'll-beat-you-blind voice, commanded Cates to hold Neecey's free hand. "Not a word," she said. "Not one damn word."

When they got to the building, she set her children in the shade of the porch. "Don't move," she said, "don't move an inch." She popped a sucker in Odessa's mouth, then removed the thermos from the back of the stroller.

The kids sat there — afraid of the tightness in their mother's voice, afraid of her usual mellow eyes, now granite brown. The thread was tiny, invisible, but each felt something cutting into them, choking them into silence. Cates fingered the pistols at his waist. Neecey, eyes wide and sweat crawling down her back, twisted the hem of her dress.

Neecey clutched the purse Marie shoved in her hands. She watched as Marie inserted a key into the lock, opened the door, and entered the vestibule. Later, she would overhear Marie telling Della what happened inside the apartment:

Girl, Louise was in the kitchen cooking breakfast for him and his ho . Breakfast!

Whatcha do?

I eased my big belly behind those big-ass plants in the dining room. You know you can see into the kitchen from there?

How?

Through that gilded mirror next to Jesse's old bedroom. Well, there Louise was in the kitchen using her best china coffee service on her special tray, like she was fixing breakfast for Miz Mamie Eisenhower or somebody. Same damn tray she used to serve my wedding breakfast.

What happened next?

She came traipsing up the hall and knocked on the door, calling, "Jesse, Jesse." All soft and apologetic. "Jesse, I done fixed y'all some breakfast. Jesse?" Then I heard his lying whorish ass: "Yeah, Mu'Dear." And I felt like all those big-ass plants was choking me. And the baby was flip-flopping in my stomach. And the walls was laughing at me. Honey, I felt like I was floating down a river of death, then I realize I was actually walking toward them.

Oh, Laudy!

He saw me first. Cussed or something and leaped out the bed hold-

ing a pillow before his manhood like every woman in that room never seen him naked before. Then Louise saw me in the dresser mirror. Trembled so hard the china was rattling like windows in a tornado. And that dark-roasted coffee bean of a woman who was in my mother-in-law's house screwing my husband had the nerve to ask me what the hell I was doing there!

Naw!

Uh-uh, trying to cover her nakedness with a sheet. Jesse pleading, "Marie now don't go to pieces." "Pieces!" I screamed. "Don't say another word, M-F; not another word." And that heifer whining, "Jesse, Jesse." That pissed me off. I can't tell you how I did it, I just moved. I yanked that sheet off that ho, exposed all that vile filth. Then I dashed all the gasoline on her and the bed, and she was spitting it out her mouth, screaming. It musta got in her eyes. I don't know. Before any of them knew what was happening I rushed up and grabbed her greasy hair and wrapped it around my hand and yanked her ass out that bed. Louise musta set the tray down, 'cause by the time I had Gwen to the door, she was coming at me.

Girl, naw.

Uh-uh, I just tightened my hand on that ho's head, while aiming the lighter at her breast. Girl, she stank. I was gonna have a good fish-fry.

You're too much.

Louise had the nerve to say, "You can't be disrespecting my house like this."

"Whorehouse, you mean," I said. Then the old heifer said something 'bout how I got children all over the world. That's when Jesse told her to shut the hell up.

No, he didn't.

Yes, he did. I dragged that ho from the bedroom into the living room. Girl, I had to control myself to keep from setting her on fire. I could hear Louise crying, "You gonna let her walk over me in my own house?" Girl, when we got to the front door the ho try to get bad. She said, "Ain't going out there. Ain't got no clothes on." I put that lighter to her head. I said, "Open it." She open the door; I yanked her into the vestibule. She got to begging and pleading. "You ain't beg me for my husband," I said and twisted her hair. Then I got the itching to set her ass on fire. And maybe she sensed it, 'cause the ho opened that door quicklike.

That story, however, was two weeks away. For now, Neecey sat in the shade of Louise's building and hissed, "Stop!" every time Cates shot his cap gun. Sweat glistened on her copper-tanned face. She was thirsty. She imagined a tall glass of grape Kool-Aid with slices of lemon. She imagined a tall glass of milk with Bosco chocolate syrup. She imagined a plain glass of ice water. Her tongue got heavy. She opened Marie's handbag and searched for a pack of Juicy Fruit.

"Wada," Odessa whined as she pushed against Neecey's leg.

"We gotta wait for Mama," Neecey said as she swallowed to wet her parched throat. She found the familiar yellow pack and removed three sticks of gum.

"I'll go get her," Cates said and jumped down.

"You gonna get us in trouble," Neecey said as she stuck a piece of gum in Odessa's mouth.

"Trouble! Trouble!" Cates shouted. "This is what I'll do to trouble!" He whipped his cap gun from its holster. "Bang! Bang! Bang!"

"Sit down and be quiet, Cates," she ordered, handing him a piece of gum.

Just then the door opened, and the gum was forgotten. The gun fell from Cates' hand, and Neecey's eyes widened as Marie and Gwen emerged from the building.

"She's buck naked," Cates exclaimed.

"Hush up, boy, and sit yo butt down," Marie said. She yanked

Gwen passed the children.

"Jesse!" Gwen screamed.

Marie put her mouth close to Gwen's ear and hissed, "Don't you get it? You ain't nothing but a piece of tail."

Neecey looked at the woman's butt as Marie dragged her down the steps. The woman didn't have a piece of tail. She had no tails. Marie shoved the naked woman onto Jesse's black Impala. The woman danced in front of the car as she tried to cover her breasts and privates.

Moments before, Peoria Street had been empty, quiet. Now, a man two doors down rose from his stoop to watch the naked woman dance. A couple of teenage boys rode by on their bikes and crashed into parked cars. Across the street, a woman in a straw hat peeped over her hedges. Soon many people filled the street. Neecey was embarrassed for the woman and for herself.

The door opened again, and Louise stepped from the apartment. "You're humiliating me!" she cried.

"You didn't think about my humiliation," Marie said.

"Mu'Dear," Cates cried as he ran to her.

"You got these kids watching this mess!" Louise screamed as she struggled to lift the six-year-old child. "What kinda woman are you?"

Odessa pressed against Neecey. Neecey pulled her into her lap. A hot flush ran through Neecey. Grown-ups fussing was scarier than the Werewolf or Frankenstein. Grown-ups fussing was like being left alone in a dark house. Neecey trembled.

"Don't you talk to me about decency!" Marie barked.

"You're fighting over a man that don't want you," Louise said.

"This ain't about him wanting me," Marie said. "It's about Gwen and me. Gwen coulda slept with him on top of the Prudential Building, for all I cared. But she came looking for trouble. Brought her skinny ass up to my door, pretending she

The Thing About Love Is...

was at the wrong apartment."

An orange-and-white polka-dot dress billowed over Louise's head. Marie grabbed the dress before it landed on the sidewalk between her and the woman. Neecey looked past Louise to Jesse, half dressed in the doorway.

"She's a ho," Marie stated. "She don't need clothes."

"Dada!" Odessa wiggled on Neecey's lap. She reached for Jesse.

"Marie, why you got these kids here?" he asked as he lifted Odessa.

"Who the hell gonna take care of yo children while you're screwing around?"

"Marie ..."

"Don't Marie me," she screamed. "Didn't I tell you to get out? 'Just leave, Jess,' I said, 'just leave.' But you got down on yo knees and swore that you love me."

"Did you know that, silly girl?" she asked Gwen, who was still bent low beside the car, trying to hide herself. "You calling me, saying, 'Jesse don't want you. He loves me.' You think I'm some stupid woman trying to hold onto a cheating man. Hell, naw!"

A siren wailed in the distance. The watching people no longer pretended to be busy. They inched closer to the scene. Somebody laughed at the woman dancing on her hunches beside the car.

"Give her the dress, Marie," Jesse said as he adjusted Odessa in his arm.

"Go to hell," she said. Marie crumpled the dress into a ball and tucked it under her arm. "Neecey, come with me."

Neecey scooped from the concrete ledge and slung Marie's pocketbook on her shoulder. She squeezed the gum in her hand.

"Marie, the police are coming," Jesse said.

"Ain't the one dancing naked in the street," Marie said.

"Just give her the damn dress," he said.

"Humph!" Marie snorted, grabbed Neecey's arm and started

The Thing About Love Is...

walking down Peoria toward Sixty-third Street.

"What about the kids?" Louise said.

"You such a good madam," Marie said, "you watch them."

Prematurely, Marie gave birth to Serenda Joy the third week of August. Jesse and Neecey cleaned the apartment thoroughly, while Cates and Odessa dabbed at dusting furniture. Laughter rebounded from the wall and drifted out the open door.

"Serenda Joy," Jesse sang as he slung the mop across the linoleum floors.

"Is she pretty, Daddy?" Neecey asked as she washed dishes.

"She's gonna be a fox," he laughed.

"When we gonna get another brother?" Cates asked.

"Maybe soon," Jesse laughed.

Whatever plans Jesse had to increase the family disappeared three weeks after Marie's homecoming. One day after school, Odessa's and Serenda's cries greeted Neecey and Cates as they entered the apartment. The apartment was ominously dark. All the shades were lowered and the drapes drawn. Marie sat on the sofa with her hair in kit curlers and in her white chenille robe with the huge pink rose. Her eyes were red and swollen. Odessa, mucous and tears running down her face, flew into Neecey's arms. Neecey picked her up. (From that point on, Odessa would spend the rest of her toddler years in Neecey's arms.)

"You all right, Mama?" Neecey asked.

"The baby is crying!" Marie said and closed her eyes.

Neecey stood for a moment, adjusting Odessa on her hip, wondering what to do. Serenda's cries whisked around them. Marie's apathy frightened Neecey. Even with a sniffle, with a fever, and with a broken arm, Marie was a woman of action.

"Mama?" Neecey questioned.

"Mama?" Cates said as he walked up to her and touched her

face. Marie looked into his caramel eyes with the thick black lashes and heavy eyebrows. "Oh, Jesse! Jesse!" she sobbed and gathered Cates into her arms.

Big Love

Michael Burke

Tom leans back and plows his long fingers through his thick, wet-with-sweat hair. He closes his eyes and here, in the darkness of his bedroom, he whispers.

"Patrick," he says, "tell me that you love me."

I catch myself groaning, then close my eyes, too. I'm on my back, and Tom is kneeling across my thighs. "Come on," he says. "Tell me that you love me."

Tom and I: We've been through this before. I sigh, open my eyes. "I love you," I say, and Tom sighs, too, lifts his chin, then shakes his head. He lowers his face and looks down on me.

"Just once," he says, "I'd like to hear that from someone who's not handcuffed to my bed."

"Yeah," I say, squirming just a bit. "Well," I say. "You better get these off. I've got to pee."

Tom starts scrounging on the nightstand for the key. He can barely see without his glasses. As he's leaning over me, I lift my head and kiss his flat stomach, which makes him giggle.

"That tickles," he says.

"Yeah," I say. "Well, you better hurry."

In the bathroom, with the door closed, standing in the bright light before the mirror above the white sink, I think about Tom and love and how I kissed his stomach, how I hoped that kiss would make him feel better, how I did, in fact, love Tom —

cared for him, felt for him — but how my love was different than the love he desired, than the loved he asked for, than the love he wanted to hear.

When I return to the bedroom, Tom is curled beneath the sheet, on his side, facing the closed window. I slip into bed behind him, pull our bodies together and kiss the back of his warm neck. He murmurs something.

Tom turned thirty-one last week, so I pull close enough to whisper in his ear.

"Tommy," I say. "Good night." I know that calling him Tommy makes him feel younger.

Tom lives with a lawyer named Victor. I have never liked Victor, which is maybe why I still sleep with Tom every now and again. Why Tom sleeps with me is his business. I suppose it has to do with love.

My current boyfriend — and I use the term for lack of a better phrase — is named Wheaty. When I met Wheaty — at a New Year's party hosted by twin lesbian painters — I asked him if everyone called him Wheaty because his pony-tailed hair was the color of wheat. He raised his thin eyebrows and just looked at me for nearly a minute.

"No," he finally said. "Everyone calls me Wheaty because my name is Wheaty."

"Oh," I said.

"It's short for Wheaton," he explained.

"Oh," I said again. "Well, how do you like the artwork?"

Wheaty and I slept together that night, and we've been sleeping together, more than less often, since. I was walking downtown after work yesterday — yesterday was really the first breezy, Spring day we've had this year — when it occurred to me that I hadn't slept with anyone besides Wheaty in quite some time.

The Thing About Love Is...

That realization might have been another reason why I called Tom.

Wheaty is six years younger than me and he's still living the part of his life in which he calls every man he meets, "Jim."

A dark-haired man at one of the bars. The guy will light Wheaty's cigarette, and Wheaty will smile his thin smile and say, "Thanks for the smoke, Jim."

A stocky blond getting off the subway. Wheaty will brush shoulders with the guy, smile, then lower his eyes. "Oh," he'll say. "Pardon me, Jim."

A new waiter at one of his favorite coffee houses. Wheaty will actually wink, then smile, then say, "Hey, Jim, what's new?"

I once yelled at Wheaty to stop all this flirting, but he merely shrugged and said, "It gives me a sort of Lauren Bacall air." Then he narrowed his eyes before I could say anything else. "A young Lauren Bacall," he added.

Tom is dressed and in the kitchen now. I'm still in bed, but Tom's closet is open and his gray suit jacket is hanging on a hangar off the doorknob. Tom is a lawyer, too.

I hear him running water for the tea kettle and opening the refrigerator door, probably grabbing a bagel, which he always eats plain. I kick the sheet to my feet, sit up in bed and stare again at the suit coat. I start wondering how much time I've spent with Tom, how many nights and mornings we've done this same thing.

"You're awake," he says.

He's standing in the bedroom doorway now, dressed except for his jacket, swallowing a bite of bagel. His eyes are bright behind round glasses.

"You look like shit," he says. "How much did we drink last night? You want some bagel?"

The Thing About Love Is...

Before I can say a word, the telephone rings. It must be seven o'clock. Whenever Victor is out of town, he always calls Tom at seven o'clock.

"Let me get that," Tom says, smiles and disappears.

Before I met Wheaty, before I met Tom, I lived for five months with a realtor named Frank. I suppose I thought I loved Frank. He was a few years older than me and he owned a condo. I was shocked, devastated, when he eventually told me that he had fallen for some new guy, some new guy who owned a condo, too.

Two weeks after Frank dropped me, I was on my brother's roof, helping my brother nail new shingles to his old home.

"We better take a break," I remember Sean saying. "This is hot work."

We set our hammers down, crawled our way up to the peak, and started passing a plastic bottle of water back-and-forth between us.

"Kathy," my brother said — Kathy is Sean's wife; I tell her just about everything — "Kathy," he said, "tells me you just broke up with that guy."

Sean had seldom referred to Frank or any of my gay friends. Calling Frank "that guy" would've normally set off my temper, started a fight; but, on that afternoon, Frank was pretty much just "that guy" in my thoughts, as well.

"Yeah," I said. I sipped some water and passed the bottle back.

Sean and I kept from looking at one another.

"Well," my brother finally said. "That's gotta be tough. You okay?"

"I'm fine," I lied.

From the corner of my eye, I could see Sean nod and take a big swallow of water. He wiped his mouth with the back of his hand, then passed the bottle back to me. Wiping his mouth like that, sitting this close: Sean reminded me so much of Dad.

"You sure?" Sean said and our eyes connected only briefly.

"Yeah," I said. "I'm fine. Really." I swallowed some more water, then turned my face to see Sean clearly. "It's just that Frank — that asshole — still has some of my power tools and disco records."

My brother nodded, his narrow face full of genuine understanding. And then he couldn't help but laugh. When he didn't stop laughing, I said, "What's so funny?"

"Nothing," Sean said, shaking and grinning and still laughing.

"What?"

Sean looked at me almost bashfully. "Power tools and disco records?" he said. "That's just something you'd never hear a straight guy say."

After a moment, I started laughing, too. But I shoved Sean's shoulder anyway, and told him to go fuck himself.

Tom returns to the bedroom, still smiling. He walks passed me to the closet, slips into his suit jacket.

"You better get up," he says. "I've got to get to work." Then he leans toward me and kisses my mouth.

"How's good ol' Victor?" I ask, then wince.

"I better brush my teeth," Tom says.

After Frank, I met Tom and we started having sex. Tom — Mr. Corporate Lawyer by day, Baron von Pleasure by night — introduced me to a variety of harmless party toys: blindfolds, handcuffs, a rainbow of flavored rubbers, which are an acquired taste, to be sure. But a little kink was exactly what I needed to forget Frank.

Tom and I both somehow knew we'd never really be more than friends, nothing other than buddies who fooled around from time to time as we stumbled through life looking for Big Love.

The Thing About Love Is...

"Big Love" is Tom's phrase, I suppose because "Mr. Right" sounds a little silly.

At a bar one night, I asked Tom if what he had with Victor was Big Love and Tom shook his head, said, "No, no, no."

Then he spoke louder to hear himself above the music. "But it's the closest I've ever come," he said. "Maybe the closest I'll ever get — and that's what scares the hell out of me."

A few weeks before Frank dropped me, my father suffered his first stroke. My brother's wife Kathy had called that morning with the news. "You better get to the hospital fast," she had said. "Sean's getting dressed."

I was living in the city, close to the hospital, and I arrived about forty minutes before Sean and Kathy. The old man was laid up in a regular room and looked better than I expected.

"Where's your brother?" he said.

"On his way," I said.

"Good," Dad said, closing his big eyes.

"How you doing?"

When Dad didn't reply, I asked again. "How you doing?" When Dad didn't reply the second time I knew better than to ask a third. His sullen silence had little to do with his stroke.

We sat in the white quiet of that little room until Sean and Kathy arrived. Sean rushed toward Dad's bed, grinning hopefully, saying, "Hey, old man, what kind of trouble are you raising now?"

At the same time, Kathy walked over and hugged me. "How are you doing?" she asked.

This all happened three years after Mom had died. From a stroke. Same hospital.

"Me?" I said. Then I realized that I must have been crying. "I'm fine," I said. "I'm fine."

The Thing About Love Is...

"Patrick," Tom says. He's standing in the bedroom doorway with his arms crossed. "Come on. Get dressed. I've got to go. I'm late."

I groan and stand out of bed. I'm feeling stiff when I stretch and when Tom tells me to hurry again I say, "I'm hurrying, honey, I'm hurrying."

I smile, hoping I sounded like Victor. Then I bend to pick up my underwear from beneath the handcuffs on the floor.

"I'm getting too old for this," I mumble.

I toss the handcuffs to Tom and he proceeds to watch as I get dressed. Tom has always gotten a kick from watching me dress and undress, and, now, he just stands there, not smiling, not blinking, just watching.

After I zip up my jeans, I sit on the edge of the bed to lace my boots. Tom looks toward the bare, hardwood floor between us.

"You and Wheaty," he finally says. "Big Love?"

I can't help but smile at the notion. But I gently shake my head, whisper, "No."

Tom nods, gives me a swift glance, then frowns. "Well," he says. "Maybe someday," he says. He clears his throat, tosses the cuffs onto a pillow and turns. "Let's go," he says. "It's late."

Dad had been worse than he looked, which shouldn't have come as a surprise. That was Dad all over. The next morning I visited him in the hospital again. Of course, we didn't say much and we looked at one another even less.

But just as I was preparing to leave, my father spoke. "Before you go," he said. His voice was much weaker. His eyes were wet.

When he didn't continue I stepped back to his bed. He raised his big hand to cover mine resting on the thin railing.

"Before you go," my father said, "tell me that you love me."

This time I was well aware of my tears.

The Thing About Love Is...

"I love you," I said. "Dad, I've always loved you." He nodded, then sighed, then closed his eyes. "Yes, son. Good night, son. And thanks."

My father didn't say another word. He died that night.

I make it through another day — thinking that maybe there is no perfect love, thinking that maybe it's "coming close" that counts. Love is really a small, fragile thing, I think, and yes, that seems unsatisfactory.

"Unsatisfactory" was a word Frank had used often.

When I get to Wheaty's loft for supper, we know better than to ask each other too many questions.

"How was work?"

"Fine. How was your day?"

"Just dandy."

Neither of us inquiries about or even mentions the previous night.

Later, in bed, in the darkness once again, the two of us naked between warm sheets, I get an idea. I try to blindfold Wheaty, but he objects. "How come?" I ask. "Doesn't it turn you on?"

Wheaty gives me one of his raised-eyebrow looks again. "I've been blindfolded before," he snorts. "It's the color I detest. I mean look at it. It's peach."

I groan and ask Wheaty what difference the color could possibly make.

"Believe me," he says. "Peach matters. If there's one thing I know, it's how to accessorize."

I laugh softly and kiss his cheek and press our legs together and pull myself close beside him. Wheaty: He smells like fresh sheets.

I turn my face into the pillow. I whisper his name. I whisper, "Tell me that you love me."

"What?"

The Thing About Love Is...

I have to wait a long time before I can get around to repeating myself. My eyes are closed. I think I am pretending that I am not really there.

"Tell me that you love me," I say again.

"Oh, Jim," Wheaty says. He's whispering, too. He wrestles onto his side so he can put his arms around me. "Are things that bad?"

Lady Moon

Freyda Libman

Her face is powdered white against the sky
whose ballroom black tuxedo holds her close
in ardent tango wedding thigh to thigh,
the moisture of two mouths in breath betrothed

She wears a gown of gossamer and gauze
embroidered with small shadows of desire
that flit across her smile and give him pause
to see her crescent lips outlined in fire

In moments just as these are passions cast
in marble white as death and bright as love:
the stillpoint arch and sway of moments past
enduring in the endless dance above

the lady moon embraces night her way
until his darkness is concealed by day.

With these New Tunes

Adria Bernardi

Haiku baby.
Wudja?
Wanna?
Maybelatah.
Baby you I coo ya.

But it's not a haiku, I said. Five seven five.
I'm a beat man, you said.
Drumroll. Ta-dum. Ta-dum.

It's so stupid, but you know my heart is tick-tock-ticking, thunking against the sternum.
Ta-dum. Ta-dum.
A song on the radio on a station I never listen to.
I was driving, sitting, and a song brought me to my knees.
Now? after all this time?
There have been others, scores of others, in that cerulean zone.

Last night was the first really hot summer night; you could see beads of moisture hanging in the air. In the middle porch of a three-decker that faces the park, a woman stood on the balcony tousling her hair, fanning it from behind. Odd, I thought, exhibitionist, to be getting ready, performing her toilette, in a public

The Thing About Love Is...

place, on a balcony overlooking the park; who was she showing off for? She was young, in her early twenties. A trigger-hair second later, I realized she was holding a dryer. And then she began to blow her hair dry. It was Saturday night. She did this with such ease, as if she were completely unaware that she was standing in public view, knowing only that it was too hot inside to be blow-drying hair and that this was the best place to do it, at least there was a breeze. She was not thinking of who might notice her from below, but thinking ahead of the evening that was yet to come.

It made my lungs contract and collapse, like an emptied bellow, and I suddenly felt old. No. I felt not young.

From a distance, I've followed your meandering trajectory. They've used one of your songs in the sound track of an off-beat major motion picture.

And whenever I hear of you, I start to feel again like clean crew socks just out of the dryer. As if I were too comfortable and new. What were you doing with me, even for a brief period in time? You knew it, I knew it, I was no bohemian, I was no hippy. If I had been a howler, more in need, it would have made some sense. If you had discovered that I had a secret addiction to heroin. Him? With her? That was what their looks said at all those parties that started at midnight. But no, when I think of it now, I smelled like shampoo, like aloe, which you, to my astonishment, inhaled.

April seeped in though the seams of the canvas tent, it was Italian-made, surplus supply cast-off by the Italian army, sold in Army-Navy stores. And it leaked, not a leak of biblical proportions, but a trickle, and the floor was wet, and the sleeping bags

The Thing About Love Is...

we had laid on the floor were wet, and the blankets on top of us were damp, and it was cold, it was Minnesota in April, of course it was cold, but it was private, out there in an open field, where a little tent city had sprung up the night before. In the interval between night and morning, with all its little wakenings, it was damp and cold, and it did not matter, because when I woke all I cared about was you, I mean each and every impulse, ten fingertips pressed against your scalp, knowing that on the left side of the back of your head, midway up, to the left of the cortex, there was a bump. I did not care about the damp, I did not care about the cold, I do not think I noticed. When I woke, above I saw a thousand beads of water hugging the taut canvas, condensation and melt, and I reached for you underneath the damp wool blanket.

We woke in an embrace.
There was frost on the lawn and vapor rose up from it.
The birds yawned and chattered sleepily.
The dawn how soon it comes.

My God, who could do that now? Who could sustain that now, sleeping always intertwined, wrapped so that neither could let go? Well, I know that I could not. Your backbone, the round corners of your angular shoulders; you said into my ear, I could feel your lips on cartilage, the reverberations in the tympanum: This is how it should be. Yes. Forever and ever and ever. I thought it, I did not say it. I tiptoed around the jinx, the hex. I knew enough to not utter it. You had a soul which would wander. And I knew better than to say it; who believed in forever? I didn't. I did. You didn't. Or maybe you did for that interval of time between the outer limits of a chord, the vibrations contained within it.

This morning, I took out the left side of the van as I backed out of the garage. A huge long gash, the metal bent crisply into a

The Thing About Love Is...

valley. The insurance premium is going to go up. See? You were right. It would not have worked. I left the house the other day with mismatched shoes. They were very nearly identical, one black, one brown, the same style of sturdy rubber-soled walking shoe. But still.

You were going to wander. *Vagabonder.*

At a physical level, I knew that I could not. I was like a pit in the stomach, a hardened oversized chokeberry, and I knew that I was not going to make any long journeys with you.

I had one chance. And my one chance was not to be waiting for you to come home from some club in Minneapolis, or Santa Monica, or New York City. I could see into the future, that was my dilemma. One of my hangups. I knew the future. And so I could not make myself be light and easy. When I looked into the future, I did not see myself there as your woman, your girl, your lady, waiting in an apartment with a porch overlooking the park, smoking cigarettes in the dark. If I had remained inside that chord, what would have happened? But I could not have stayed within it, because what I saw outside the diapason of that perfectly imagined chord was whiskey and cigarettes stubbed out in saucers, half-filled cups of beer, a lingering haze of pot. I saw you sitting in the dining room, on a sofa with the stuffing coming out of the arms, playing your guitar, writing down words and notes in a little spiral notebook. I did not reject this part of my envisioning. You were smooth and long and perfect. Your eyes translucent. But mainly, when I looked ahead, what I saw was a kitchen table at dawn, in the back room of an apartment, and me looking through the want-ads.

Era.m combat sobre-volers,
E sobr'amars e loncs dezirs
Now over-wanting assails me

The Thing About Love Is...

And over-longing and long desire;
And overboldness and folly and unseemliness
make me pursue that which befits not my worth.
And if I want too much, in my folly,
my sense appears somewhat paltry,
but I remain noble and true.

This is what I went on to do. I teach this. One semester every other year I get to teach what I want, troubadour poetry. The rest of the time it's grammar.
Je suis un rock-star.

One semester every other year.
Sobre-volers and sobr'amors e lonc dezirs.
Over-longing and long desire.
The poem is by Giraut de Borneil.

It was later in the morning, after I took out the side of the van, that I heard your song on the radio. I don't listen to the rock 'n roll station much anymore, ten drippy songs for every one with something. But I had it on because they were fund raising on the classical station. I was going to the municipal dump, taking brown bags filled with dead branches and grass clippings. When I heard it, my tire bumped off the side of the curb.

I wanted to be your one and only, but you, even then, needed lots of women surrounding you. Even now, there are several. They have good hair, long legs, lips that can pout and let through song that sounds like angels; it's true, their voices do stir.

The dawn how soon it comes.
A man in bed with a woman who is not his wife, nor is he her husband. This is one of the stories in the poems that I get to

teach one semester every other year.

I hardly know how to begin a poem which I want to make light and easy.
Un vers que volh far leuger.
Light and easy.

A foolish thing was my presumption.
*Folors
Fo ma sospeissos*

The folly returns every so often. In the latest version, I am on the verge of running off with a man from Galicia because of the language he speaks.

My fantasies are so domestic, but you knew that then, and that is why you pulled away; I would have pulled away too, but I was stuck with myself.

Your fantasies always end with marriage, you said.

How could you have known that? I didn't say that. I denied it.

I was inhaling a Marlboro. I was drinking a Grain Belt beer. Jerry Garcia was on the juke box singing "Stella Blue." It was snowing outside. And I felt a stab in the depths of my left temple. Migraine. And I said to you, What do you know about my fantasies? I stood up and nearly passed out from the nausea that was just beginning. I walked past the other tables into the barroom, and I ordered a shot from Bear the bartender and I drank it. My head grew larger and the throbbing got stronger. I said some good-nights, then I walked out the door. I remember the ice squeaked beneath my feet at such a high pitch that it caused a knock inside my head each time I stepped.

I walked back to campus, and I could hardly see. It was snowing but that was not the problem, it was my eyes. I heard footsteps behind me, and it was you, and you had brought me my jacket.

We went to bed. We slept.

You said that you were sorry.

So you've escaped, haven't you? Forty-two years old and you've escaped. Found all those escape clauses.

One of my closest friends said to me, as I sat on the edge of the bed at mid-term, "He's never going to marry you."

It hadn't crossed my mind to marry you, or anyone else, I was twenty years old, that state of being was so far away, a maybe, that had nothing to with me. Who was thinking of marriage? Not me. It was not what I was angling for, fishing for, and this was what she implied in her voice, that I was trying to snag you.

"He's never going to marry you."

But you know, she was absolutely right.

Let's go, let's meet in Santiago de Compostela, where it will rain and rain and rain, a woman will rent us a room and rattle the door handle every two hours to make us come out during the day, saying, You can't stay in bed, I've rented you the room only for sleeping. And we will have to go outdoors and walk and walk and walk in the rain; the poor saints on the cathedral walls will be all covered with lichen and moss, stone made smooth by water and fog, this is the rainiest part of the continent, and we will go into a bar to dry out, to warm up, and we will drink hot chocolate made with heavy thick cream that is sweet, so sweet, it is like drinking a melted bar of chocolate with a dollop of whipped cream.

Folors
Fo ma sospeissos

The Thing About Love Is...

A foolish thing was my presumption.

But then it was so different.

All the debates about a life devoted to activism, social justice, revolution versus a life devoted to art. Which would it be, which would it be?

You could plead rock 'n roll. They forgive the troubadour anything. Even if he likes really expensive cars.

You were granted a certain dispensation.

You didn't have to picket the governor's mansion, you didn't have to collect recyclables, you didn't have to engage in a discourse on the ethics of private property or the way in which women are objectified, repressed and silenced by a culture dominated by white middle-aged men.

Middle age. We're getting close now, aren't we? Depending on how long you think you're going to live. What's your actuarial prediction? It must not be so long for rock 'n rollers, even those devoted to lyrics, but I imagine that since you've made it to forty, this has significantly increased the chances that you will live to old age, whereas, at age nineteen or twenty, it was a very risky proposition. I, myself, keep upping the ante; I'm at eighty now. But by the next big milestone, the floating half-way point, the middle, my life's path will have to be shifted upwards again, extending my life to ninety. This I can imagine and still avoid calling myself middle aged. But after that, it gets tricky, the revising upward. One hundred? I am reluctant to push it so high. Do I want to live to one hundred and twenty, like Jeanne Louise Calment of Arles, the lady in the newspaper who gave up cigarettes at ninety-five because she could not suffer the indignity of not being able to light them herself? At some point soon, I will be middle aged, but you? Another dispensation? You could always get them. You said twenty was your middle point, but you

The Thing About Love Is...

were not correct in your sensitive young man poet projections.

Your stature, you were tall on top of it, aloof, allowed you to be part of the discourse yet kept you out of conflicts. But me, I was pounced on, sitting in that living room chair, inhaling a Marlboro, hoping to outdistance migraine. How can you think of art, of literature, when there are so many starving people, so many tortured prisoners? someone started in on me. I had said I was thinking of going to graduate school for French. Someone asked if that meant I would then go to French-speaking Africa to do hunger work. I said, no, no, if I am very lucky, I'll end up at a Big Ten university teaching French literature.

"The literature of the French Revolution." Richard Fallon said this, and began to lecture everyone else. He was wearing his navy blue proletarian fisherman's cap.

He was talking about the evolution of the French Revolution. The lessons of the French Revolution. The betrayal of the French Revolution. "This is what she will be dedicated to."

He said it in a patronizing tone, as if he had bailed me out of an ideological fix, some reactionary hole I had dug myself into as a result of my inarticulateness. That made me resist.

Liberté. Egalité. I said I didn't foresee myself concentrating on the French Revolution.

Richard Fallon was stunned silent.

I love the lyric poetry, I said.

Elaine Leonardi called me bourgeois and elitist. She always carried the torch for you. She worked herself up into a self-righteous little frenzy and said, "Don't you think you'll find it irrelevant to be counting syllables while babies in Third World countries are dying from dehydration because multinational corporations are forcing baby formula down their throats?"

At that point everyone else mumbled in agreement and drifted off to other parts of the room. Mark Robinson flipped through a

The Thing About Love Is...

stack of albums leaning against the wall next to the television set and picked out Bob Marley. *Lively up yourself because I said so.*

This was his way of defusing the situation.

Patricia Early filled up a bong with water at the kitchen sink.

William Krebs chopped up dill pickles and made himself a tunafish sandwich.

My eye sockets hurt I was so stung. There was an empty Grain Belt on the arm of the sofa and I picked it up and started to peel off the label.

Did you know Elaine Leonardi was diagnosed with breast cancer two years ago; she is a nurse and works in an AIDS clinic in Humboldt Park in Chicago.

Richard Fallon, most radical man, is a lawyer for Disney, dedicated to the Disnification of Europe. I saw him at a wedding at a country club not too long ago.

We were standing underneath a crystal chandelier in the center of a ballroom with parquet floors. I was holding a glass of Pinot Grigio, trying to catch the eye of the waitress who was serving jumbo shrimp marinated in soy sauce and ginger.

He said, "My work is an extension of the revolution, the left extends so far it becomes the right and forms a circle."

He was an ass at nineteen and he's still an ass at forty-two.

Yes, Richard, I said. It's all become Mickey and Donald.

Yes, exactly, he said.

So, see what you missed. You had to go and become a rock-star. I'm sorry, I know you are not a star-star, you are an anti-star, a reclusive one who gives no interviews, and frankly no one asks that often, you're a musician's musician. But oh, I have not thought of you for such a very long time; I have two children, one miscarriage behind me. A near-divorce. I was a landlady, but we have no tenants now because we took over the upstairs apart-

The Thing About Love Is...

ment. I am teaching at a small Catholic college and every other year I get to teach the course on Troubadour Lyric Poetry. I have not thought of you in a very long time, but when the tune tumbled out of the speakers, I knew from the first few glycerine chords that it was you. After the tire bumped off the curb, I pulled the van over next to the park, and I listened. I listened, I suppose, to see if there would be me in there somewhere. I could not hear your voice distinctly; it was the ageless angels who were coming through. How futile to envy angels. So I listened to the words and there was something in each line. The lyrics were obscure and slightly out-of-reach, the melody was halting, and I remember thinking for a second, is he playing a guitar or a lute?

I don't want you thinking I have been walking around for the past twenty years mooning after you. No. It is very, very far away, those very early dawns. Very sweet and sad. But it came upon me like a thwack, unexpected and painful.

> Thwack. There you were.
> Now, it behooves me to think on something else,
> for I love such a one to whom I make no entreaty
> because in the thinking itself I know well I'm at fault.
> What shall I do? for a bold urge comes to me
> that I should go and plead
> then fear makes me renounce it.
> *E paors fai m'o lasser.*

I read somewhere that Neil Young cut his finger while trying to slice open a package of turkey wrapped in sealed-tight plastic and he had to change his plans. Has that ever happened to you?

> *A penas sai comensar*
> *un ver que volh far leuger...*

The Thing About Love Is...

I hardly know how to begin a poem
which I want to make light and easy.
Yes, this was always a problem. I could never make myself easy.

Tunes! someone howled a long time ago, in a living room
where there was silence. We need tunes!

You need the rub, you need the wound,
otherwise the line is just too smooth,
your song came through the speakers.

Minstrel, now, I say to you, with these new tunes be off.

Last Word
Edward J. Underhill

The Curtain Rises: We see a table set for two, including a white, linen tablecloth.

Sound: Offstage there is noise from unseen diners and waitstaff suggesting the lunch hour at a fine restaurant.

At Rise: On stage is BARRY. *He is in his mid-thirties, wearing gray slacks, an expensive sport coat and a white shirt, open at the collar.* BARRY *is seated at the table, fiddling with a glass of wine. He is relaxed, almost bored.*

JENNIFER *enters, hurries to the table. She is in her mid-thirties. She wears a professional-looking skirt and blouse, carries a large purse. As* JENNIFER *takes a seat, she begins...*

JENNIFER Sorry, I'm late. I'm doing a market study for Sunshine Foods — you know, my best and damn near only client. I spent all morning with a focus group in Long Island. Then I'm on the phone with the company for an hour trying to explain why people don't like a chocolate pudding made from tofu.

BARRY The people have spoken — the bastards.

JENNIFER I can send you a case of the stuff, if you want.

BARRY That's okay. I already have a refrigerator full of food that looks like chocolate tofu.

JENNIFER Have you been waiting long?

BARRY Just long enough to order a glass of cabernet.

JENNIFER A glass of wine? Planning to take the afternoon off?

BARRY No. Thought it would help me relax.

JENNIFER Wine in the afternoon would make me horny.

BARRY I'll order a bottle then.

JENNIFER As if you ever had to get me drunk in order to ...

BARRY Things have changed.

JENNIFER Yes. Sex is out of the question. I have appointments all afternoon. Owning a marketing firm is like having a baby that never grows up. Besides, my therapist would kill me. Two years of counseling gone for naught.

BARRY That's the trouble with women. They get sex all wrapped up in emotions. This is my latest discovery. Women are too emotional. Or else, too calculating.

JENNIFER Bitterness is such an attractive quality, Barry. Can I at least order before we start bashing the sexes.

BARRY Sorry. Didn't mean to start off heavy. Besides, you're excluded from my general observations on women.

JENNIFER Thank you, I think. Ah — the waiter. Ready? I know what I'm having. (*To the waiter*) Caesar salad, dressing on the side. Mineral water. No lime; too depressing.

BARRY (*To the waiter*) I'll have the steak sandwich. Fries.

JENNIFER You know, eventually I would have had to kill you if we'd stayed married. You eat so much, and still you look the same as in college — one eighty?

BARRY One-ninety, now.

JENNIFER An extra ten pounds on a man looks good. Says he's not trying so hard.

BARRY Hey, I work out. Twice a week. Usually.

JENNIFER Yes. I still remember how you used to eat potato chips on the stairmaster.

BARRY I did that once.

JENNIFER Once that I saw. Meanwhile, my body is turning to ooze. Salad for lunch. Every day. Aerobics classes, running and still...

BARRY I think you look great!

JENNIFER My clothes, Barry. My clothes look great. You wouldn't recognize me naked.

BARRY We could have sex, to find out.

JENNIFER No. I want you to remember me the way I looked in college; the NYU marketing major you would do anything for ... to do anything to.

BARRY I remember the 'you' from the summer before grad school. When we worked for that resort in Vermont. I particularly recall how you looked that rainy afternoon we spent in the boathouse.

JENNIFER Hold that thought — for the next twenty years.

BARRY Really, I don't know why women in their thirties get so worked up over their bodies. I dated someone for three months, and I never got to see her naked. I mean, in the full light, standing up.

JENNIFER Congratulations to her. You can bet your ass no man will ever see me naked in the light of day again. From here on out, it's all smoke and mirrors. I've discovered all kinds of maneuvers to prevent full body disclosure.

BARRY Look, you're a knockout. You always will be. I'd forgotten how crazy you get on this issue. Like the time just after we were married when we spent four hours in that store on Fifth Avenue...

JENNIFER Saks. How can you never remember the name of a store?

BARRY Saks, then. We spent four hours looking at every black dress known to mankind, and you ended up buying the first one the girl showed us .

JENNIFER I still have that dress. I can't fit into it anymore, but if I ever get a fatal illness, and lose a lot of weight, I'll wear it again.

BARRY Well, that's something to look forward to. Good, the food's here. (*To the waiter*) I'll have another glass of wine, thanks. (*To* JENNIFER) So, now that we've covered the relaxing chit-chat, why did you call me?

JENNIFER That can wait. You said you wanted to talk to me, too.

BARRY Yeah, but you called me ... so, I guess, this is your meeting.

JENNIFER Is that what we're doing? Meeting? Of all the things we've done with each other, meeting is the one thing we've never done before. We dated for two years; slept together for all but two weeks of that time; finished college together; got our master's degrees together; worked together; smoked pot together — once; married each other for six years; traveled together; made each other miserable for a year; and divorced each other. But we've never had a meeting together. Well, its about time, I say.

BARRY God, you talk so much. I forgot.

JENNIFER It's a compliment, Barry. I only talk to people I like. You don't have to listen. Just tune me in when you hear something dirty.

The Thing About Love Is...

BARRY I'm sorry, did you say something?

JENNIFER Very fucking funny. Your wit must be what makes you the star writer of American Business magazine.

BARRY Actually, I left the magazine about six months ago.

JENNIFER You're kidding? You finally quit? I think that was smart. Are you...

BARRY Working? Yes; for my uncle — the one that sells office furniture in East Rutherford. I'm in charge of the house accounts. Which means I have an American Express card, Knicks tickets, a car and a salary that's about twice what I made as a writer.

JENNIFER Sounds great.

BARRY Sounds easy. Most of my customers are here in New York, so I haven't had to move. I sleep late, eat late, drink late.

JENNIFER How long can you hold out there?

BARRY Until my pride kicks in, or I retire, whichever occurs first.

JENNIFER What made you finally decide to quit the magazine?

BARRY I just got tired of writing the same bullshit profiles of self-absorbed businessmen. I did one on this guy who's developed a new paint-can lid; where the paint won't get all gunky in the rim...

JENNIFER I'm in favor of that. Does he need a marketing firm?

BARRY I'm sure you don't mean to interrupt. So, I did this one-thousand-word article on the guy. You'd have thought he slept with Mother Teresa twice the way he was going on about this stupid lid.

JENNIFER Well, at least he's excited about something...

BARRY Yup. And that's why I quit. I decided that there was no point writing about these people if I couldn't get up for them. I thought, if I'm gonna be a whore, I might as well get paid for it.

JENNIFER Ah, the pioneer spirit!

BARRY I could pretend I quit the magazine and took a job selling office furniture as part of a plan...

JENNIFER No. Don't pretend anything. I see you're in a funk. You always give everything the worst spin when you're in that kind of mood. You were at the magazine for what? Six years? I'm sure you got everything out of it you could.

BARRY Except a career writing books, which is what I intended.

JENNIFER Everyone needs a break once in a while. I was a lesbian for two months in college, remember.

BARRY That was before me. What was her name? (*Pause*) I don't know. Some days, I feel like I've given up on myself. Some days, I think I'm finally looking into the headlights of reality — I'm not gonna be a writer.

The Thing About Love Is...

JENNIFER Her name was Aurora. What does your family think?

BARRY Ecstatic. My mother started to cry when I told her I was going to work for her brother. My dad. Well, my dad said, 'You can still type up things if you want. I'll read 'em.' My father thinks that going from business writer to furniture salesman is a logical career move. So ... what I consider to be the second biggest act of cowardice and failure of my adult life is celebrated by my family as a show of ... maturity and good sense.

JENNIFER Families are supposed to be wrong about things like this. The drug companies count on it. I assume you consider our divorce as your number one act of cowardice and failure. Are you doing any writing now?

BARRY Yes and no. Yes; divorce is number one failure; and no, I've resisted the urge to do any writing. I just think it's time to admit I'm not going to be a writer when I grow up.

JENNIFER Don't give in yet. You've gotten a lot of articles published. You did that thing on the sewer system I saw in *New York* magazine last summer.

BARRY Did you read it?

JENNIFER I started to. (*Pause*) I intended to. (*Pause*) I still have it. (*Pause*) I'm sure it's great.

BARRY The only thing worse than not getting an article published in *New York* magazine is getting an article published there. Then all your friends expect you to be on the Pulitzer Prize track,

The Thing About Love Is...

and when that's the only piece you get published in two years, you look like a loser. Worse, you look like a loser who wrote an article about the sewers that everybody saw and nobody read.

JENNIFER Nobody thinks you're a loser. People think writers are cool.

BARRY People who think they're writers in their twenties are cool. People who think they're writers in their thirties are losers. Let's face it; my anticipated double-barreled publishing career never went off. It's okay. There's a lot to be said for selling office furniture. Jesus Christ sold office furniture.

JENNIFER He did?

BARRY Well, he was a carpenter. Presumably, he made at least a few desks, credenzas ... file cabinets. And I assume he also did some selling. It was a family-run business from what I understand.

JENNIFER Spoken like a true salesman.

BARRY Thanks for the compliment — I think.

JENNIFER At least at the end of the day, you know if you've accomplished something. You have the tale of the tape to confirm what you did. In my job — my career — it's all so soft. Trying to figure out what people like by what they say they like. I spend half my time in a dark room looking through a two-way mirror at teenagers and housewives eating crackers, cookies, cereal — none of it tastes or looks like real food. It's called qualitative research. The opinions of six pimply kids from Livingston you

The Thing About Love Is...

wouldn't trust to return a movie to Blockbuster are the basis for a twenty-million-dollar product campaign. Yesterday I spent two hours trying to figure out what a teenage girl meant when she said she liked our candy because we never tried to "deflavorate" it. Deflavorate it? Since the candy comes in fourteen flavors, ranging from shit to puke, I don't even know where to start. The housewives say they love the "cheesy tidbits" in the blue package, but hate the Cheesy Chunkies in the green package, even though they're the same artificial, cheese-flavored product. They all agree the bite-size candy is better than the bar, but everything we know about sales says consumers buy bars, not bite-size.

BARRY Maybe the consumers are wrong?

JENNIFER They can't be wrong. The consumer is always right, by virtue of being the consumer.

BARRY Then the people on the other side of the glass are wrong.

JENNIFER Maybe. People can't be wrong about what they like, but that doesn't mean they know why they like something. But if somehow they can lead you in the right direction, then...

BARRY Then Third-World nations are eating fudge tofu in glow-in-the-dark, Michael Jordan glasses.

JENNIFER You joke, and yet you're wearing a seventy-five-dollar tie. You can't eat a tie, you know.

BARRY A focus group tell you that?

The Thing About Love Is...

JENNIFER My point is that we make buying decisions on a mix of needs ... desires ... drives. My job is to figure out what motivates people. And for better or worse, I'm good at it, and I like it. (*Pause*) You spent seventy-five dollars on a tie, Barry, when you could have bought one for ten bucks because that tie says something about your identity. The question is, what does your tie say?

BARRY Dry-clean only, I believe.

JENNIFER I'm serious. You're a salesman now; you need to ask yourself, why does somebody buy a chair?

BARRY So their ass doesn't hit the floor when they sit down.

JENNIFER That's the first need. But why a particular chair? What are they really buying? Importance? Credibility? I bet you could write a great article on the subject...

BARRY (*Enthusiastically*) You know, that might not be a bad idea ... There's these two old guys at the company, the ancients we call 'em. They can give a complete profile of somebody based on what kind of pen they carry. The thing is ... (*Pause*) Ahhhh ... clever girl, what? The young man innocently believes he is in the midst of a genuine conversation, only to discover that he is, in fact, the subject of a little motivational marketing by his ex. Your two-way mirror is showing, Jenny. I may have to include your name on my list of women who are too calculating.

JENNIFER Add my name to whatever demented little list you want. I'm only trying to help — it's my personal philosophy; always tell the truth, even if you have to lie to do it.

BARRY Well, I appreciate your concern and deceit. But until further notice, I'm a furniture salesman, not a writer.

JENNIFER I think what you need is a girlfriend.

BARRY Oh, please. Don't start on that.

JENNIFER Ah — struck a nerve. Let's hear.

BARRY There's nothing to hear. What about you? Are you seeing anybody?

JENNIFER Not really. I mean, I'm seeing somebody. But I'm trying to take it slow.

BARRY Who is it?

JENNIFER Do you remember Clyde Mandera?

BARRY The guy who owns the ad agency? Oh, I hate that guy. I hate that guy so much. Please don't be dating him. Please, please, please tell me you're not dating him.

JENNIFER I'm dating him.

BARRY Jesus, Jen, you are so much better than him. I would never have asked for the divorce if I knew you were going to date Clyde Mandera.

JENNIFER Why have you always hated Clyde? He's been great to me — His agency is doing well, and he refers me clients whenever he can...

The Thing About Love Is...

BARRY Fine. Then, send him a fruit basket, but don't sleep with him.

JENNIFER Clyde has been a terrific friend, especially right after the divorce. I can't understand why you hate him so much.

BARRY He's so fake. That phony British accent; the rep ties ... the sideburns.

JENNIFER The sideburns are real, so is the accent. Clyde was born in England.

BARRY As I recall, he only lived there 'til he was six.

JENNIFER And that's when people learn to talk — when they're children.

BARRY Yes. They learn baby-talk. If Clyde says he has to go wee-wee, and he says it in a British accent, that I understand. But the rest of his talk, the "petrol for the auto," his weekly "shed-you-all." Ugh, I wanted to throw-up whenever I had to talk to him.

JENNIFER You only met him twice that I recall.

BARRY More than enough... Let's not talk about him. Except, and this is the Last Word — I claim Last Word on this subject: You can do better.

JENNIFER Barry, you don't know him...

BARRY Nope. Nope. I called Last word. Even divorced, we still

The Thing About Love Is...

have Last Word, and I claimed it. You are prohibited. Prohibited. From saying anything further on the subject. Under the rules, you can now claim the Last Word on any subject of your choosing. But for this subject, I get the Last Word, and this is it — You can do better.

JENNIFER Then tell me who you're dating?

BARRY I'm not sure I want to talk about this.

JENNIFER Is it somebody I know? How about Margaret from the magazine? She seemed like your type.

BARRY Margaret Barnes? You think she's my type? What makes you think that?

JENNIFER She was smart. And very funny.

BARRY That's my type? Smart and funny? How about good-looking? Most men want to hear that their type is good-looking.

JENNIFER Men have such depth. Anyway, Margaret Barnes is good-looking.

BARRY Well, I never went out with her. She was too ... too much like a guy. I mean, the way she stood, and she walked like a cop.

JENNIFER Alright, Margaret Barnes is disqualified. Who is it, then?

BARRY You don't know her.

The Thing About Love Is...

JENNIFER Then, for Christ-sakes, tell me!

BARRY Her name is Rebecca. Actually, it's Becky. Becky Leland.

JENNIFER That sounds young. She's not young, I hope.

BARRY Don't get mad.

JENNIFER Oh, God — how old, young, is she?

BARRY Twenty-four.

JENNIFER Oh, God. I'm so sick. You're dating a twenty-four-year-old.

BARRY It's not serious.

JENNIFER It's just so depressing. The last twenty-four-year-old I'm ever going to have sex with is you. And that was more than ten years ago. And we were married then, so I didn't appreciate it. Life is so unfair.

BARRY Look, it's not a big deal. Becky and I are not serious. It's just ... (*To the waiter*) No, we're fine, thanks.

JENNIFER How do you know her?

BARRY She's ... She's the receptionist at my uncle's company.

JENNIFER You're dating a twenty-four-year-old receptionist from New Jersey? I bet she has perfect breasts and the face of an angel.

The Thing About Love Is...

BARRY Well...

JENNIFER That's the story of Barry Fitzdonald. At the self-proclaimed lowest point in your life, you've got it ten times better than anybody else.

BARRY Thanks for understanding.

JENNIFER Whatever you do, don't get her pregnant.

BARRY Christ, I won't get her pregnant.

JENNIFER You're having sex, aren't you?

BARRY Yeah, but...

JENNIFER I know you. You'll leave it all to her.

BARRY That's bullshit.

JENNIFER We had sex for almost nine years — two of those were unmarried. The only safe sex we had was of the oral variety.

BARRY Becky's not much into that.

JENNIFER Now, I understand why you're so bitter. Is Becky one of those women you recently discovered is too emotional? Or is she one of the calculating ones?

BARRY Neither.

JENNIFER But if you had to choose one category or the other?

The Thing About Love Is...

BARRY Emotional.

JENNIFER That's the most calculating kind of woman — the emotional kind.

BARRY Don't be bitchy.

JENNIFER You're right — I take back what I said. But just as a matter of market study, how is it having sex with a twenty-four-year-old?

BARRY I'm not sure if you've noticed this, but sex is not what it used to be.

JENNIFER To what part of the anatomy are you referring?

BARRY Not the anatomy. I mean, this whole safe sex thing. Condoms. And AIDS tests. And personal histories. I always feel like I'm Madonna.

JENNIFER Sounds like you've been a busy boy.

BARRY I wish. I don't have the patience to make the small talk, and women our age are highly focused on finding husbands.

JENNIFER And you're not?

BARRY No. I am not. I just want to meet somebody interesting.

JENNIFER It's difficult to meet interesting people if you're judging them by the width of their ass.

The Thing About Love Is...

BARRY Hey, give me some credit.

JENNIFER Then why are you dating the receptionist if what you want is interesting? Why don't you date the paint-lid guy?

BARRY First of all, don't knock Becky. She is interesting. She likes to read. Likes basketball. Likes to cook...

JENNIFER Okay, okay. I've heard enough. I'm not against her. You'll have to admit this is a confusing subject — the love interest of your ex-spouse. Creates ambivalent feelings.

BARRY Sort of like not getting invited to the party of a friend you don't like.

JENNIFER Actually, I'm sure Becky's nice, and, no doubt, head over heels for you. And I mean that figuratively. (*Pause*) Just don't accidentally get her pregnant. And that, my boy, is the Last Word on that subject.

BARRY If the safe sex lecture is over, why don't you tell me why you wanted to get together?

JENNIFER Before we come to that, I'd like to ask you a question. A serious question. Something I've always wondered about. I really don't have the right to ask. And it's okay for you to lie. But, here it is: Did you ever cheat?

BARRY What?

JENNIFER Did you ever cheat during our marriage? I mean, toward the end. That last summer.

BARRY When we were fighting all the time?

JENNIFER Or, after that, when we stopped fighting. Stopped talking.

BARRY And we were both looking for excuses to stay away from the apartment?

JENNIFER I remember you were traveling a lot. We stopped having sex. I thought maybe you were having an affair.

BARRY No, no affair. I came close — once. During a trip to San Francisco.

JENNIFER Tell me.

BARRY No. Too embarrassing. Besides, it's history.

JENNIFER It's important for me to know. C'mon. Let's hear.

BARRY Okay. If you have to know. It must have been September of what? Nineteen-ninety-four? Anyway, it was a couple of months before I finally filed for divorce. I'd been at the magazine for about three years. The whole writing staff was covering this huge week-long business consortium. You and I were in the "not talking" stage of our marriage, so I doubt you remember this trip. I was still in awe then of Cal Markum, the owner of the magazine. The old man was in Frisco with us, schmoozing all these advertisers and CEOs. Most of the staff spent their time getting loaded at free parties and receptions. I was too depressed and confused to be drinking. So, I really worked hard. I began to hang out with another writer: Terry Kenney. She'd just started at

The Thing About Love Is...

the magazine.

JENNIFER Terry Kenney? I don't remember her.

BARRY Terry was nice. Short, blond hair. Very athletic-looking. A little thin. Kinda freckly, if that's a word. The corner of her left front tooth was chipped. And she smoked like she was on death row. But she was funny, and took her job seriously. I could tell she was at least a little interested in me by the third day. I wasn't hanging out with the rest of the staff, and I noticed she wasn't either. We ran into each other a lot in the communications room. Anyway, on the last day of this spectacle, Markum meets Bill Gates. Somehow gets him to agree to an exclusive interview. Maybe because we're the best writers at the magazine, or maybe because we're the only people on the staff still sober, Markum wants Terry and me to do the interview. Gates can only talk to us at eight that evening, so Terry and I spend all afternoon working out our questions. Very "Twenty-first century, I-understand-business" kind of stuff. At about six, I decide to go for a run along the harbor-front — toward the bridge. I was trying to figure out what I should do about us, and somehow get my head straight for this interview. (BARRY *pauses — sips his wine.*) When I get back to my room, I find an urgent message from Terry. I call her back, and she says the interview is off — that she'll come up to explain what's happening. I'm still in my running clothes soaked in sweat when she gets there. She right away kicks off her shoes and takes one of those little bottles of wine from the mini-bar. She throws herself into a chair, puts her bare feet on the bed. She's wearing very tight, ripped jeans, and a sleeveless t-shirt.

JENNIFER Virgin-white, I suppose?

The Thing About Love Is...

BARRY Like snow. I ask her a few questions while I pull off my shoes and socks. She's all business-like. Disgusted that the interview has been canceled. An emergency has come up, and Gates has to leave for Seattle early. He's supposed to call Markum in case there's a change. But for now, the interview's off. I start throwing out ideas — "Can we meet him at the airport? Or fly with him to Seattle?" I mean, I'm all business, too. Still, in two minutes of undressing, I'm down to my underwear. Terry looks at me; I look at her. I say, "I'm taking a shower. Just in case." She simply watches me. I go into the bathroom. But I don't shut the door all the way. I run the water; study the mirror for a moment; take a second to catch my breath. Decide what to do. I get into the shower, and kinda wait. She's coming in any second, I'm sure.

JENNIFER And you're hard as a rock, of course.

BARRY Of course. And I wait. And wait. And she doesn't come in. So I shower, dry off, and return to the room. I'm wondering, "Is she in bed waiting for me? That'd sure make things easy." (BARRY *pauses — sips his wine.*) I go back in. She's still in the chair. Still dressed. Only she's on the phone. Talking to Markum. She hangs up. "It's definitely off," she says. "Missed opportunity." She gets up; stretches, gives me a long look. "Markum says to meet him in the lobby in fifteen minutes. He wants all of us on the eight-thirty flight." Then she grabs her shoes and walks out. And that's my only near miss in four years of marriage.

JENNIFER Would you have? If she'd made it easier. I mean, she made it as easy as she could. But if she'd gone to your bed?

BARRY Probably. I think, probably. But you know, the fact that she didn't climb into my bed wasn't an accident. She knew I couldn't do it. I certainly wanted to, but I couldn't.

JENNIFER That was decent of you. I would have understood, considering the circumstances.

BARRY Now you tell me.

JENNIFER No one can give you permission to break a vow, Barry. You can only cheat on yourself.

BARRY I would never cheat on myself. I'd be too worried I'd find out. (*Pause*) So. Why did you want to know if I ever had an affair?

JENNIFER Because I was sure you hadn't. And I just wanted to know if I could trust my instincts about something like this.

BARRY That sounds ominous. Are you worried that Clyde might be fooling around?

JENNIFER I think so. I mean, I think I'm worried. Although I don't think I have any reason to worry. I just wish I could trust my instincts when it comes to my personal life the way I can in business. I don't know why none of my professional skills help in my personal life.

BARRY What is your relationship with Clyde? Mostly personal or mostly professional?

JENNIFER I told you. It's personal.

BARRY But it wouldn't be anything if he didn't help you get clients?

JENNIFER Now you're the one who sounds bitchy. I'm dating Clyde because I like him, not because he's good for business.

BARRY You can't possibly separate your feelings for him from the knowledge that he's important to your company.

JENNIFER That's ridiculous.

BARRY You said it yourself; the choices people make are based on a complicated mix of drives, desires, needs. I'm sure you like Clyde in part because he's kind and smart, and likes the same movies you do. But you also like him because he's successful, right?

JENNIFER I suppose.

BARRY And because he's smart and successful, he helps you get clients. And you like that about him, as well.

JENNIFER I'd like to think I'm not that superficial.

BARRY It's not superficiality. It's just part of the whole equation. I dated this woman for a while who lived on Central Park West. Unbelievable apartment. Looked like it was decorated by Winston Churchill. The place belonged to her father, who lived in Italy most of the time. She was just okay, but I coveted her apartment. It had fireplaces in every room, a huge-screen television, marble bathtubs. Every time I was ready to call it quits between us, she'd invite me back to her place, and suddenly she didn't seem so bad.

The Thing About Love Is...

JENNIFER And you think women are calculating? That's the most calculating theory I've ever heard. Dating somebody because they have big fireplaces — no wonder you're having trouble finding somebody. You don't want a relationship; you want *This Old House* with tits.

BARRY Face it: When you date somebody, you date the person, their car, their job, their taste in music, their shoes, their friends, their kitchen. The whole package. If somebody's good-looking, you don't notice a whiny voice so much. If the sex is good, it's easier to accept somebody who's cheap. At some blurry point a person is what they own. You can't dispute that — your whole life is devoted to the principle that people define themselves by what they buy. I'm just taking it a step further — people are constantly weighing all the physical and personality stuff, and all the other lifestyle issues. It's just that people don't acknowledge it; like you said, people know what they like, but they don't know why. Or don't want to know why.

JENNIFER So you think the only reason I'm dating Clyde is because he helps me get clients.

BARRY Not the only reason, but it is a reason.

JENNIFER It's not healthy to think that much. Even if I am exploiting my relationship with Clyde — and I'm not saying I am — I'd rather not know it. I already have too much unearned guilt. Besides, if you're so skilled at unmasking people's secret desires and motives, then why don't you tell me what Barry Fitzdonald wants?

BARRY Well, I'll admit that I'm confused about things right now. I'm not sure I'm interested in any kind of serious relationship. It would have to be ... somebody who's strong and funny and ...

JENNIFER And twenty-four?

BARRY Or was twenty-four. I want somebody ... like you. Somebody I could never cheat on. I guess I want what we once had. Sometimes I look back at our break-up, and I can't figure out how I ever let the thing get away from me. Other times, I think our marriage broke up for the same reason I didn't go for it with Terry in that hotel room.

JENNIFER How do you figure that?

BARRY I'm a coward, by nature. I probably should have had the balls to screw Terry, and the balls to fight for our marriage.

JENNIFER So, now we come to what you consider your single greatest act of cowardice — asking me for a divorce.

BARRY Bingo.

JENNIFER Oh, man. You are wrong on that. You're wrong on both things. You could never have lived with yourself if you'd slept with that woman. And your asking me for a divorce was probably the bravest thing you ever did.

BARRY Bullshit!

JENNIFER No. You forced us to get on with our lives. I could never have confronted our problems straight on. I was grateful

The Thing About Love Is...

you took the lead. I mean, I was sick about it for awhile. Really depressed. But it was the right thing to do.

BARRY What makes you think we couldn't have worked it out?

JENNIFER I don't know. Because we didn't, I guess.

BARRY We shouldn't have stopped talking.

JENNIFER I think maybe we talked too much. We were such good friends, and the sex was always good. I think we just assumed our marriage was a sure thing.

BARRY You think that's why our marriage failed? Because we got along great?

JENNIFER I think a person needs something from a spouse. Something unknown and unknowable. We worked great as friends, but on a deeper level, something was missing. I don't know what it was. But we weren't able to give it to each other. It's useless to blame anybody.

BARRY I think things between us were so good for so long, that when things started to go bad, we didn't know what to do. We had no experience at failing. So we just gave up.

JENNIFER Maybe that was the right thing to do.

BARRY Giving up is never the right thing to do.

JENNIFER You've given up being a writer.

The Thing About Love Is...

BARRY It's more complicated than that.

JENNIFER Everything is. That's the compelling and scary part about life. Maybe you're right; maybe we should have fought for our marriage. Maybe you should have slept with that woman in San Francisco. Maybe you should have started selling office furniture ten years ago. Who knows? Nothing is at all certain. I only know, or I think I know — one thing. You have to keep moving forward. Not make the same mistake twice. I think I'm just beginning to understand how random life is. That's why I wanted to talk with you. I've made a decision.

BARRY About what?

JENNIFER About my life. My career. I've been thinking about this ever since my Uncle Billy died.

BARRY Your Uncle Billy died?

JENNIFER Yeah. Last April.

BARRY The uncle you were so tight with? The one who took you to the prom and Italy, and all that?

JENNIFER Yeah. He had cancer. It was a pretty horrible thing, but he only lived with it for about eight months. He was just fifty-six. Never sick a day in his life. So it was a big surprise.

BARRY I can't believe you didn't call me.

JENNIFER I'm sorry. I didn't know you felt close to him.

BARRY I don't mean that. I just know how important he was to you. It must have been a terrible time.

JENNIFER Worse than anything I've ever known. I was only four when my father died, so this was my first encounter with death up close and personal. It was a sickening experience. I almost gave up my business, I was so depressed.

BARRY You should have called me. I feel bad I didn't help you get through it.

JENNIFER I thought about calling you. Too many times, really. Anyway, I was in Rochester with him when he finally died. I had been there about a week, watching him move farther and farther away.

BARRY He wasn't married, was he?

JENNIFER No — well, he was once. A long time ago. My mother and I took care of the funeral arrangements, and we thought about finding Uncle Billy's ex-wife, but nobody knew her name, or where she was.

BARRY How long were they married?

JENNIFER My mother couldn't remember. She thought two years, maybe three. It was right after he got out of the army. They lived in California. After the divorce, he came back to New York. I never even knew he had been married. After he died, I looked for a marriage certificate, but couldn't find it. I felt very strange going through his drawers and closets. I could smell him in his clothes and papers. It was depressing. And exhilarating. Afraid what I might find. Kept looking for the one thing that would explain his life.

BARRY Rosebud?

JENNIFER Yeah. Rosebud. No luck, though. Except I had to pick out his clothes for the wake. He only had one dark suit. And only one tie that wasn't stained. I went to Macy's and bought him a white shirt. It was the first shirt I ever bought him. I almost got one that was on sale, but it looked a little cheap, like the collar wouldn't hold up to a half-dozen dry-cleanings. (*Pause*) I know it's crazy but I didn't want the last thing I bought for my uncle to be cheap. So, I got him a hundred-and-ten-dollar Armani shirt. (JENNIFER *takes a sip of water.*) I brought the clothes to the funeral home, and the guy there made me go back to the apartment for underwear and socks. I always wondered about that, but it turns out they bury you in all your clothes. But no shoes. As I was leaving, a guy from the back came out, and brought me the stuff he found in my uncle's pockets. I had forgotten to check. He handed me a quarter and a book of matches. The matches said, "Thanks for coming to our wedding, Jennifer and Barry. September twelfth, nineteen eighty-eight." The last time my uncle had worn that suit was to watch us get married. Back at his apartment, I went through the envelope of photographs my mother brought to show at the wake. There was a picture of Uncle Billy and me at our wedding reception. He was wearing the suit — and the same tie I'd picked out for the wake. I realized then how everything changes. Even if you don't want it to, even if you don't recognize it. Not usually for the better, either. I decided that the only good things that happen, happen because you do something to make them happen.

BARRY You don't have to tell me. Six months ago, I was a writer. Now, I'm selling metal chairs.

JENNIFER Then do something, Barry. I am.

BARRY You are what?

JENNIFER I'm doing something. I'm moving my office. To a funky building off of Twenty-eighth Street. Twenty-eighth and Sixth Avenue. It's where all the agencies are. And I'm hiring a receptionist. And an assistant.

BARRY That'll cost a fortune.

JENNIFER I know. But I have to do it in order to make it clear to my clients and myself that I'm in this business for keeps. And that's why I called you.

BARRY To borrow money?

JENNIFER No. Do you remember that AT&T stock my uncle gave us for a wedding present?

BARRY Yeah.

JENNIFER Well, it's worth about thirty grand today — of course, half of it is yours.

BARRY You want to sell the stock your uncle gave you?

JENNIFER Gave us; not me. Us. That's why...

The Thing About Love Is...

BARRY You can't sell that stock. Don't you remember what you said during the divorce. You said, let's never sell the stock. That way we'll always have something that's ours. Something we can talk about — a reason to call. A chance, a small chance, that maybe, maybe someday we'll get back together. I can't believe you've forgotten...

JENNIFER I...

BARRY If you need money, I can give you some, or lend it, if you want. I just can't believe you forgot...

JENNIFER I didn't forget, Barry. I didn't forget what I said about the stock.

BARRY If you didn't forget, then why... (*Long pause*) (*No, even longer than that*) Do you have the stock certificate with you?

JENNIFER (JENNIFER *takes an* ENVELOPE *from her* PURSE. *She opens the* ENVELOPE, *removes the* STOCK CERTIFICATE, *puts it on the table.*) You're a great guy, Barry. It's just ... for better or worse, that part of my life is over. I don't want to live in the past. And I don't want you to, either. (BARRY *nods, takes a* PEN *from his pocket, signs the* CERTIFICATE. *He hands it back to* JENNIFER.) I'll send you a check for your half.

BARRY Is that the Last Word on our marriage? "I'll send you a check for your half?"

JENNIFER No. This is the Last Word: I wish you a great life ... No, I wish you a happy one. (JENNIFER *puts the* CERTIFICATE *and* ENVELOPE *in her* PURSE. *She gets up, puts her*

The Thing About Love Is...

HAND *on* BARRY's SHOULDER. *Then she leaves.* BARRY *remains at the table.*)

Lights fade.

Forgotten Note

Nikki Lynch

your whispers tickled every hair on my neck
sending goosebumps firing across my skin
i miss your smile so soft and confusing
but a simple touch of your hand made my whole body glow

the sun's clouded in   winter's still winning
and i promise you a new spring
new memories if you let me in
but you can't   not this time

i knew leaving that night i would never
feel your eyes electric shock   flash of
something someone new beneath you
under your skin, did i ever sink in?

i told you everything inside my head
every stupid word accusing me
incriminating me instead
confessing love and forever and etcetera

Free Fall

David McGrath

We are not exactly Romeo and Juliet.

The digital voice of the operator instructs me to insert "eightee cents, please," into the pay phone at the Dominick's supermarket. I am holding a white plastic bag containing a pound of Puerto Rican coffee and a Booth's frozen dinner, when Lee answers the phone.

"Do you..." she begins to ask, the rest of her sentence obliterated by the crashing of the shopping carts being herded through the doors by an employee, a boy about sixteen — his cheeks grated fiery red from acne. I lean closer into the phone.

"Do you miss me?" she asks.

"Yes."

"Say that you do."

A child, a girl — short red hair, pink shirt — is led screeching out the door by an iron-faced woman who reads her register receipt while pushing the shopping cart, yet she still manages to stare at me. I switch the phone hand with the hand holding the grocery bag that shows I am shopping and not just here to make a call.

"I miss you," I say.

"Tell me you miss my pussy."

"Lee, I'm in the Dominick's for crissakes."

"Is someone watching you?"

The Thing About Love Is...

A look through the glass doors shows moderate activity at the checkout counters. A gum chewing cashier with a mound of blonde hair, swirled like frozen custard, chats with the acne boy. The boy, glancing towards the doors, is sporting the latest style haircut—the sides and back of his head shaved to the scalp, with waxy black hair covering the top of his head like a lamp doily. A gold stud glints from his earlobe. I rotate my right shoulder away from them and am now nearly inside the above-the-waste enclosure for the telephone. The warm, nutty smell of the coffee, which earlier I ground in the machine that sits in the coffee/tea/cooking oil aisle, envelops my senses like an anesthetic.

"Someone's always watching."

"Are you touching yourself?"

I smile, shake my head.

"You're smiling and shaking your head, right? Now, James, tell me how much you miss me."

"Okay," I laugh. "I want to make love all night, till we're both comatose."

I smell something else — wool, perhaps — and I spin to see that an old woman clutching the handle of a shopping dolly is standing right behind. Waiting to use the telephone. Her eyes, gray pebbles, peer at me from underneath the lines of her red framed bifocals.

It is an Illinois summer day of rain and cold and wind, but I crank open the window while driving home, to smell the air sweetened by chlorophyll from the wetted roadside trees and grasses.

The radio is playing "alternative rock" — a slower tempo, minor chords — a sound I lately search for with the radio scan button, and I think how it may have something to do with this secret affair I am having with Lee. I am divorced, but she is mar-

The Thing About Love Is...

ried to a man who sounds like, from her side of the story, a dangerous mistake. He suspects she is straying.

Not really sure we're in love. More of an arrangement. More Mickey Spillane than Shakespeare. She loves sex and says she's never met anyone like me. But that's what they do. Like my ex-wife Nicole before everything changed. She had me believing I was someone extraordinary. She must have been laughing inside the whole time.

I lift my foot off of the accelerator, am doing 55 mph in a 30. It's what happens sometimes when you get a pulsing beat on the radio, the erotic snarl of an electric guitar, lyrics sung by a woman addressing a former lover, asking, "Do you think of me when you fuck her?" She explodes the F in fuck, says it with no shame. Like Lee. Nicole would say Lee's "indecent."

The first time I saw Lee, she was like a blade of crabgrass in a garden of flowers, consisting of the idle spouses of the lawyers and investors who lived in the suburbs of Lake County — spouses who dressed "casual" at evening, in their six-hundred-dollar cashmere sweaters which they perpetually smoothed and adjusted — politely impatient — with hands that showed off their fifty-dollar manicures paid for by their husbands. I know how much because it's what my ex-wife used to pay.

I see a photograph in my head of that roomful of women, and Lee is wearing faded jeans and brown Keds, a long-sleeve plaid shirt — could have been a man's shirt, or at least a boy's, as she sat only as tall as an eleven-year-old — with drab, blonde hair, gathered in a pony tail that was off center. She wrote in a notebook, with some apparent urgency, and when she looked up, I remember having had little reaction to her closed mouth, and her attentive face, remarkable only for its absence of makeup in a meeting room filled with other women manifesting hours of earlier mirror time.

The Thing About Love Is...

I had just concluded a slide presentation of my photo essay on my trip to the Lac Dulambeau Ojibwa Reservation. I do freelance photography. Well, I am trying to make a living doing that, and whatever else I can, which is why I accepted an invitation to speak at the Ironwood Estates Improvement Association meeting. It seems that women are big on Native American culture these days.

I used to write news for a suburban newspaper but switched to what I really love; the loss of a regular salary didn't please Nicole all that much. "You men are all alike," she said, when she realized I wasn't going to change my life back to fit her plans. I tried to tell her this was my calling, that I even think in photographic images; but she dismissed me as "unambitious." Our marriage went bad after that, like garbage that's been standing in the kitchen too long.

"How has your experience changed you?" asked one woman. She had long brown hair — very brushed — a Mickey Mouse sweatshirt, and a pearl necklace.

"I've aged a little." Some laughter.

"Really," I said. "Seeing first-hand the consequences of poverty, corruption, unemployment both saddened and exhausted me."

"What I mean," the Mickey sweatshirt continued, "is your feelings. You know, being around the holy man, for example. Could you feel his spirituality?" She put on a pair of gold, wire-rimmed glasses to look at my response.

"Again, there was some sadness. I was reminded of Karl Marx' dictum about religion. The 'opiate' of the people."

The very next image in my head is a distance shot of Lee in that room, as she looked up from her notebook; then I zoom in on her Hollywood smile and a pair of gleaming, root-beer candy eyes. She rolled those eyes and shook her head, smiling as if she were in on the joke, with her mouth open so that I thought she would laugh out loud. A smooth, turquoise stone, about the size of an almond, hung from a strip of leather around her neck.

"So, Mr. James," she said, in a voice smooth, cold — like milk. "You felt sorry for them."

"Uh, no. Not exactly. Your name is?"

"You felt superior?"

"Not at all."

"Bull*shit*," she said.

Other heads swiveled from her to me, anticipating some drama. She had bowed over the notebook, and I could not tell if she were still smiling. I started to walk across the front of the room in her direction, to try to distinguish her scent amid the gaseous clash of expensive perfumes.

"You just said, let's see, I have it here," she said. "You just indicated that somehow they're fooling themselves with their spiritual beliefs."

Before I had reached her place in the front row, she stood up, stopping my approach. She seemed to look into me, grinning with a closed mouth, rocking slightly from side to side, clearly straining to withhold or, at least, temper her indictment of me. The turquoise stone caught the light, a blue flame at her neck.

"Yes, Miss... Yes. It was a bad analogy, the Marx thing. Didn't do much for Marx, either, as I recall."

She sighed, released my eyes by looking down, and shivered peristaltically. The last action shot of her in my head, reminded me of a perched mourning dove that rises slightly, expands its wings, then shivers, gathering the wings back in tightly. I am not a bird watcher. Sometimes I go with some friends who shoot doves in the fall. Anyway, I thought I had felt that shiver — I felt this warmth inside, some chemical, hormonal reaction.

The mental photograph and her voice stayed in my head. The next day I was able to contact her by trying all the phone num-

The Thing About Love Is...

bers on registration slips from the lecture. I recognized her voice after the eighth call: different on the telephone — clear but with a thick, texture, like Drambouie. She agreed to meet me for lunch near her home.

That's when this thing, this "it" took off. We took turns shedding parts of ourselves — a hat, a scarf, one glove, one truth at a time: her marriage of three years, her childhood in Wisconsin. When she had said her mother had been one-half Ojibwa Indian, my eyes had searched for the turquoise, but saw just the leather necklace — the stone nestled under her shirt. She had said she'd wanted to "go home," to the reservation in Wisconsin, that she felt "fucking disconnected" with all the noise and people and concrete. She said that her Ojibwa gift was that she often knows things which "voices" tell her.

I had told her about me, about my divorce, and I don't remember much else, except her reaction when I had offered that I was a low-key person, a "thirty-three-and-a-third," you might say, while she seemed more of a "seventy-eight." A second's pause, and then her explosion of laughter, alto pitch. She said I was showing my age since no one knew from vinyl records anymore, and an old woman at a nearby table turned and looked at us to quiet down.

I am not in any swoon or anything. She's, well, fun. Of course, it's what I thought I was getting with Nicole ten years ago, too, like that feeling that there's a prize at the end of every day; but I am guarding against being fooled this time.

The only bad part in this is her husband Charles. He drinks. He pushes her. Or pulls her off balance and lets go, so she hurts herself on the furniture. She had to call the police once, but he successfully denied everything. Later he told her she'd have "regrets" if she called again. His suspicions led to his purchase of a Caller-ID device so that I have to make my calls from the pay phone at the Dominick's. Small price to pay for a good lay — 80 cents. I shouldn't say that. She means more than that, I guess.

A wet summer evening following the Dominick's call, in an older, grain-mill town beyond the suburbs. The mud and the farm fields are not visible from Main Street, but their faint ripeness and warmth hang in the air.

"Pick one," she says. Her head tilts upward and coyly to the left, and as the wind blows back her yellow hair, my eyes follow the long graceful ridge of tendon sloping down her neck, ending just above the breastbone. She watches my mouth for an answer, maternally bunches her lips in order to coax mine.

"I see Chinese," I say, "Mexican, Italian, fast food, and, I guess the steakhouse is American, and then that greasy spoon at the end. Any is fine. As long as, well, never mind."

She snarls in mock exasperation at my reticence, steps forward and reaches up to grab the hair on the back of my head.

"Tell me," she says.

Her deep brown eyes search my face. They shine with "what next?" excitement, and, I think, affection. I don't know. I shouldn't count on that.

"As long as there's liquor, is what I meant to say. Wouldn't you like a drink? There'd be none at the fast food or at that "Eat" cafe. Probably none at the Chinese place, either."

"I should have known — forgot about my rummy's needs," and she swats the side of her head with her hand. I am no alcoholic or anything, but Lee claims she "sees" alcohol abuse in my past. The problem with her husband is not mentioned, but it clings to us like mustiness to clothes.

She lowers her hand, and the curve of her forearm could be that of a small child's, and I feel this inexplicable sadness. She's standing right here with me, yet I miss her. It's as if I am lonely for some part I can't get at. I try to remember if this sort of senti-

The Thing About Love Is...

mental stuff happened when dating Nicole, but no prints materialize.

Lee wears an ankle-length cotton dress — Hawaiian flowers — which she calls her hippy dress. It loves her body, caresses the youthful symmetry of her torso, of her school-girl waist, of the soft, sculpted contours of her hips.

She takes a quarter from her small bag, and with a compact, child-like spasm, flips it into the air, the top row of teeth biting her bottom lip as she watches it fall and then roll on the sidewalk. She stops it with a stomping of her foot and laughs at her game. She reminds me of a sparrow, flitting, stopping, on the verge of flight.

"Heads. Mexican. Cervesa for you."

I draw apart from her as we enter the restaurant and am not unhappy that the dining room is empty. I smell nothing cooking; just a whiff of old plaster, and soapy dishwater. A bell rattles above the door as it closes behind us, and although I don't replace my arm around her waist, we effect several gentle collisions on the way to an interior table against the wall. We've not been here before, but it's our regular table.

The waitress is a young Mexican girl, early twenties. She is speaking Spanish on the telephone in front of the cash register. She acknowledges us with her dark eyes, and then they flash briefly through the rectangular window to the kitchen.

"Do you see that, Lee, her smile?"

"What?"

"Not brash. Tender. That's how you talk to a boyfriend. "

"Fuck you, James."

"Oh, don't worry. I'm not your boyfriend."

"You're my sex toy."

The waitress comes over and asks if we're ready to order. Lee is staring at the menu but not reading it. I order a beer and say we

The Thing About Love Is...

need more time for food.

"What is it?' I say.

"Charlie."

"Tell me."

"That's what I like about you. You listen."

She lowers her head and leans forward, so that the blue stone swings away from her throat.

"We had a bad one this morning," she continues. "I told him I made up my mind to go home. He said like hell I was, that I was nuts. That the Reservation was a 'fucking ghetto.'"

I do try to listen, but watching that gemstone bounce about her neck and roll along her skin has me breathing in her smell — lanolin, must be baby oil — and remembering the first time we had sex. I had just brought her a glass of orange juice as she sat in my living room, wearing a red dress with one of those blatant slits in the front, open enough to show her right inner thigh, the color and smooth texture of chocolate malt, disappearing in a slight pucker beneath the elastic of pink panties. Didn't even make it to the bedroom—started in the hallway. I'm kissing her lips, her neck, the cottony skin on her belly; and biting, but not too hard. It's like I want her for herself, even more than just wanting to get off, as it used to be with Nicole. That was after lovemaking got to be some kind of favor she was doing for me.

Lee, while she isn't exactly the dainty type and talks like an ironworker, she's all quiet when we're done, her eyes closed tight with this angelic smile, like a little girl dreaming about Christmas. She knows how to make a man happy.

"I don't know if I like this place," she says suddenly.

She gets "feelings" about places, forebodings triggered by some ominous image, such as a subject's expression in a painting, or the heaviness of the draperies. It's some kind of Indian thing. Places and spirits. I'm not sure. We once had to leave a Chinese restaurant because something told her it must have been built on sacred burial ground since she could hear the restive spirits.

She is looking around the room, the tip of her tongue peeking out of her mouth, tasting the air.

"Do you want to move to another table?" I ask.

She shakes her head, more shiver than shake, squinting her eyes, as if to show that whatever is bothering her will be withstood. She is wearing silver earrings, miniature dream catchers, those circular, sieve-like Indian fetishes that intercept nightmares from violating the sleep of children. The blend of her blonde hair, turquoise necklace and the silver, and her umber eyes that look like the darkest of rubies and I get this flash of one of those Egyptian queens that they'd carry on a pallet.

"We can move to another restaurant," I say. "Another planet, if you like."

"I wish ... I wish," and she holds up both hands and proceeds to grasp fistfuls of air, one hand then the other. "I wish the lights were different. You know?"

"Too bright?"

"That buzzing. Those fucking florescent lights make me insane." She crosses her eyes and sticks out her tongue.

"Do you want a drink?"

"This water is good. But would you quit looking at me that way!"

"Sorry. You look really good today."

"It's just one of those 'good hair days,' all right? And my water weight is low, and I didn't wake up with a zit this morning."

"Oh, my Juliet, you move my heart when you talk so."

"Oh, Christ, don't call me that. Talk about a couple of dopes."

"Us?"

"Romeo and Juliet."

"You didn't finish about Charles."

The Thing About Love Is...

"I did the worst thing you could do to a man, I suppose."

"You lost the sports pages?"

"He told me to sit. To air all my grievances. Anything but the drinking, that is. So I made several complaints. Financial stuff. The house, uh, problems. His temper. Then I told him I needed more than one minute of sex."

"Smart."

"I know. It's bad. I cringed, but he didn't touch me. Just walked out. I dread tonight."

"Stay at my apartment."

"Sure. And tomorrow?"

"Leave him. Next month I'm going to Texas for a project. I'd love to have you along."

"Right. That will solve my problem. You fucking guys are all the same."

"What do you mean?"

"Just get the waitress. Order me a wine. I'm going to pee."

"Goddam kids, that's what does it," said Rich. He's around 75 and is the night manager at the Traveler's Rest. He peers over his bifocals at the pegboard for the No. 11 room key. We have been here dozens of times. It's close to Lee's house, and it's cheap.

"The chain probably just needs readjusting, Rich," I say. "I'll take a look at it."

I am carrying a Hasselblad 501 with a zoom lens, hoping that he'll ask me something about them. I've been wanting to photograph him. The old guy is tall and incredibly straight for his age. He has these steady blue eyes.

I sneak a peek through the window at Lee, waiting in the car in front of the office. She sticks out her tongue when I catch her eye.

"That would be good, Jimmy," says Rich. "I call the plumber in here, it costs five times what those kids, what broke it, what, you know, what they paid."

I hand him money, and he hands me the key.

"I'm only charging you the single rate," he says. He hands me the change and I thank him.

Room 11 has one lamp with a 40-watt bulb that barely illuminates the cigarette burns in the carpet and in the bedspread. The mud-brown rug, imitation walnut paneling and thick scarlet curtains retain a sweet, rancid blend of air freshener and cigarette smoke.

"Home," I say.

We undress and huddle under the sheets, and the scent of her skin — faintly like vanilla, faintly like salt — fills my head.

Somehow she seems new, as if that first time in my hallway, she were someone else. Or I was. She is small like one of those pubescent Olympic gymnasts, but not hard. The graceful curve running from waist to hip to her lean leg is not from body building but from pedigree — her mother had been a dancer, her brother a Triple-A baseball player, her ancestors a tribe of Ojibwa hunters — lean, fast forest predators. But I have to say her most exceptional feature is her ass. I tell her she has a DaVinci ass.

"A physicist couldn't plot a more perfect projection," I say. She smiles slyly and juts it out in an exaggerated fashion.

I kiss her palm, take her forearm ceremoniously with both of my hands. Her skin is a deep tan, as if from a winter weekend in the tropics. I remember Nicole's veins as delicate and purple just beneath the whiteness of her wrist; Lee's are invisible, her blood coursing deep.

My hands, like those of a blind man, re-learn her body. My tongue finds its way in the dark, circling her navel, pushing inside. I hold my hands beneath her.

"I like the way you lick me, sir," she says. "I ought to just chain you down there, chain you to my pussy."

Her pleasure intensifies mine, quickens my breathing. I slide roughly up and over her body, finding my way inside. She pulls the hair on my chest with her teeth.

"Did you ask permission?" she says.

We are in safe darkness, but I can see the teeth in her haughty smile. She enjoys my agitation, like a walleye fisherman's pride in the writhing and twisting of his prize.

"May I, mistress?"

I enter slowly, must resist the biological reaction to come immediately.

She raises her hips to take me deeper, and I hungrily comply, shivering involuntarily from the increased pressure.

"Am I hurting you?" I ask.

"Shut up, please."

There has been this zone between us, a zone that usually separates men and women even when they're together. Like at the restaurant, when we had sat next to each other in the booth, rather than across — hips touching — holding hands, joking, listening to each other's words, and trying to guess what the words could be hiding. But there was that zone, a place of knowing each other truly, that we cannot seem to meet in. Like I'm seeing her image in a mirror, yet when I try to touch her, my finger is ridiculed by the cold hard glass.

But in bed together we seem to break through. We meet in one brain, and I stop pushing to freeze this moment. My mouth is against hers but not kissing. I inhale her breath. We are silent. For a moment I think I know what it feels like to be her — knowing and loving me.

Stupidly, I start to reach for the camera. It's a life segment which I want somehow to save. But such segments defy description with words or logic; you are just in them and then out of

The Thing About Love Is...

them, and they cannot be recreated, only awaited.

The dizzying moment before climax is like the parachutist's pause in the open bay of the airplane. Then we plummet. She cries out softly. Ice cold waves surge improbably upwards from my calves through my chest and into my brain. The free fall is more spiral than vertical, the two of us pushing and pulling in a whirling, dream-like dance.

When I regain my equilibrium enough to look at her, she's bemused by my expression.

"Did I hurt you?" she asks.

"Shut up, please." I kiss her left eye. I lift up to focus my eyes on her face. The turquoise stone has slid just behind her left shoulder.

"We were there, weren't we, Lee?" I say.

"We were somewhere," she says.

I am breathing hard, but I nuzzle my face between her neck and shoulder. With Lee, I don't have that sudden need for space.

"Just a 'piece of ass,' right, James?" she says. She laughs.

Light suddenly outlines the heavy curtain with illumination, and I rise from the bed to look through a slit through the window. She doesn't move. There is no car, but I can see that a cloud has just vacated the front of a three-quarter moon. Lee is also out of the bed and at my side.

I cover the slit and turn, feel for her, hold her a few inches away. In the darkness, I hold my breath. She seems to, too, and we listen to the silence. But I smell her hair — sweet like fruit — and I gather her up. She's warm. Suddenly, a chill passes through my chest, like a slow moving gust of wind.

"Did you feel that?" I ask.

"What?""

"Like someone else is here."

"A spirit, probably. Someone from your side to inquire why I

The Thing About Love Is...

don't trust you."

"You don't?"

"Only so far."

I drive her across the parking lot to her car. Asphalt and lights and engine sounds wake us up to the rest of the world, and we are silent. She kisses me shyly and drives off alone.

I look in the rear-view mirror, and I try to see what Lee sees. Red eyes, shaggy mane. An old horse loathe to leave its range.

As I drive across town, I notice her necklace on the passenger seat. I pick it up and can smell her on it — a fragrance like apricots — must be her hair. At the intersection of Channel and Lake, I remember her address and turn left.

On her block, before I get to the cluster of houses where her number would be, I see a lighted two-storey house with white siding. The light shines from a side window on the first floor. Her car is in front, so I pull over and turn off my lights.

She must be in the kitchen, and I strain to see movement on the first floor. I picture her running water at the sink. Reflexively, I lean forward towards the mirror, but I pull back. For now that my eyes have adjusted to the darkness, I see him standing in the shadow of the living room. Waiting.

Yellow light fills the front window, as she has flicked on the switch on her way in. They are both in my view, and as she tries to walk past him, he grabs her hand and twists her arm.

Through the telephoto lens of the camera I see her cry out in pain, though all I hear is the high-pitched ratcheting of the auto-rewind on the 35 millimeter. He pushes her against the wall, and I click again. Her arm looks very small in his grasp, and now she is shouting back, stops to cry when he pushes her own wrist and his forearm into her chest.

He isn't much taller than she, and he is wearing a brown, long-sleeve shirt. I've yet to see his face but have several shots of his back and of his head with a shiny bald spot, like a Franciscan monk.

I open the car door with my left hand and start to slide out, but she has stopped crying and is saying something with her eyes closed. He twists around, coiling a backhand blow, and I snap two of his dark face just as he strikes her about the head.

I am out and running toward the house — the camera and the turquoise stone both left on the front seat of the car. I try to think of words to use as I ring the bell. But all that come to me in the semi-darkness are black-and-white photos in the morning mist — of the last time I was in Minnesota. I was 8 years old, in the back seat of our car, speeding across the bridge that arches over the Mississippi River.

Vecchio

Richard V. Russo

Of all the tales of Sicilian immigrants in the new land that I heard as a child, playing about and under the tables and chairs while the adults talked, shouted, argued and laughed, there is one in particular that remains lodged vividly in my memory as a dark, malignant and somehow inexplicable horror. I first heard it — first and last heard it, for the story was never, I am sure, repeated outside that one time — on a gray afternoon in late October. I was sitting on the old wooden porch behind the house, vaguely bored, watching the rain which had interrupted my play as it fell on the neat, orderly rows where the tomato plants and squash had been, watching as it disappeared into the dry brown grass, and listening to the irregular rhythm the drops made as they plopped and splat from the roof into small puddles along the edge of the porch. Two of my uncles and a neighbor sat in chairs that creaked, clad in light sweaters or old jackets. They were at home on this dreary weekday because men who worked with shovels and hammers and trowels did not earn their daily bread when the rains fell.

And so they sat, these swarthy, wiry, grizzled men who lived by their sweat and their backs, steeped in the odor of garlic and cigar smoke, men who could not afford the luxury of self-deception, they sat and spoke in subdued voices of the rain, of the new wine fermenting in the cellar, of the dry brown earth, the grape arbor,

The Thing About Love Is...

their work, and of course, of men. And all the while the rain fell, gently, undisturbed by any wind. And when there was a certain lull in the talk, it was my Uncle Salvatore who first noticed the dark figure, almost a silhouette against the ashen, diffusely lit sky, crossing the fields beyond the yard.

"Look," he said softly, barely nodding his chin. "Out there. In the rain. There is a man who has always been a mystery to me. If any man has cause to curse God and hang himself, it is Vecchio. Yet he lives. He lives, and says nothing."

"*Ma che?*" asked Uncle Frank.

Uncle Salvatore said nothing, but kept his eyes fixed on the figure slowly making its way in the rain. Then he dropped his gaze.

"Vecchio's story is a story of earlier days. He lived at the edge of the fields outside town, in a small brick house his father — God rest his soul — had built."

Alone now, with a wife everyone knew about but few ever glimpsed, he had worked with Uncle Salvatore on the new school building. Despite the fact that they had been on the same work crew for several years, Vecchio — he was not then called by that name — had kept a distance between himself and his fellow Sicilians.

"Oh, but understand, he was not unfriendly, or aloof, but somehow different, somehow *estraneo,* not in any remarkable way, but real enough to force you to notice it, little by little. He was always on the fringes of the company of men, on the invisible line between the light and the shadow, which is both but is neither, content, it seemed, to be something less than a participant and real member. He did his job well, though — he could lay a row of bricks as clean and straight as any of us. And if you'd ask him for advice on masonry, for a tool, he would give you what you asked for. But no more, no less, and say nothing if he did not have to. He was solitary, unfathomable, looking out at the world from a place so deep inside himself that no one of us could see or reach or understand. He was a mystery, even though we knew his history. He was a shadow in the brilliant light of day where no shadow could possibly exist.

"But Vecchio's story is also the story of his wife. For years now no one has seen her, except sometimes as a dark figure peering through a crack in the window curtain. She has not left that house for more than forty years, has not known the sun on her face since she was young. But when she was a young woman ... she had, in those days, a reputation as a *malatesta,* a headstrong, willful creature with an eye for any man in long pants. They said she lived alone, on Convent Avenue, near the harbor. Who her people were, when they came to this country, these things no one seemed to know. It was rumored that she came from the north, but her history was murky, like the water in the harbor. But about her, about the things she did, everyone knew the stories, one wilder, more scandalous than the next. Of course, the gossips no doubt exaggerate, but in spite of any lies her reputation was as black as a nun's habit, black as her hair, black as her wild, piercing eyes as deep as the ocean, eyes that were said to swallow men's souls."

She was called, interestingly, Angela.

"Vecchio first saw her, so the story goes, at a dance hall near the docks. He had gone there one Friday evening, dressed in his only suit, poor fellow, his rough hands hanging from his sleeves like artichokes. For most of the night he stood at the bar, watching through the smoke and the noise as the sailors and the merchant seamen went from woman to woman. First this one, now that one, getting drunker and louder, stumbling around the dance floor, fat sweating necks, whiskey breath, hands no longer discreet.

"In the center of it all was Angela, beautiful Angela, shuttled from one to another like some cheap toy, laughing and shrieking, her wild hair flying, her hips moving to encourage the men. And then she saw Vecchio.

"What made her do it, who knows? Perhaps she wanted to make fun of him for her friends, to tease that poor wiry man in an old suit that didn't fit him properly, his artichoke hands. Who knows what moves some people? But when she saw him, so the story goes, she pulled away from the sailors, grabbed Vecchio by the arm, and dragged him into the thick.

"They began to dance, her white hands back of his neck, her arms bare and perfumed. She winked and smiled and stared at him, stared with those wild, hungry eyes. Poor Vecchio, he stumbled along, his boots heavy and clumsy, his artichoke hands on her waist, trying his best not to make a laughing-stock of himself.

"And then it happened, the mysterious way these things do. He was hooked, like a poor dumb fish.

"When the music changed she pushed him away and laughed and went back to the crowd of men. He followed her, grinning like a jackass, and when she saw him she pointed and laughed and the men laughed, and she made an obscene motion with her hips and they all laughed again, she the loudest. Poor Vecchio, red with embarrassment, left the dance floor, pushing his way to the door, and went outside. But he did not go home. He couldn't. That wild thing had swallowed him, and he no longer had a will of his own.

"They say he waited all night for her to come out. And when she and a sailor stumbled through the door he followed them through the dark alleys to her house, and watched as they went in, locking the door behind.

"Who can say what was in his mind as he stood there? What did he want? Was it her body, her eyes, his stolen will, a lost soul?

"Here, more wine. Anyway, to go on, after that Vecchio was at

The Thing About Love Is...

the dance hall every night, watching her. And each night he would follow her home, with roses, or perfume, or gifts he must have starved himself to buy. He offered them like prayers; she took them all. And each time he pressed his question: Would she? And each time she winked and laughed. For months this went on, his gifts, the question, her laughter. And then one day, she said yes.

"They were married on the feast of Saint Anthony that same year, married in the dance hall because Father Pascal denied them the church. He condemned their union, railed against it, even tried to stop it. But it could not be stopped. Vecchio was hooked — swallowed, and Angela ... who knows what she was?

"Vecchio took her to live with him in the house his father had built on the edge of the fields where they live even now. For several months it seemed there was a kind of peace in his world. We saw him each day as he came to work, just as he had done before, and his life had the routine appearance of the normal life of a married man. We watched, expecting to see his face smile, his stomach increase. But we saw nothing like this, like what we had expected. He was as distant and as unreachable as ever. Yet little by little he did begin to change, and we saw that something was wrong. His eyes, which had never been expressive, had never drawn a second glance, were now growing tired and sunken, hollow and dark, like the exhausted eyes of a man near death. No one could say for sure — we did not know it then — but he was being drained of life through his eyes, sucked empty by the wild creature who was now his wife.

"Then, one night, Angela appeared at the dance hall, drinking and dancing wilder than ever. Soon she was there every night, like before. But it was worse now, for she was Vecchio's wife. At first, when he found out where she was going he would go after and wait outside for her to come out, too ashamed, perhaps, to

The Thing About Love Is...

go in after her. They say he tried to talk sense into her. To remind her of what she was now. But she only laughed at him. Then the poor man began to plead with her, his artichoke hands held out to her as if she were a saint. And Angela? She mocked him.

"Finally, something happened, something snapped — who knows what? — but Vecchio was no more what he was. They say he had crazy eyes that night, wild eyes, as he went into the dance hall looking for Angela and elbowed his way through to where she was dancing surrounded by a crowd of drunken, cheering sailors. He stood there, watching, unable to move, watching. And then, above the noise and the whiskey and the sweat, he began to bellow, to bellow like a wounded animal. He kept on and on, louder and louder, until the eyes began to turn toward him. When Angela saw him standing there with his crazy eyes, the awful bellowing, she began to laugh. It was the last time.

"Suddenly, Vecchio stopped making that horrible sound. He grabbed Angela by the wrist and dragged her away from the stunned crowd of men, dragged her outside, into the darkness.

"No one knows for certain what happened then. The police later said there were no witnesses. But the rumors say that he dragged her around to the side of the old building and shoved her to the ground. He stared at her, his crazy eyes. And she glared back, her eyes wild like never before, glared at him with hatred and rage and contempt. And then, Mother of God, she spit in his face. Vecchio, they say, stood there for a moment, her spittle dripping from his chin. Then, with his artichoke hands, he slowly reached into his pocket and pulled out a small glass jar. He unscrewed the top and let it drop. He leaned over toward Angela, who was still glaring at him. And then, with one muttered word, he threw the acid into her face.

"She screamed, they said — people heard it — but by the time anyone came out to see, Vecchio had dragged Angela halfway

The Thing About Love Is...

down the road to his house. One drunken sailor stumbled out and began to lurch after them, but he soon gave up and went back to the music and the lights.

"The next day two policeman went to Vecchio's house — someone must have told them about the screams. He let them come in and sit down, but did not utter a single word, not even when they showed him the jar cover. He just sat and listened to their questions and stared at them with his terrible eyes. One of the policemen tried to talk with Angela, but through a crack in the bedroom door she whispered to them to go away, that everything was as it should be. And so they left, for despite what they might think, there was nothing they could do.

"No one saw Vecchio for some time after that. Then, one day, without warning, he turned up on the job, and everything was as it had been, as if nothing had happened. But there were two differences. Where before he was quiet, now he said nothing, asked nothing, answered nothing. And his eyes, *Jesu*, his eyes. They were dead, like the eyes of a man who has lost his soul. And Angela..."

Uncle Salvatore began to drift, his voice lowering.

"They say she is disfigured beyond recognition, that she has lost the sight of her left eye. For years now no one has seen her, except sometimes as a dark figure peering through a crack in the window curtain. She has not left that house for more than forty years, has not known the sun on her face since she was young."

"Salvatore!"

My aunt's voice shouted to us from inside the house.

"Salvatore, *vene ca! Venite a mangiare!*"

It was time for supper. The figure in the rain had long since disappeared. Slowly the men rose, their chairs creaking. My uncles bade good evening to our neighbor, all saying they hoped they would see the sun tomorrow. Then they gathered up the

The Thing About Love Is...

glasses and went in, the screen door creaking behind them. I stayed sitting where I was, and continued to look at the rain and the brown fields and the puddles. Then, my small body roused by a shudder, I got up and followed the men inside.

Many years later, long after Uncle Salvatore and Uncle Frank had died, longer still after Vecchio and the dark woman had ceased to act out their drama on this earth, I happened to find myself one day, on a return visit to that town where I was born and grew up, walking near the harbor. There wasn't much left of the old waterfront, for the tentacles of time had reached even here. The old piers and tin roofed sheds were being torn down and replaced with modern cargo-handling machines. The old frame houses that had once bulged with ship chandlers' stores and the generous caverns of sail lofts had been demolished. Gleaming glass towers were being raised in their places. A new world was rising on the dust and ashes of the old.

I wandered about for many hours, wandered until evening blanketed the murky water, until I was jolted from my musings when, with a start, I realized where I was. The old wooden building I had been staring at without really seeing, that had somehow miraculously escaped the general destruction, was the dance hall I had heard about many years earlier. In an instant the memory of what I had heard that afternoon on the porch behind the house began to flood my consciousness, and for some strange reason I could not fathom, could not account for, I felt like a pilgrim at journey's end. Unable to contain my curiosity, I went inside.

The room was dimly lit, but I could see there were few people inside — it was early yet. I walked over to the bar and ordered a drink, and I stood there, surveying the room with the kind of frightened awe one feels upon encountering a childhood fantasy in the flesh, watching as the place slowly began to fill. Music

The Thing About Love Is...

started blaring from the jukebox glowing in the corner — the bands had long since disappeared — and couples, mostly sailors and local women — began to move out onto the floor and gyrate wildly. The din grew, and the crowd swelled, and soon the room was shoulder to chest with sweating men and shrieking women.

I lingered at the bar for what must have been hours, drinking, watching, held by the spectacle, when I was dimly pricked by the realization of how long I had been there. And so I was about to order one last drink when I noticed in a corner of the dance floor a crowd of men surrounding a young and beautiful woman. She was being flung from one to another, her wild hair flying, her hips pawed by their drunken hands, teasing them with her laughter. A small shock of recognition and fear kicked at my groin and began to shudder up my spine. For an instant I stood transfixed, like a spectator at a ritual. And then, against my will, I craned my neck for a better glimpse of that wildly moving figure.

It would have been better if I had not done so, for to this day I am haunted by what happened. The woman, who had been oblivious to everything except the men around her, suddenly caught my eye. She stopped moving, and stared at me as if in puzzled recognition. And then she smiled, smiled at me with her wild eyes, eyes as deep as the ocean. I froze in cold terror, for now I knew. She pulled away from the crowd of men and began walking toward me, her eyes fixed on mine, smiling.

How I was able to do it, I have never known. Perhaps it was the crash of the glass as it slipped from my hand and shattered on the floor. But somehow I broke my gaze. I knew I would not have another chance. With no other thought than to flee, I pushed through the crowd, making my escape at the door, and began to run, my fear faster than my legs. I was running for my life.

Here, more wine. Just one more thing, the strangest of all. I remember having an hallucination as I ran, no doubt caused by

The Thing About Love Is...

the whiskey and the running and my confused imagination. I thought I heard in the distance behind me as I ran a faint and beautiful laughter. And then a voice — the same voice. It called out a name, a name I knew as I know my own. It called again, and then there was silence, no sound except the sound of my own harsh breathing.

But come, let us go inside. The wife calls us in to supper. And you, nephew. Come. No, the rain has not stopped. Perhaps tomorrow the weather will be better.

Insurance

Scott Mintzer

I had the strangest dream last night. The Devil appeared, and told me he would make me famous. But there was a catch: I had to die in the process.

"So you have to kill me when I become famous?" I asked him. He didn't look like I would have expected: towering, flaming, fiery red, sharp horns, forked tongue. He had the appearance of a young man with a strong jaw and cheekbones, thick dark hair, dark eyes, wearing an Armani suit of the kind my boss's boss wears. He was a handsome devil.

"They're inextricably linked," he said. 'The act that kills you is what makes you famous."

"Don't I have to sell you my soul too? Isn't that the usual deal?"

"No no," he said, "I've got plenty of those. The crop is good. I'm actually doing a favor for my friend Death. We help each other out sometimes. He's a little short these days, what with the drop in smoking and all."

In the dream I tried to take a look around at our surroundings, but I couldn't really see much — just some clouds everywhere. There were no buildings, no other people, not even a landscape or a backdrop; nothing at all for reference. We were in dream-space.

"And if I decide to take you up on this offer," I said, "how will I contact you?"

The Thing About Love Is...

"When you have truly acquiesced," he answered, "I will know." I felt suddenly very chilled, even started shivering, and noticed a cold breeze blowing against me. It was right then that I woke up and realized that Matilda had once again tugged the entire blanket over to her side of the bed.

"Tildy," I say. She is sitting up in bed, reading Danielle Steel.

"Hmm." She does not look over at me.

"Tildy, I had a very frightening dream."

"I never remember my dreams," she says.

"I saw the Devil."

"Tell him to pick up the dry cleaning on his way home from work," she says. She turns a page.

Getting up each day is hard, but the morning shower is my privileged time — to forget my worries, to think about nothing at all. Hot water pelts my sore back, steam rises in great clouds, and everywhere around there are white tiles, blue curtain, pale soap bubbles that slither and burst. Everything slides down the drain in the end, all except the scum that gathers on the slopes of the tub, looking somehow like it belongs there. Every so often Matilda gets irked and attacks it with a scrub brush. I miss it when it's gone.

Then I shave, confront my own face of fifty-five years: hawk nose, narrow eyes, cheeks like road maps, chin like a pointed star. I have to chuckle; because even more than my father I resemble great uncle Murray, Murray the criminal, the womanizer, alcoholic. The traitor to the faith. What on earth am I doing with his face, Murray the great Jewish gangster? I am nothing but a little *pischer* in a big pond.

Murray was big. Every exploit of his was reported in the newspapers, became the source of my family's greatest shame. They used to speak of him and shake their heads, though it looked like

The Thing About Love Is...

they felt good to shake their heads about him, because every Jew needs something to feel guilty about, right? But then it came out that in order to convince the aldermen to overlook his questionable business dealings, he was giving a large donation toward the construction of the Church of St. Mary the Divine, and that was the last straw. Racketeering, numbers, protection, this was one thing; building a church was unforgivable. Overnight his name disappeared from conversation. Nobody acknowledged that he existed. I was young enough to be ignorant, but old enough to figure out that I shouldn't ask any questions. The only one who would ever mention him after that was my cousin Sheldon, the taxi driver, a tall, gaunt man who had brown-stained fingertips from chain-smoking and looked twenty years older than he was when we ended up alone at a table at a family wedding. I remember him tapping his cigarette on the table and saying, "They all hate him."

"Who?" I asked.

"Your uncle Murray. They all hate him." I pulled uncomfortably at the cuffs of my teenager's suit jacket. I was not used to wearing one. "They all treat him like shit. But the truth is, they're jealous of him, Jake. And you know why? 'Cause everybody in this city knows his name."

I sell insurance. Commercial, mostly small business. I do a lot of road work, visiting the customers, selling on-site. It pays the bills. I am no hypocrite, either; I own a good deal of what I sell. Insurance on the house we live in, even though it is more space than we need since David went off to college ten years ago. Insurance for my health, to guard against the rupture of my appendix, cancer in my prostate. Insurance on my life, and Matilda's. Insurance on the car that I drive downtown everyday to sell insurance. Insurance on the jewelry that Tildy keeps in the

The Thing About Love Is...

velvet storage box on her dresser, gold-and-ruby stuff that she puts on once a year when Shirley Dubler invites her along on one of her high society functions, then comes back and for a few days doesn't feel much like talking. I don't press the issue.

It's a basic April day — almost warm enough to wear just the jacket and tie, but still a little blustery. On the way out I grab my lightweight overcoat, and throw it in the back seat of the Oldsmobile. It's dark green, not a flashy car, but it gets me there. Really, it handles pretty well for an eight-year-old machine. Some other men my age drive Cadillacs, but I can't see what for; they don't look or handle a bit better than this car, the gas mileage is horrendous, and they cost a small fortune. I think it's pure ostentation, nothing more. I'm happy with this car, and I particularly like the color. Every spring I notice how close the color of this car is to that of the trees that lift their leaves up to the sky, as though they were thanking God for something. They are obviously enjoying the season. I wonder if a man can be jealous of a tree.

Business has not been great for me lately, and they've told me that maybe I should try selling insurance in my own neighborhood, but I don't see how I could. The neighborhood is largely one- and two-family houses packed closely together, at the edge of the city limits, a low-middle to middle-class ethnic place. The neighbors are old Jews and Koreans and Indians and Italians, mostly second-generation, some first. It used to be predominantly Jewish before waves of immigrants moved in, and most of our friends, tired of seeing street signs and posters that they couldn't read, of being crowded out of the place that was their home, picked up and *shlepped* out to the suburbs, or to Florida, there to rest in peace. Two years ago, after our best friends, the Schimmels, moved, my wife sulked and said that maybe it was time for us to go too. "You want to leave our home of twenty-five years?" I said. 'Tildy, where would we go? Where else do we

The Thing About Love Is...

belong?" She didn't answer.

The commercial strip is on a major street that leads to the highway, made up of mom-and-pop stores with their own separate awnings: the Jewish tailor stands next to the Korean grocery, and on the other side is a sari shop, and next to that is the Dairy Queen, which is owned by Filipinos. They bear no relation to each other; the owners probably cannot even communicate except for the barest pleasantries. And I am no better; from shopping in the local supermarket I have learned to say "excuse me" in five different languages, but that's about all. Nobody can talk to anybody anymore. I'm feeling very tired this morning, for some reason. But I'm sure I'll be all right.

I slide into a gap on the highway like an egg settling into a carton. It's a nice road; it winds through the northern part of the city, with high-rises and hospitals and other notable buildings around it, including the one I hate that looks like a giant pinball machine, which Matilda thinks is positively breathtaking. Then it winds up along the shoreline downtown. All the cars on the road have their windows closed, their stereos on. I myself never listen to the radio, preferring instead to let my mind wander in the silence. With the windows closed it's as though each car is its own little traveling cell not connected to the world around, not even driving on the same road, because you can't hear anything outside except the noise of the road, and all the other cars hear the same nothing, like one of those nightmares where you see people screaming all around you but nobody makes a sound.

I can't help thinking about that dream. Why did I dream such a thing? In truth, I've been having some upsetting dreams for about a year-and-a-half, ever since my younger sister Ellen got sick. There was one where I went to the cemetery to visit our parents' graves, but I couldn't find them. In the dream it was Fall, and there were brown leaves like a carpet over everything, and all the gray stone slabs looked alike, and I just couldn't find them. Of course, this has nothing to do with real life, you understand; I know exactly how to get to the gravesite. Another time, I dreamed that Ellen was standing at the top of a tall building, one of those downtown high-rises, and she was either threatening to jump, or somebody was about to push her, I couldn't tell which. She had this terrible look on her face, and there was a huge crowd assembled in front of the building, and I was trying desperately to make my way through all the people to save her, I was planning to catch her when she fell, but I couldn't push through all the people, there were too many gathered around. That's how it ended, with me stuck in this huge crowd, not getting there. And in the dream I had the thought that if I were a doctor, I could have saved her. Do you think it's possible, in real life? That I would have realized about that pain in her belly? My parents had wanted me to be a doctor, you know. It was their fervent hope. They bought me books. They used to have my pediatrician give me pep talks when I came for check-ups. I was considered the smart one in the family, the one who would get somewhere. I almost think that they neglected the education of my two younger sisters in their zeal. Then too, they were girls, and in those days girls did not aspire to such heights. They both married young, one to an architect, one to an accountant. Ellen died too young too, may she rest in peace. And I was in no position to help her, having been kept out of the medical profession by poor grades in physics and chemistry. But that was a long, long time ago. I got a business degree instead, went straight into insurance, and have been there ever since. But really, I've done all right.

    The one thing that bothers people about this road is the large number of trucks that ride on it. This is a main thoroughfare for interstate traffic running through the city, so there are always big rigs hauling produce, furniture, machine parts, and anything else

The Thing About Love Is...

that needs transporting, not to mention moving vans, delivery trucks, car-carriers, and other traffic that is not permitted on some of the other roads. I can't decide whether it's the sheer size of them or the thundering noise they make that scares most people. They don't bother me, though. They are good drivers, and they stay in their lanes. For a while the road burrows down to run twenty feet below the street level with the walls made of brick and the buildings and billboards just barely visible over the tops of them, and then as it rises up from its long trench it bears left and comes up along the shoreline, next to skinny city beaches and miles of glinting blue water. It takes a very, very sharp right turn, preceded by some flashing lights, with the sidewall striped yellow and black like a bee; I call this the Big Bend. Then it follows the coast to the towers of downtown. The one where I work is not far from the road; when I get off the exit I drive just a few blocks to a plain blue-grey building, not very different from all the other office buildings except that it has my company's name on it, dip quickly down into the underground garage, and park in my usual space. Other people in suits are doing the same. I don't know any of them. They must be from other departments. Together we walk past the newsstand and the breakfast vendor to the elevator bank, without speaking, and ascend to our respective floors.

In a minute I am at my desk. Bill who has the cubicle adjacent to mine, is already there. "Morning," I say.

"Somebody named Panarelli called for you." Bill and I share a phone line. It is one of the company's latest cost-saving measures.

"Frankie Panarelli," I say, more to myself. "What did he want?"

"He said he wants to cancel."

"Cancel? Why?"

"Didn't say." He turns back to his own desk.

"Damn. Now I need to go see him." I hang up my coat, turn to

The Thing About Love Is...

my own desk. It is small and crowded with papers, a piece of modular office furniture attached to gray fabric partitions with metal edges. I have had many of these over the years; periodically everyone gets moved, to fit someone's idea of an efficient arrangement of personnel. This one is near a window, but the view is only of a building that looks like this one with another company's name on it. The lighting is poor, and the fixtures flicker a lot. In the winter there is a terrible draft. I used to dream of one day getting my own office, with real walls and a big wooden desk and a door I could lock, but I gave up that pleasant notion many years ago. It takes the company a very short time to decide how far you'll go.

"Jesus," Bill says over my shoulder. It is one of those exclamations that is alleged to be to yourself, but is really meant to cause other people to inquire. I turn and actually notice him for the first time this morning: he is wearing blue striped paints, a red shirt, and a polka-dot tie. He is a decent enough fellow, but *oy*, who taught this man to dress? He is one of these men whose wife you actually root for to dress him in the morning. I also notice that, although I assumed he had gotten in early to get things done and would be well into his workload, he is actually reading the newspaper, which perhaps explains in part why he has been in this business about as long as I have and has come about as far. "What?" I oblige him.

"You know that serial killer, the one who raped all those young girls?"

"Yes."

He drops the punchline with satisfied disgust. 'They're bringing out a book of his poetry," he says. He shakes his head.

"Don't know who would want to buy that."

"The publisher can't keep up with all the stores' orders." He shakes his head again. "These people are sick fucks." There is a

The Thing About Love Is...

silence while he waits for my reply, but I have nothing to say. I am tired, and my belly hurts. So he goes on. "Guess the guy's famous now, so he's a commodity. Maybe that's the business I should be in. Selling poetry from psychos. Guaranteed money, long as you hitch your wagon to a star."

I am thinking about that dream again. Really, I am disturbed to have had such a dream. I have been a good man, worked hard all my life, supported my wife and son, respected my parents, stood by my sister in her time of illness. So what have I done in my life to deserve a visitation from the Devil? Or maybe it wasn't any evil of mine; maybe he came to me because he thought I might take him up on the offer. Though really this is foolishness, because a man's dreams are the product of his own mind, no matter how strange. But that would mean that I thought I might take him up on the offer, which is even more disturbing. Who would make a deal like that? Some *meshuganeh* who watches too many talk shows, who'd gladly confess to being a wife-beating vampire just to be on TV for ten minutes, that's who. I cannot understand this fascination with being famous. I think it's all about money, really; if you're famous then you must have money, or else you can sell a book of poetry and make money, so people are interested in you. Then you have to put up with being snooped on by those *shmata* tabloids Matilda reads, while they make up stories about your weight problems and your illegitimate children. It is not all glamour. And I think I know something of what I say, because in my humdrum life I have met several famous people, believe it or not.

Once I was checking luggage at the airport and who should be ahead of me in line but Lefty McConnell, the pitcher. Now since you may not be a big baseball fan, I'll inform you that this is one of the finest pitchers in the game I am talking about, and a local product too; he's at the peak of his career, and is widely felt to be

The Thing About Love Is...

a future Hall of Famer if he keeps it up. When I recognized him a little jolt went through me, just to be standing right next to a real major-leaguer of such stature. In person he looked a little ragged, with a face full of stubble, bushy black mustache, faded baseball cap, and stooped shoulders, as though he had some great burden. He was talking on one of those tiny cellular phones that weigh about three ounces, in hushed tones that I couldn't overhear; when he finished he flipped it closed, slipped it into his back pocket, and stood staring, at nothing. I looked around then, as though I were expecting cameras, reporters, lights, fans — something to mark the occasion. But there was nothing of the kind, of course; nobody seemed to recognize him but me. As it happened I had just seen him pitch on TV a few days before; he threw a good game, but the closer came in in the ninth, let two runners score, and lost it for him. "Tough loss, last time out," I said to him, trying to be friendly. "They're all tough," he said, not even looking back at me, not wanting to be bothered. Then they called him to the counter. He was not a particularly nice man.

The other celebrity I met was Gustav Hinman, the actor from Austria who does all those adventure movies. I was at a basketball game with a friend from work — we were using the company boxes, so the seats were terrific — and there he is, sitting right in front of me and one seat over. He was wearing a sport jacket and slacks and an open-collared shirt, but even still you could tell what a well-built man he was; the shoulders on that jacket were just immense. With him was this absolutely stunning woman: long dark hair, eyes like a cat, perfect red lips. He looked relaxed and happy, enjoying himself, paying more attention to the woman than to the game. Everyone around us kept looking over at them, and for some reason it gave me a gloating, almost prideful feeling, to be sitting closer to them than anyone else, as though in looking at them they must be looking at me too. It

The Thing About Love Is...

even occurred to me that they might show him on camera, and that if they did I would surely be in the picture too; but I checked the screen throughout the game, and they never did. At some point I think he and the woman may have been having a fight; they were pretty quiet, but the tone of their voices was strained, and they seemed to turn away from each other. I wanted to say something to him, something sympathetic maybe, I don't know what, but the only thing I could manage was, "You dropped your program." He reached under the seat to grab it and said, 'Thanks." Nothing to extend the conversation came to mind. They left shortly afterward, midway through the fourth quarter, both looking peevish. I almost wanted to leave with them.

There is a pile of work on my desk. I start sifting through the files, trying to decide what to do first, but nothing seems to focus my attention. I glance around my desk, but there isn't much on it, aside from the work I am ducking: a small digital clock, a coffee mug, a little plastic desk accessory that holds pens, paper clips, rubber bands. In the corner are a few pictures in attached, jointed frames: one of Matilda, one of my son and his wife, and one of my sister Ellen, which I put there over a year ago when she got sick and have yet to remove. I don't believe I have mentioned the cause of her death, which was ovarian cancer. By the time they discovered it the tumor was the size of a grapefruit, and had spread all over the inside of her abdomen. Sometimes, like now, when I look at her picture, or think of her, I can almost feel it myself: a dull ache in my belly, and a feeling of heaviness, of weight burgeoning, pulling me downward. I'm sure it's nothing.

I decide to call David, who works about eight blocks away. I haven't seen him in over a month. I dial his investment banking firm and am connected to his secretary, who tells me that Mr. Kappell is busy at the moment and inquires as to my identity.

"It's his father," I say, and a few moments later he picks up the line. His voice is loud and a little brash, so unlike mine. "Hi Pop. You picked a bad time. I've got a meeting in five minutes. But anyway, how are things? Is something wrong?"

"No, I'm fine."

"How's Mom?"

"She's fine too," I tell him. "What's this meeting about?"

"New deal we're trying to swing. It's big, really big. Major player is attempting a leveraged buyout, and he wants us to finance."

"Who's the major player?"

"Can't tell you, because it's strictly confidential right now, everything's still in the planning stages. But he's very big, a guy you've probably heard of. Every time he breaks wind *The Wall Street Journal* sends a reporter. He's been on the cover of *Money* magazine twice. A major, major player. Pop, are you sure there's nothing wrong?"

"No, I'm fine. Nothing's wrong." Outside the window a siren gets louder, recedes. "I just had quite a dream last night."

"Oh Jesus, not one of those," he says. "I've told you that maybe you ought to see somebody about those."

"Oh, I don't know. This dream was different. Anyway, I'll be all right."

"Look, Pop, you know you haven't been yourself since..." He stops, not wanting to mention it. In the background I can hear shuffling noises, the scratching of a pen on paper. He is a very industrious man, my son. "Corrina thinks maybe you should see somebody too." Corrina is his wife, whose picture sits on my desk: a pretty little *shikse* with a nose like a gumdrop. She is a social worker, works in administration for a big city program. He has done very well for himself.

"It just seems like so much trouble," I tell him. There is an awkward pause that stretches out for several seconds, when neither of us says anything. I hear him open his desk drawer, put something away, close it. Then he is hitting some buttons on his computer keyboard. "How is Corrina?"

"She's okay. A little stressed out since they gave her the orphans' program, on top of everything else she has to do. Freakin' city won't hire enough people to do the work that has to be done."

"She going to continue on?"

"I don't know," he says. "We don't really talk about it much."

"Well maybe if she doesn't, she'll have time for other things." There is a pause. "You know those baby clothes your Aunt Ellen gave us to give to you? We still have them."

"Yes, I remember," he says.

"You guys have been married three years."

"We're trying, Pop." He sounds a little testy. I can hear an adding machine over the line, little clicks and whirs. "But it's tough sometimes, when you have a lot to do at work. We've both been very busy lately."

"I notice," I say. "You're even too busy to talk to me for five minutes without doing work at the same time."

"Look, Pop," he says, and he is angry now, his voice rising with it. "I *told* you I have a big meeting in five minutes. I *have* to be on top of this stuff. I'm not gonna just sit here keeping my head above water. With a job like this there's always tons to do and you have to be working all the time. *That's* how I got here, and I don't intend to stop now, or else I'll end up..." He stops short again. But it's all right, because I know what he was going to say anyway. "I have to go," he says. "Bad time for me to talk. But listen, maybe I'll stop by this weekend? Maybe Sunday morning we'll go for bagels and lox. As long as I'm out in your neck of the woods. Okay?"

"All right," I tell him.

"Give my love to Mom."

The Thing About Love Is...

The employees' kitchenette is not far from my desk, and with the phone no longer pressed tightly to my ear I can hear people laughing there, intoxicated with their morning coffee. I myself have never been a big coffee drinker, preferring to let my energy level take its own course. I drink a lot of coffee only when I really need a boost. The smell is very tempting right now, but I am too worn out to make myself get up to get a cup. "I don't feel so good," I tell Bill.

He looks up from the newspaper that he had been scribbling on — probably doing the Jumble, or the Find-A-Word. He looks me over, as though noticing me for the first time this day. "Yeah, you don't look so good," he says with his usual tact. "Maybe you should go home."

"Can't. Too much to do. And I need to go see Frankie Panarelli now."

He makes a face, the meaning of which is not clear to me, and goes back to his paper. He spends the longest amount of time reading the gossip columns, and the interviews with film stars. He is like a child in many ways, has the bald manner of one, the simple look at life. In early childhood everyone seems larger than life, the entire world is made up of a small circle of people, your family, your schoolmates, the other kids on the block and their parents, and all of them know each other, and you talk about them all with the assurance that everyone knows who you are talking about, so that in a way everyone is famous. When you grow up the circle widens, people at its edge no longer know each other, and so you make small talk from the covers of magazines, from TV interviews, from the lives of people we all know of, as though fame were a language that all of us speak. And it is a language with dirty words too, like Leona Helmsley, or O.J. Simpson. In my childhood the name of the only person in our family with genuine notoriety was profane too, and I knew by

The Thing About Love Is...

instinct that if I spoke it something bad would happen. Even when Murray died, gunned down with a bodyguard while walking his dog, and the newspapers boiled over with gangland speculations, nobody in my circle would mention his name, no one except cousin Sheldon, whom as it happens I ran into a few weeks after the shooting. It was summer and I was eighteen, working the register at a drugstore between school terms, the store was nearly empty, and out of sheer coincidence the customer in my checkout line, waiting to buy a pack of Pall Malls, was cousin Sheldon. He was sincerely glad to see me, in the way that only a person who wouldn't bother to put on an act if he wasn't glad can be. He asked about my plans, and I told him that I was starting college in the Fall. I asked him how the taxi business was going. After a few minutes the conversation flagged, and Sheldon said to me, "He knew it would happen."

"Who?"

"Murray," he said. He opened his newly-purchased pack, crinkling the plastic wrapping. "He knew he was a goner."

"How did he know?"

"He was not a stupid man. He knew what kind of a life he was getting into when he started. It might be this year, next year, maybe it should have been last year. But he knew it had to happen."

"Then why didn't he do something about it?"

He lit the cigarette, took a deep drag. "I don't think he cared," Sheldon said. Then he let out a burst of coughing that rattled in his bony chest and left him short-winded.

"Jesus," Bill says behind me. He has found something else in the newspaper to remark upon. I myself rarely read the paper, as it is full of nothing but bad news, and isn't there enough trouble in life without the paper to bring all that *tsores* right to my eyes?

"You know that German guy, Gustav Hinman, the one who

The Thing About Love Is…

makes all those shoot-'em-up flicks?"

"I've seen him," I say.

"He just signed a deal for his next movie," he says. He stretches out the words for emphasis. "*Te-e-en m-i-i-l*-lion *do-o-ol*-lars. Can you believe that?" He waits for my reply, but I don't feel like having this conversation. I am tired. "Plus, he's getting married, and you should see this girl. They got a picture of her in here. What a looker."

"I've met her," I tell him, but my voice comes out much softer than I expect, and Bill doesn't hear me.

"Who wants to pay to see his movies, anyway? They're all the same. I've seen the last three on cable, and they were all the same."

David, when he was a boy, used to like movies like that. They appealed to the brash part of him, the part that gave him a voice so different from mine, that makes him talk loudly on the phone. He has plenty of his mother in him too, the way he leaves things unsaid. It never matters, though, because I always know what he meant to say. For instance, near the end of our conversation a few minutes ago, he left off in mid-sentence. What he was about to say was: or else I'll end up like you.

"I tell you, that guy's got it made," Bill says, shaking his head. Then he stops, puts the pen in his mouth pensively. "I wonder if he writes poetry."

On the way to Frankie Panarelli's I decide to stop off and get a haircut. Why not? The barbershop is on the way to Frankie's, and anyway, I have the notion somehow that it will make me feel better, might take some weight off my head, so to speak. I have been a customer of Mickey's for quite a long time, long enough that I don't need to tell him how to cut my hair when I come in. He is a customer of mine too: I sold him insurance on his place many

The Thing About Love Is...

years ago. The quote was so low that he couldn't turn it down. It didn't need to be high, though; what's going to happen to a barbershop? There's no physical damage; nothing to start a fire; nobody robs a barbershop; there are no earthquakes or floods around here. Basically the coverage is for vandalism, or some kind of accident. And there's not much to cover either; the only major capital expense to reopen the shop, aside from restoring the room itself, is the barber chairs. And for Mickey that would be a major improvement. His chairs are very, very old. The whole place is very old; in fact, the place looks older than Mickey does. The chairs are a little rusted around the edges. The mirrors facing them are scratched. The wooden counters in front of the mirrors are chipped, and the tonsorial equipment that sits on them — scissors, electric clippers, brushes dipped in baby powder, combs in clear cylinders filled with blue stuff — is largely worn and outdated. The tiles on the floor, white dirtied into gray, are littered with locks of hair in many colors. On the opposite wall are several dull orange plastic chairs, a brown Naugahyde couch that looks like it was evicted from a frat house, and some gouged end tables piled with magazines. Basically it is a place where nothing ever changes, like an old, frail man who figures to be dead the next time he catches a cold, but instead looks exactly the same, year after year, whenever you see him. This can be either comforting or unnerving, depending on what kind of mood you're in.

Mickey is a little guy with a mustache, large ears and a balding head, prone to laughing and idle chatter. He has a peculiar habit, though: he will not converse with you, more than a sentence, until you sit in the chair. I think that maybe he views the talk as part of the service he provides, and feels it unfair to talk to someone standing by while depriving the current customer whose time it most properly is. As a result of this you walk into Mickey's Barbershop, where you have been coming for haircuts for the last

The Thing About Love Is...

ten years, and receive only the barest acknowledgement from the proprietor until your turn comes and you climb into the chair, at which point he talks to you with the endless, familiar, aimless nosiness of an in-law.

"So did you take the wife or the girlfriend?" He asks while snipping the current occupant of the chair, a beefy guy, mess of dark curls for hair, dressed in coveralls, with grease ground into the spaces under his fingernails, clearly a mechanic of some kind.

"The girlfriend," he says. "The wife'd never appreciate nothin' like this. And the seats we had, Mick. Three rows from ringside. You could see the sweat flyin' off their heads every time they threw a punch."

I am glancing through the stack of magazines, mostly *People* and *Sports Illustrated,* but underneath these a few issues of *Cosmopolitan.* I am puzzled by the presence of a women's magazine until I pull out one issue and notice the cleavage of the woman on the cover, at which point I reflect that Mickey is a shrewd little businessman.

"Did she like it?" Mickey asks, while I start reading about the new complexion-enhancing diet.

"Oh, man, she was in heaven. Smilin' at me all night. She couldn't believe it. In the seventh round a piece a King's tape flies offa his glove and lands right in her lap, and she nearly passed out. Held it f'the rest a the night. Says she's gonna sleep with it under her pillow."

"So I guess it paid off to take her then." He pulls out the electric clippers.

"Did it ever, man, 'specially when we got back to her place." They share a hearty laugh, held back in no way by the presence of a third party. "Take her on a nice date an' that girl can go at it like the devil," the mechanic concludes.

I look up from my magazine and there is a man staring in

through the front window, silhouetted in the sunlight. He is a handsome young man with a firm face, jaw and cheekbones that look like they were carved out of marble, dark eyes above these and a shock of dark hair above those. I am jolted to see him; I recognize him from somewhere, but I can't place him. He presses his face up to the glass and raises his hands sideways to ward off the glare, and as his arms go up I see the striped cuffs of his sharp gray suit. He scans the inside of the shop as though trying to decide whether to come in, or as if he were looking for someone. Then he finds me (as I had somehow been afraid that he would), and he stares at me, without blinking. My heart flutters, and a feeling of dread welled up in my chest. His dark eyes seem to leap out of his head, like hot coals. The blood is draining from my face. I feel myself under the force of his gaze being pulled from my seat and sent ... somewhere, I couldn't imagine where. He is staring, and I feel myself sailing away, slipping, *Gott in Himmel*, it is so tempting just to slip away, so warm and soft and earthy and inviting ... when I can no longer stand it my eyes close, and when they open a moment later he is gone and the buzz of Mickey's clippers is deepening to a halt.

"Gave you a scare, didn't I?" Mickey says to his customer. "You thought I was gonna cut it too short."

"Nah, I never worry wit' you, Mick. You'll be cuttin' my hair till I kick the bucket." He gets up from the chair. I realize that I have slid down quite far in mine, and I pull myself up. I do not understand what has just happened. Mickey rings the mechanic up, thanks him for the tip, then dusts off the chair and ushers me in with a big smile. "Step on up to the plate, Jake. How's my old insurance man? How's it hanging?"

"Pretty low," I tell him, climbing into the chair. I feel a little unsteady.

He looks closely at my face. "Jake," he says, "you don't look so good. Is something the matter?"

"No, not really."

He looks at me skeptically. "You been thinking about your sister again?"

"No, it's not that," I tell him. My voice is not strong, and I feel detached from everything, the shop, the world. "I just don't feel too good today."

He stares at me a little more, and then he wraps the bib around me and gets the spray bottle. "How's your son and his wife? They expecting yet?"

"Not yet," I say softly, and there is silence. I sense that Mickey is perturbed, as this is not our usual pattern of engaging, and I recognize that I need to start a conversation to avoid any bad feeling. "Mick," I ask him, "you ever think about being famous?"

He stops cutting for a moment. "Famous?" he asks, and his lips curl up a little, as though I had guessed some secret fantasy. "You mean, like, what would it be like?"

"I mean, like, would you want to be."

"Oh sure I'd want to," he says, and resumes cutting while he talks. "I mean, who wouldn't? See my face on the TV, pictures of my shop in the magazines ... course, I guess I wouldn't have this place no more. I'd have a bigger place, a nicer one. Marble floors or something, paintings on the walls, nice wood for all the counters, maybe a chandelier. Ha! Wouldn't that be a pisser? A barbershop with a chandelier. Then I could prob'ly charge fifty bucks a haircut. And a little nobody like you couldn't even get an appointment." He chuckles.

"Nah, but really. I don't even know if I'd have a shop anymore. Then I wouldn't have to worry about getting new supplies, about cutting enough heads to pay my bills. I could prob'ly just make a living giving interviews, being on talk shows. You know, I heard about this one real famous artist used to drink coffee in this fancy

The Thing About Love Is...

cafe everyday, and instead of paying his bill he would just make some little doodle on a napkin and leave it for the owner. Could you imagine that? If every little thing you laid your hands on was worth thousands of dollars? And there'd be so many things you wouldn't have to worry about anymore, 'cause eveyone would know you, and eveyone'd want to be next to you, be your friend, so's if you ever got into some kinda jam there'd be all these people to help you out. Heck, you prob'ly wouldn't even need insurance anymore, right Jake?"

He gives a hearty laugh. I try to laugh too, but it comes out a weak smile. I am tired and drained, and I am still thinking about the man in the window, trying to recall where I've seen him before, but it will not come.

Mick fills in the silence. "It would be so different. People asking after everywhere you go, everything you do. Looking at you all the time. Though I suppose that's not always such a good thing, everyone knowing your business. Like that actor, whatshisname? The guy's just looking to have some fun for the night with a hooker, no big deal, and then somebody finds out about it and before he knows it he's a laughingstock. And that old movie star, she just locked herself in her house, never went out, never spoke to anyone, never let anyone in. Greta Garbo, that's the one. Lived like a total hermit. Because she couldn't stand the fame, couldn't take all the attention, that's why. Not everybody's cut out for it. I tell you, sure everybody wants to be famous, but it kills your life I think. Sometimes I wonder what these people are really after.

"Like I was saying to the wife last month when we were on our vacation in Niagara Falls ... y'ever been, Jake? It's a beautiful place. You should see it sometime. Anyways, we're lookin' down at all this water coming down so hard on the rocks, and we're reading about all the people who've gone over the falls in a barrel, and Rosie says, 'My God, who would be so crazy, to do something so dangerous just for a little attention?', and I says to her, 'C'mon, Rose, those kids you see on the MTV with the guitars and the long hair, they'll all be dead in ten years with needles sticking out of their arms, is that any different?'"

He pauses to assess the job he's doing on my hair. "But this is a funny conversation. You didn't even say anything about what I would be famous for. Not that it matters any. I mean, famous is famous, right?"

Frankie's Place is in a part of town that used to be very Italian and is now fast becoming less so, in part because others are moving in, and in part because the whole neighborhood is receding, like a wave drawing back from the shore. It feels very empty here. The bar is at the intersection of two residential streets, and for several blocks around there is little but quiet, plain houses needing paint on their walls and children on their porches. Many of them are for sale.

Directly across the street from Frankie's Place is a park, consisting of a weed-strewn grassy field, wooden benches the color of turds, rusted water fountains, an asphalt clearing under two basketball hoops without nets. I park the green Olds in front of it (it seems right; its color matches the worn grass so well), and as I step out of the car that feeling of heaviness rushes into the pit of my belly, so strong it is almost painful, a little nauseating, and a wave of fatigue rolls over me. It is a bit frightening, the way it comes on so suddenly, and I feel sick and nervous at the same time. I manage to slam the car door, stumble up onto the curb and into one of the brown benches that, incongruously, faces away from the park, directly into the large front window of Frankie's bar. There I sit.

Though many people are well accustomed to this sort of thing, I myself have never been good at working while ill; so I breathe

The Thing About Love Is...

deeply and wait for the sick feeling and the *spilkes* to subside. It is still around me, and although it is Spring there are not even bird noises in the air. Through the front window I can see that the bar is empty except for Frankie, wiping off the countertops with a rag. I can recall the inside of the place from the last time I was there. The furnishings are mostly wood, with dull brass edging; the tables have gouges, and the chairs slant toward uneven legs. The floor is hardwood too, but without the luster it once had. The walls are stucco. Covering the walls are autographed pictures of sports figures, mostly baseball players, posing with Frankie. Many of these were taken in the bar, and some on baseball diamonds or at dinner engagements. Frankie had a very brief career as a minor league third baseman, followed by a more prolonged career as a minor league coach. He once had a tryout with the Yankees, which he will tell you within five minutes of meeting you. I, of course, have already heard about it.

It is a little sad, really, seeing a man whose moment of glory lasted three days thirty years ago, watching him wipe the tables with his *shmata* in preparation for the lunch crowd that may never materialize. He has a kitchen in the back that serves food from a small menu: minestrone, garlic bread, a few pastas. He used to run a full-service restaurant in an adjacent room, but as the business dried up he closed it and used the space for storage, since it is accessible from the outside driveway. The door between the two rooms stays locked and they do not communicate. This place has been forever changed by abandonment, may be changing still. Frankie even looks more bald, as though the hair has chosen to abandon his head.

He wants to cancel his policy. I need to talk to him, to get rid of this sick tired feeling so that I can be convincing. I summon my mental energy, gather my arguments. He will tell me he cannot afford insurance anymore. Business is bad, he will say. And I

The Thing About Love Is...

will say, Frankie, you can't afford not to have it. This is a bar, not a barbershop. Things happen here. People get soused. They have fights. They spill things. Somebody spills his beer, slips on it and cracks his skull, and guess who's liable? People do stupid things in bars, Frankie. This place is all wood. One drunken idiot puts his cigarette in the wrong spot and your whole livelihood is up in smoke. And what will you do then? Sit at home and watch "Pride of the Yankees" on videotape? Move to the suburbs or to Florida like the rest of them? Or to Los Angeles, to rub noses with the rich and famous, to see pictures in the magazines of celebrities at dance clubs where the people have decided they would rather be than at a place like yours?

I don't feel very persuasive.

The pain in my stomach has now moved to my head, as though it decided to take a bus uptown. It pulses in my eyes. I close them against the bright day and fall asleep.

In the dream I see Murray. He is seated in a great armchair, in a den of some kind, like the one where Nixon used to have his fireside chats on TV. He wears a grey suit and a fedora, and he holds a cigar with fingers thick as sausages. He looks big, much bigger than I remember seeing him; the shoulders on the suit jacket are the size of the actor Hinman's. He takes a deep drag on the stogie, breathes out a big cloud of smoke, and smiles, like a big, well-dressed teddy bear. "Jake," he says, "good to see you." I know I am dreaming, because in real life Murray and I never met. "Cigar?" he asks, offering me a Cuban from his pocket.

"No thank you."

He replaces it. "One of the fringe benefits of being dead is that I can smoke as many of these as I want. I don't have to worry about cancer, and nobody complains about the smell. So what brings you to my place?"

The Thing About Love Is...

"I came to see you," I tell him, hesitantly. "Because I've heard so much about you. I wanted to meet you. We're kin."

He chuckles. "To you I am little more than kin, and little less than a king." I am confused by this conversation; my understanding was that Murray had no more than an eighth-grade education. "You aren't what I expected," I tell him.

"And what did you expect? A tall, fiery monster with pointy horns and a tail?"

"Last I heard," I say softly, "Jews still didn't have horns."

His face is blank for a moment. Then he bursts out laughing, his body rolling back in the chair, his arms gesturing out widely like a god in an act of creation. "Oh, Jake," he says, pointing at me with the cigar, "you always were such a kidder. You should display it more often than you do. Your humor adds even to heaven."

For some reason his great munificence is getting on my nerves, and his praise does not warm me. How can a dead man be so smug? "You are fortunate to have gained entry to heaven," I tell him. "No doubt a product of your good connections."

"Oh, I had good connections in my time, son," he says with a certain gravity. "I think at some point every man in this town who amounted to anything either owed me a favor or paid me back for one. But that had nothing to do with all this. You talk about my connections as though I don't deserve this."

"Well, with your track record ..." I begin.

"My track record? It's nothing short of superb." He takes a great puff on the cigar. "I was a great benefactor to the community, a good neighbor, admired and respected by all. You should be proud of me, Jake. I can sense that you are, somewhere deep within your heart."

"You spent your life breaking the law."

He smirks. "I just made my own rules from time to time. But

that's what greatness requires. And what else is heaven but a repository for greatness? The people we write articles about, take photographs of, make movies about, follow like lemmings while alive, visit the graves of when dead, and afterward claim to have seen in a Burger King in Kalamazoo, Michigan. *They* have an afterlife, and so make up the population of heaven. The rest make no more impression when they die than a stone dropped in a lake."

"And you are not such a stone?"

"*I* was a great man," he says with indignation. "I had an army of men under me, and an army of women willing to be. I had a stretch of town on the west side that was indisputably mine, never mind who held the ownership papers. People curried my favor like royalty, me, who started out a little Jew-boy from the *shtetl*. The paper had a reporter just to cover me! And when times were good I had more money than God ..."

"And the drinking, the theft, the coercion ..." He does not stop to listen.

"... why, I heard the other day that Geraldo Rivera wants to do a special on me. And he'll have a lot to talk about. You're looking at a man who slept with movie actresses! You should see my gravesite sometime, Jake, see the marble mausoleum erected over me. Liberace is buried right next door, and his is smaller!"

"That isn't the only religious monument you're responsible for."

"Oh, you're not going to pester me with that damn church, are you?" Here his face becomes angry. He emphasizes his point with the cigar. "That church was an absolute political necessity. It was just the way the dice rolled. Besides, they were going to build it anyway. What's one more *goyim*-house to me? And by the way, Rebbi Kappell, I think the last time I saw you in *schul* you still had all your hair."

"At least I'm not a traitor to our faith."

The Thing About Love Is...

"And what exactly *are* you?" he jumps in, now positively wrathful. "Who are you to be admonishing *me*? Some great moral force, some great thinker? You're no better than the rest of that damned family, who made themselves my judge and jury!" His voice becomes progressively louder and louder, climbing toward a shout, as his face looms closer and closer to mine. "And then they all shook their heads about me, bent over a little lower, as though they were suffering for my sins! Is that what you think, you self-righteous little peasant? That just because you disappointed your parents, buried your sister, just because you have a wife who's miles away from you and a son well on the way to it, that you can tell yourself you're suffering for my transgressions?! Well let's not kid ourselves, Jacob, neither one of us is Christian, and we both know that if you suffer for anybody, it's yourself! So can you live with the measly little life you've carved out for yourself, you pathetic little insurance peddler?! And the measly little death that you have in store?! Can you?! Can you?! Aaawoooooooo!!!" Here, with his face inches from mine, he suddenly rears up and lets out a piercing, bestial howl, like a wild animal, a sound that came from something deep and primitive, that sets me to quivering all over and fills me with dread and panic.

I wake up with a start to find that the high-pitched noise in my ears is the whine of a large garbage truck speeding by on the street in front of my bench, and the shivering is from the cold breeze that comes in its wake, blowing in through my open coat. The breeze stings my eyes as it kicks up pebbles, dust and wrappers, the debris of a decrepit city park. Into my lap blows the body of a dead insect. It is small diamond-shaped, and green, the color of my car; it has six legs. The legs stick up stiffly into the air. I stare at it for a moment; it seems to belong there, in my lap. It is my familiar. I get a brief sensation of being pulled away from myself, looking down upon myself, as though I were momentari-

The Thing About Love Is...

ly an omniscient force looking over my own shoulder at me, but it is the insect that is me. I stare self-consciously at the insect that is me. Its body is a dull shade, as though worn down by years of wind gusts. Its tiny, jagged black mouthparts are silent, refusing even to speak bug-words that I would not understand anyway. Its legs are motionless, and rigid as flagpoles. I wait for it to move, hoping, but it does not. It remains completely still. A gust of wind comes then, and blows away my familiar, and I am snapped back into my own consciousness. I look up, see Frankie's Place across the street, and I know that I will not go in. I get into my car and pull away.

I start heading toward the office and another wave of fatigue comes over me, and that feeling of pain and dread in my belly, and I decide finally to go home and call in sick for the rest of the day. It will not matter. Another account lost; this is not new. Bill will have to find someone else to read the entertainment section to. He would have no trouble, I'm sure, if he would just stand in line at the supermarket, or go to a hairdresser and stick his head under one of those *gezuntah* dryer-things. It all makes my stomach hurt.

I pass through Frankie's bleak neighborhood on the way to the coast road. The street widens out to four lanes, dotted by bus stops, and becomes commercial; there are small shops, bakeries and hardware stores, plumbers and pizzerias. Nobody is going in or out. There is a real estate office with whitewashed windows and a sign saying, "For rent. Build to suit." There are plenty of metered parking spaces. There are fat, middle-aged women with shopping bags sitting on benches, and young men with mustaches standing on the corners, cigarettes tucked into T-shirt sleeves, striking poses of masculinity. None of them seems real to me. They feel like mannequins in a Disneyland ride, or extras on a

The Thing About Love Is...

movie set, placed there for the benefit of my attention. I have trouble believing that any of them continue to act, continue to exist, after I drive by. I expect that any moment now they will flip the switch and shut the ride down, or yell "Cut!" and strike the set, pay everybody their twenty bucks each and send them home, and this place will cease to exist, and I will be left alone, in the void, in my car.

The entrance to the highway comes, and for the second time today I slide on, this time into much lighter traffic, as it is not rush hour. The sun is a great cantaloupe in a fruit salad sky of mottled reddish-purple, bluish-gray clouds. The water to my right is the color of steel. There are few other cars around. I think about turning the radio on, then decide to leave it off and let my mind go where it will.

My eyes start to close, and I abruptly snap them open, as much from fear of dreaming as from fear of crashing. I know that many people have trouble sleeping, but I myself had never suffered from insomnia until about a year ago, when Ellen passed away. Now I know its curse, and I am tired all the time. I am not sure whether it is the insomnia that gives me such awful dreams, or the awful dreams that make it difficult to fall asleep, or maybe they are part of the same problem. But with dreams like I've had today, could you fall asleep? I can still see Murray glowering over me, feel his hot breath in my face. Why did I deliberately enrage him so? And that episode in the barbershop, was that a dream too? Everyone has been trying to frighten me today, starting with the Devil this morning. That one's been on my mind all day, in fact. Funny: it was so disturbing to me before, but now it seems less threatening, even comforting a little, like a new friend. It's not such a crazy offer, really. For a younger man it would be too much to give up, but I am no spring chicken, I. I have lived on

The Thing About Love Is...

this earth for over half a century, just missed being drafted for two different wars, seen the Cold War come and go, Neil Armstrong land on the moon, movies go color, television take over. I've seen athletes beat up their wives, actors overdose on drugs, rock stars die in plane crashes. I have seen a lot, really. Enough to know what I think of things. Enough to see the down side of life coming, the failing vision, the stiff joints and fuzzy memory. At this point I'm more of an autumnal turkey than a spring chicken, I would say. But not to worry; I'm in the piece of mind business, and have dutifully provided myself with poultry insurance.

The pain in my stomach is a little better now, but I am still so fatigued that I nearly drift off to sleep while thinking these things. The road is more crowded now, and many trucks have appeared, little ones for local jobs, and some big rigs for distance hauls. The drivers always look so tired. I feel sorry for them. They have hard lives, and have to contend with long hours and sore backs for years and years. I hope their medical coverage is good, at least. They get no recognition in that job, locked up in their little cabs practically for days at a time, anonymous behind a platform of chrome and steel where hardly anyone is even aware of them. Really, is it so crazy to want something more than that? Just to come out from behind a steering wheel or an insurance policy, or a bar counter, that's what I'm speaking of. To wake up every morning and know that there are thousands of people who know you are alive, and that some of them even care. To have an effect on the world, instead of being the one the world makes its dull, gray, clay impression upon. To be the one Bill reads *about*, instead of the one he reads *to*. Wouldn't that be something? Tildy might even notice. And David would talk about me in the office. Wouldn't that be something?

Certainly there would be things that I would miss. The glint of

The Thing About Love Is...

the water in the sunlight on my morning drive. And the smell of falafel from the street in front of this one little Middle Eastern place in my neighborhood that keeps its front door open eight months of the year. And the way my car matches the leaves on the trees in the spring, around this time. The flicker of the menorah on the eighth day of Hanukah, when all nine branches are filled with narrow candles whose flames wriggle with the lightest currents of air, randomly but in perfect synchrony, like tiny dancers in a holiday stage show, that I would miss. The feel of hot water on my tired skin in the morning. I think I would even miss the useless chatter of my barber, that stupid little leprechaun. I know I would miss being a grandfather, knowing my child's children, if he ever has any, seeing the big green eyes of a little bowl-headed boy with skinned knees, or the long brown hair of a little princess in a new dress for her big visit to grandma and grandpa's house. That I would miss deeply. But she would at least have me to talk about when she got old enough to learn, could look at my picture and say, that's my grandpa, he was a famous man, and everybody knew him, and he is a part of my family, and do *you* have any famous relatives? And the other middle school girls would sit respectfully and shake their heads no, which is something, you know, because those middle-school girls are a mighty tough crowd. So it might be worth it. And besides, they would have Tildy, and God knows she could pinch their cheeks and spoil them and annoy their parents enough for the both of us.

And who's to say there wouldn't be plenty of other good things to enjoy in the hereafter? Murray seems to be having quite a nice time of it, I would say, with his Cuban cigars and fine furnishings. He knew what he was doing, the way he lived his life. He made just this decision, really, opted for stature, standing, for notoriety in a dangerous business. He had to know how it would end. It couldn't end any other way, in those circles. But he knew that if he had to live the ant's life, the life of oblivion, one speck in an inseparable mass of billions, that he might as well be dead. And he is. But what a death! They talk about him still years later. And he had the last laugh at the world, too, because there is still in this very city, a building with a plaque bearing his name, his, and not just any building, not a trendy restaurant, or a dreary hospital pavilion, but a Christian house of worship! Our Lady of Murray! The Church of the Sacred Heart of Murray the Yid! Victory for us all! If only the Spanish Inquisitors could see it.

I am north of downtown now, on my way to my home to rest my tired soul, and the traffic is much heavier here. Sedans, trucks and taxis, minivans and motorcycles, all of us in different colors but really just blending together, like jelly beans in a jar. Behind me and one lane to the right is a little red sports car, and looking hard through the rearview mirror I can see the driver, a man with a baseball cap and a bushy mustache, holding a cellular phone in his right hand. Next to him is a clattering school bus filled with children and a driver who looks like she has a splitting headache, and behind them is a massive supermarket truck filled with I can only imagine what, artichoke hearts and band aids, hot sauce and roach traps, things I have no use for. A hundred yards away I can see the Big Bend looming, with its thick walls, blinking lights and brazen stripes. My eyes are watering from trying to hold them open. The image of my parents comes to mind, and my sister, Ellen, and I think of how much I would love to see them again, and so maybe the water in my eyes is from tears, I cannot tell. The clear sky overhead gives way to a sheet of gray clouds further north, and as I watch them approaching me in the high wind I decide that I would take the Devil up on his offer after all.

The pain in my belly disappears, and my vision begins to darken, as though somebody were playing with the contrast knob.

The Thing About Love Is...

The fatigue now is irresistible. I can see the sports car to my right is gaining on me, and it will momentarily be beside me. Behind him the truck still roars, and next to the truck is the school bus, which is easing up for the curve. As we approach that ninety-degree leftward bend I catch the sports car's license plate, which says "LEFTY." That's the last thing I see. It is not the last thing I think of, though, with my lids meeting, and my hands drifting ever-so-slightly to the right, because it occurs to me that I forgot to tell the Devil to pick up my wife's dry cleaning.

Family Album

Freyda Libman

You are there as lovers
in the album collecting dust,
buried quietly under books.

Smiling up at me,
eyes crinkling in the sun,
you defy the daylight
of an endless May
with your round mouths,
your arms entwined,
awaiting the coupling of
your tennis match.

In dishabille, you lean
against a balustrade,
hair ribbon untied,
shirt sleeves rolled,
the shadows on your faces
like the inscrutable script
of Yiddish news.

I rub my fingertip over
your full breasts, mother,

The Thing About Love Is...

over the swell of flesh where I
will sleep until you bid me wake.
I stroke the wavy obsidian of your hair,
father, trace the wire circles
of your glasses in the light.

I know it is rude to stare at
young strangers, at the
careless creases and tiny lines,
at the furrows that spread
across your startled cheeks.

Still my finger smudges the gloss
of your smiles. Half in homage
to your youth, my lips repeat
the ancient Kaddish, mourning
not your death, which has not come,
but the beauty of your bodies
like a bright promise
I once believed.

Finding Momma
Jotham Burrello

The radio was broken. No static, nothing. And I needed a distraction between my ears. Even a sappy love song by the latest one-hit-wonders would have done the trick. I had not seen Momma in fourteen years, and the quiet forced me to tally every Christmas, every birthday, every day I had been away. I now regretted leaving my husband and daughter at the Super 8 in Gallipolis. I have never felt so alone. Like the man on the moon.

I passed Daddy in the town cemetery on Howland Road. The regular dead had flat stones that could be easily mowed over. I wondered if Momma ever visited. I never saw the plot the town assigned him but I'm sure it had a flat stone. Though even if I had known I wouldn't have stopped, maybe before, but not now. Driving by was enough. I could feel the prickling of his heavy beard against my face and smell his Old Spice aftershave inside the rented Hertz. Whenever he wore his blue captain's hat on the river, he'd roll his sleeves up over his Navy tattoos and march in place on the orange Astroturf deck of the fishing boat with his hands on his hips barking out orders. My sister Tammy and I would scurry around coiling ropes and pretend to hoist sails like we were crewmen on that double-masted brig stenciled on the front of his white bottle of Old Spice.

I followed Tammy's directions to the dirt road running along the Kanawha River. The modest homes and wide trailers were

The Thing About Love Is...

nestled in a plush ravine of greenery and wild flowers about ten miles south of where the river bled off the mighty Ohio. Tammy said the man Momma had taken up with, Cyrus Blitz, worked on the barges that needed service before the watery haul down to the Mississippi.

The cluster of homes was more of a neighborhood. Many were trailers, but there is no shame in trailer living in these parts of West Virginia. The majority were canary yellow or robin's-egg blue, faded but tidy, some had jungle gyms out front, others semis. The homes were permanently parked on either side of the water, brown and polluted from factories upriver.

I repeated the number 24 in my head as I rolled by Momma's mailbox. The dirt road dead ended into a huge pile of earth. I turned the ignition off and sat for a moment. The forecast called for light showers so I had worn a yellow slicker and boots. I wished I hadn't. I wanted to arrive unnoticed, not as a sunburst, a laughing stock. More Garbo and less Rosanne.

I walked passed number 24. Cyrus had a canary-yellow trailer. It wasn't as long as some others, but Momma never needed much. White lattice surrounded the concrete foundation. There was one of those shiny metallic satellite dishes poking off the backside like a beak. I was surprised by the dog run latched between two oak trees; we were never allowed pets. Behind the trailer the river ran low and green grass poked through cracks in the newly beached brown rocks. I walked to the end of the road, passed two trailers and a weathered A-frame, then turned back. On the side of the trailer three sunflower windmills, each about two feet high, spun around atop a mound of topsoil. I wasn't ready yet. Thunder cracked off in the distance, and it began to sprinkle. I pulled up my yellow hood and went back to the car and reclined the seat.

My Daddy spent half his savings on a new eight-millimeter

The Thing About Love Is...

film camera the month I was born. From Day One I was immortal. I thought most of those old movies were sold with the old place, but then a few months ago when Robert and I were packing for our move to the suburbs, Sally found some of the reels with Daddy's meticulous handwritten labels. (I had forgotten I'd taken them with me when I left.) We rented a projector from the library and watched them against a cement wall in our basement. Sally wanted to watch my seventh birthday first because she had just had one herself. She wanted to see if my Barbie doll had a pink Fred Flintstone type car back in the Stone Age.

The old film flickered like moths in a summer porch light. A fine dust on the lens sent jittery black lines over our polyester jumpers, long straight hair, and high, white, fake leather boots. We watched two reels before seeing Momma. When she came on, Robert, eyes riveted to the wall, slid Sally off his lap and walked toward the screen. He had never seen her. The same red hair and freckles he said, and pointed at the wall and back to me.

"She's pretty, Jos," Robert continued, now blocking the majority of the picture. "That's your grandma, Sally." He turned toward her and the picture played across his chest. The people looked warped like in a fun house mirror; their faces out of focus with five and six chins.

"You're in the way," Sally said with a huff and folded her arms across her chest.

Momma was cutting birthday cake in the kitchen. The film looked slightly overexposed like the first two reels. She had on a scoop-neck white jumper with a pink flower pin on the left shoulder. Her fire-engine-red hair looped down her back. She squinted under the hot lights mounted on top of the camera and waved her hand to stop filming. My party guests ran behind her out of focus, fuzzy heads with blue and green plastic barrettes tacked to them swung in and out of the kitchen doorway.

The Thing About Love Is...

Suddenly, the camera fell on a diagonal, and I saw Daddy's hand come up from the bottom of the frame as he smacked Momma's behind with a yardstick — one of the old thick ones from his woodshop. Her knuckles jerked into the cake. She turned and waved the knife at him. Her lips twisted into a queer smile I had never seen. When the camera swung back straight, she turned to continue cutting but with her free hand now guarding her behind. Then the camera fell off kilter again and the yardstick rapped Momma. She dropped the knife and walked toward the camera. I read the word sonofabitch form on her lips before the camera swerved down wildly and cut to black. The picture returned a second later with my little girlfriends kneeling around our old brown couch. I stopped watching the washed-out light on the wall. It was all too real, seeing a childhood I had locked out of my mind. I rolled an imaginary ball under my foot till the end and went to bed. I found out the next morning Sally had fallen asleep in her bean-bag chair as Robert finished the remaining twelve reels.

The next weekend Robert lied about a leak in the basement to get me back down to our makeshift theater. I had watched the old reels before to quiet Sally, who by now had already forgotten they existed. Robert knew how difficult it was for me to see my father, but he insisted on showing some selected shots of my childhood.

Because of our pending move the basement was empty except for the projector and two metal folding chairs. I sat on my hands. The birthday scene played twice. I watched with one eye closed, assigning sound to Momma's silent words.

"Watch your mother here," Robert said during our third run through. He stood behind me with his hands on my shoulders. "Watch her holding her back. Right there!" He ran up to the screen, blocking all of the picture except Momma. It was as if he were standing next to her.

"She's supporting herself on that girl's chair." He pointed. The shadow from his index finger consumed three heads. "And her other hand is clutching her back."

She looked tired from preparing the party, like she usually did at the end of a long day. There wasn't much money around, and she did all the chores and worked part-time at the A&P.

"Her eyes," he continued, "they weren't puffy like that before. And the light sort of glistens off them."

"That was what the woman looked like," I said, "she had some terrible allergies."

He quickly rewound the film to the cake cutting scene. As it rolled he walked back to the wall. I watched between my fingers.

"See, no bags here." He tapped the image with a pencil. "Now this all could be exhaustion or allergies, I suppose," he said, "but watch this." I couldn't sit still; the metal chair squeaked. My bare feet warm on the cement floor.

"Now honey," Robert began and knelt in front of me. The pencil tucked behind his ear. He took my hands away from my face and cupped them to his chest. "Watch the next piece. It's right after the cake-cutting scene where your mother got hit on the butt. The camera will pan past you opening presents, but look closely over the little girl's shoulder on your left, look into the trash can in the kitchen." He narrated the action. "There you are, opening some sort of doll, and now here goes the camera, moving, moving..."

The camera trucked passed a little girl in an orange dress, stopped, then turned back the other way.

"Did you see it?" Robert asked. He rapped the pencil against the wall.

"See what?" I snapped, growing more irritated. "I'm not enjoying your little game."

The Thing About Love Is...

"Let me play it once more. Stand up here with me. I'll put my finger on it."

Again the camera panned across the party scene to the girl in the orange dress.

"There!" Robert said jabbing his finger against the wall. I saw it. Sticking out of the trash can were the two broken halves of my Daddy's yardstick.

We watched the old films until three that morning. My arrival home from the hospital to Tammy's eleventh birthday, just a few months before Daddy's fall. Robert kept backing up the film, forcing me to watch. He had unraveled another tragedy of my family, pointing out the clues of my parents' violent relationship. Their marriage had seemed like others I knew, but I suppose I had pretended they loved one another. Robert catalogued the domestic abuse at each event my father had thought worth filming: Momma's limp at Tammy's second birthday party, the bruises on the back of her arms at the Charleston boat show, her swollen nose and heavily made-up eyes at the Bryan Park Easter egg hunt, and the whipping scars, probably from a leather belt, Robert said, that ran up the backs of her legs like rungs on a ladder. Momma had played them off as sunburn every summer at the county fair.

The films made a lie out of my life, made me doubt the reliability of my own memory. Everything I had said and done to justify my leaving home became a joke.

I was physically ill for more than a week and lost ten pounds. I spent my mornings crying in front of the film projector and my afternoons in bed, watching soaps without seeing, thinking of what I hadn't noticed all those years, thinking of all the lies I had been told. The destructive side of my father had always been shielded from my sister and me, and Momma had hidden her pain. During the seventeen years I lived with her, I was as blind

The Thing About Love Is...

as she was dumb.

Sitting at the wheel of my rent-a-car, the rain slowly chipping away at the mound of dirt facing me, I wondered how Momma knew that I would lie to the police about the accident. She had looked at me differently during the questioning, so full of aplomb, and quick with a satisfied smile and reassuring wink like we had a secret, a bond between us that no jury would understand. During the investigation she told us that we would get along fine without a man around. They're only good for fetching high dishes and hauling trash, she'd say and pinch our cheeks.

But I lied for Tammy, not Momma. I didn't want my baby sister to be a latch-key kid, a foster-care runaway. So when they put me in that white sound-proof room, and the policewoman asked how Daddy had fallen, I told her that I had waxed the cellar stairs just that morning. Too slick for even a cat, I said. I didn't tell her how I saw Momma drive her broom handle into the small of his back. The cops believed our story and I ran away four days after his tumble.

I walked back to number 24 and rang the bell. The door had dents in it like it had been beaten with a rubber mallet. I heard a television and a man's voice followed by heavy footsteps. The door opened. It was Momma's new man, Cyrus. He held a torn knot of bread in his hand.

"Whatda'ya want?" Cyrus said, as if he had marbles in his mouth. "Cuz I got enough of them Girl Scout cookies from last year." He chewed a wad of bread, his large mouth rotating around like a bull.

"Momma?" I said passed him into the trailer.

"Huh?" he grunted as he took another stab at the bread.

I cleared my throat, "Is Alice here?"

He hunched down and poked his stubby finger around the rim

The Thing About Love Is...

of my drooping yellow hood. It smelled of grease and borax. He stopped chewing. I gave him a sheepish smile and he leaned back in the doorway and wiped the rainwater down his leg. He was a big, bearded man, barrel-chested with blue trousers held up by a tarnished copper belt buckle. It read Evinrude and was in the shape of an outboard motor. Two-Hundred Horses, it proclaimed.

"She's here," he said coarsely, as if annoyed a person would come to his house asking for someone besides himself. I heard a toilet flush, followed by the scampering of many feet. A gray German shepherd ran by Cyrus catching him behind the knee. His mighty belly cast him forward into the door frame. The dog stopped before me and growled.

"Damn it, Duke," Cyrus hollered, then began to choke, but not before kicking Duke's hind leg. The dog yelped and ran back into the house. Cyrus stood up too straight like he had a board up his shirt and pounded the hole in his white tee-shirt to dislodge the bread.

"Gosh darn, Cyrus, you bucket-head," Momma said loudly, "that's what ya get for nipping at cooling bread." She passed over me with a quick nod and turned to Cyrus. She slapped his back with her open palm. She wore a white apron over a red t-shirt and gray slacks.

Cyrus gagged as his esophagus opened and his cheeks blew out like a couple of spinnakers. He started chewing again and shooed her hands off of him.

"Damn it, woman," Cyrus said.

"Gimme that." She swiped the bread from his paw. Cyrus frowned and disappeared into the darkness. Momma watched him go and sighed heavily. I recognized the pose, the shoulders a little more round and the arms slightly more bony but still the same. She ran her hand over her short hair. It was cut down like a celery root with the stalks loped off. She curled her finger around a damp red wisp stuck behind her ear, then slumped down ever so slightly as if a tiny battle had been won.

"Momma," I whispered and touched her shoulder. She stood up straight. "It's me, Josie."

There was a pause. I heard the rain running down the aluminum gutters. She stepped forward out of my grip. "Whatda'ya doing back in these parts?"

"I came to see you."

"Thought you'd had enough of me."

"Will you look at me?"

"I remember ya. That sweet freckled face could make a catfish wanna walk outta water."

"Please, Momma ... please." I stepped under the short aluminum awning. She turned around slowly and stepped back into the trailer, her arms at her sides. Duke sneaked up behind her and ate the bread out of her hand, then forced his nose into her palm. She clamped her fingers around the dog's snout. The tendons in her arm flexed as she tightened her grip. Duke jerked his head side-to-side. His collar rattled.

"Never thought you'd have one of those," I said and nodded toward the dog.

"That was your father." She released Duke and he scampered away.

"And your hair. It's so short, I remember—"

"I hated it long."

I started to speak but stopped. I had an unfair advantage, and I waited for her to catch up. I had been rehearsing what I'd say and how I'd move for two months. She'd had two minutes.

"Can I come in? Just for a minute?" I said and stepped forward. "I want to show you something." She shrugged and threw her hands in the air as if she didn't care if I came in or dropped dead

The Thing About Love Is...

in her petunias.

The trailer had four sliding windows facing the road. Each was slightly ajar and the breeze pushed through the faint smell of wet mud from the river bank. Drops of rain pooled on the metal sills. There was a couch, coffee table, doggie bed, worn leather recliner which I could imagine Cyrus sleeping in, and a book case full of playing cards, photos of Tammy and her girls, mechanic manuals, romance novels and snow domes with captions like, *Newport News Shipyard, Daytona 500* and *Old Iron Sides*. I heard a refrigerator door open followed by the pressurized snap of a beer or soda tab.

"Be right back," Momma said and walked around to the kitchen on the other side of the wood paneled wall. The TV volume suddenly went up, and I heard her talking to Cyrus, though couldn't make out a word over a baseball announcer's fiery voice. She came back a minute later. She smelled like pot roast. She held two glasses of iced tea, both had spoons. The brown water swirled. Fine crystals of sugar gently fell to the bottom of my glass.

"Thanks," I said and took a sip. She clanged her spoon, wiped it down her apron and gently placed it on the glass coffee table.

"I like your place," I said, somewhat at a loss of where to go. My rehearsals in front of the bathroom mirror never got passed the front door.

Momma looked up from her tea and paused. Her blue eyes were a cleaner version of mine, which had a hint of my Daddy's green. "So whatda'ya got to show me?" she asked.

"Well Momma, I got married."

"I saw the ring."

I had turned the diamond around, but it had surfaced back into the light. "Nice piece," she said, "who'd ya marry? A doc?"

"Robert is a salesman," I said.

The Thing About Love Is...

"Of what?" She said quickly, "Gold mines?"

"No, microchips."

"Same thing now-a-days." She took a long sip from her tea. She didn't wear any jewelry. Thunder cracked outside and we both looked toward the window.

"I work for a radio station," I said, "in promotions."

"You the one that sets up those DJs at shopping malls and Shoe Carnival openings?"

"Among other things."

"I listen to the news shows on my clock radio, catch Limbaugh sometimes."

"You like what he says?"

"It's just entertainment, Missy," she said slowly and shook her head heavily like she did when I brought home a report card full of Cs. "So whatda'ya gotta show me. Got a roast cooking, you know."

I took out a picture of Sally from the top pocket of the rain slicker and handed it to her. She took it out of my hand as if she'd been expecting nothing less. She looked up at me then back to the picture and frowned.

"So Bob has got 'im a big Jew nose!"

"Momma," I said and laughed.

"Sally Ford Stein," she said and met my stare. Ford was my Daddy's middle name. "Ya live in Chicago, little girl is in the third grade. Tammy tells me the important stuff."

"But—"

"She promised ya she'd keep quiet, right? Well that Tammy's a talker. Whatever ya write in them letters leaks outta her mouth under the curlers down at Sissy's. You remember Sissy, don'tcha?"

She went on to recall our recent move to the suburbs and talked about how Sally found her new gym teacher, Mr. Fletcher kind of weird with the girls. Her voice was bland; her body

The Thing About Love Is...

relaxed. It was as if she were giving a school report, saying what she needed for a passing grade but not retaining a word.

I stopped listening after a while and thought about the films. The room darkened as the rain fell a little harder and in a dim nook, below the far window, I imagined I saw her waving the frosted knife at my father. After a few minutes I cut off her rambling.

"Momma, do you remember my seventh birthday?"

"Hell, that was twenty-five years ago, Missy," she said slouching back into the couch. "I'm an old widow now." Her voice trailing off. "Waiting for my maker."

"Don't say that."

"It's true." She looked down at Sally's picture resting on her knee.

I wondered if she saw my Daddy's smile. Or if Sally's blue dress reminded her of the one I had worn minus the white lace around the cuffs and neck. I wanted to tell her that Sally's gummy smile was no more, that her two front teeth had grown in straight. And finally, I don't know why, but I wanted to apologize for the hair. She probably noticed that first. My red and Robert's black had made caramel brown.

After a few minutes I said, "Well then do you remember our trip to Virginia Beach when I was fifteen?" I pulled my hair out from under my yellow slicker. I parted it in the middle, wound each half around my fingers and pulled the strands down over my shoulders in makeshift braids like I had worn them that summer. "Remember the camp site we stayed at by the beach? We rented that camper that smelled like moth balls and cigarettes."

"What about it?" She said looking up at me. "Tammy got sun poisoning on her face, and you balled your stuffing out over some dope-smoking lifeguard."

"So you remember?"

The Thing About Love Is...

"Where ya going with this, Missy? You know I'm not one for family reunions and such."

"How about the shower in the camper," I said, "do you remember that?"

"I don't remember no shower," she snapped.

"Sure you do," I said, "the one with the really hot water. The one that burned you."

"Whatcha getting at?"

"It's okay, Momma," I said and inched down the couch until our knees touched.

"Smell that?" She turned her head toward the kitchen and stuck her nose in the air. "Think my roast is burning."

"Smells fine to me."

"Nope," she said sniffing the air. "It's burning." She started to stand but I placed my hand on her shoulder. She didn't resist. Slowly we faced one another.

"It's okay, Momma," I said, "I know all about it now."

She made a start to speak, then looked down at her tea and rubbed her thumb in her palm. Her shoulders fell as if someone had deflated them, and I knew the memories had returned from that dark space within her. For seventeen years of my life she had endured Father's beatings. I hated to stir the demons, but unless I did, she would never know that I was sorry for banishing her from my life. That I now understood our secret bond.

I placed her left hand in mine and ran my fingers over the three purple scars that bubbled up across her palm.

"Momma," I said softly. The both of us looked down at the scars nestled in her hand. "I know now the water wasn't that hot in the shower." I paused and lifted her chin. After a minute I said, "Only the grate on top of the grill was that hot." Her wrist went limp. Her freckles shining brightly on her paling skin. She crossed her arms over her chest and shook like a child stepping

The Thing About Love Is...

out of a cool bath. I wrapped my arms around her.

A glass crashed in the kitchen, followed by the sloshing of water. I heard Cyrus cuss. He and Duke walked around the corner a moment later. Their were feet wet. Cyrus wore a Boston Red Sox hat with the corners of the bill curved so far around his face the edges almost touched. He held another piece of steamy bread. The dog licked flakes from the floor.

"She awright?" He asked.

"In a minute," I said.

"Is the beef ready?" He pointed at Momma. "Ask her if the beef's ready."

"It's ready," I whispered and placed my cheek on her shoulder. "The beef is ready."

Cyrus took another jab at the bread. "You can stay if ya like," he grunted, "but there ain't enough for three." As he turned back into the kitchen with the dog sniffing his fist full of crumbs, the television erupted in cheers as Mo Vaughn clubbed one over the Green Monster. Through the announcer's jubilation, I heard the oven door whine open and immediately smelled the sweet baked beef.

The Barbecue

Janice Tuck Lively

Everybody was twisting — grown folks and children alike. Even Aunt Mary, who was seventy years old and too old to twist, twisted. It was September, the last barbeque of the summer, and the sound of Chubby Checker wailing, "Come on baby, let's do the twist," filled the air.

If Bacchus was the god of revelry, then the washtub grills were his altars. The smell of crackling hickory and cherry wood roasting pork ribs, chicken and possums smothered in spicy honey and beer-flavored barbeque sauce rose from the huge homemade washtub grills in a fragrant cloud that hovered in the air like a big gray canopy and scented our hair, clothes, and skin. All eyes watched and waited for the tubs, through the power of fire and smoke, to transform their offerings into finger-licking, bone-sucking, face-diving, grease-flying, tasty barbeque. Laughter and loud voices mingled with the smoke as Mary's homebrew, made in her very own basement, was passed around in quart mason jars. Children were never allowed to drink the strong homebrew; we settled for soda pop and kool-aid instead.

While the grown folks laughed, ate, drank, danced, swapped stories and — as my grandmother would say, told lots of lies — the children played games and wandered invisibly in and out of their conversations like small garter snakes in tall green gypsy

The Thing About Love Is...

grass. We lingered close by waiting for the time to come when the grown folks had drank enough homebrew. Then they would pay us pennies or nickels to come dance or sing for them. Then center stage was ours as well as the nickels and pennies. If we performed real well, we were also given extra bowls of homemade ice cream that had been hand-cranked in a big wooden tub surrounded by rock salt and ice. The men took turns at the heavy crank churning the ice cream as they told stories and played the "dozens" with one another. Their stories and laughter drifted out of their throats in deep husky tones, while Lucky Strike cigarettes hung from their thick plum or pecan colored lips.

Mr. Ellis, who worked at the plant with my grandfather, was at the barbeque. He had left the laughter and conversation with the men and was sitting off in the garage by himself, surrounded by a group of small children. Mr. Ellis was usually surrounded by children. He always had time to spare for us and seemed to like playing with us, especially the little girls. He tickled us and let us sit on his lap, like a thin brown Santa Claus, while he told us stories. You felt special if you were the one he chose to sit on his lap. Mr. Ellis would take us for rides on his back, bouncing us as he walked, or perch us high up on his tall shoulders so we could see everything, as our small brown legs dangled against his chest. He never seemed to mind or say that we were too heavy. Some times he gave us nickels afterwards. I didn't like being tickled and I only sat on my daddy's or granddaddy's lap. Usually, I just sat on the ground and listened to Mr. Ellis's stories and watched him play with the other girls.

"Let's go play with Mr. Ellis," my cousin Rose said.

"I don't want to," I answered.

"Why?"

"I don't know. I just know I don't feel like it."

"But he's a lot of fun and there ain't nothing else to do. Come

The Thing About Love Is...

on let's go see what he's doing. All the other girls are over there. Besides, he may be giving out nickels for singing and dancing," Rose added.

Reluctantly, I went along with Rose because she was right. There wasn't much to do, and we were tired of eating and jumping rope. It was still too light outside so we couldn't chase the fireflies, and none of the other grown ups had drunk enough homebrew yet to start paying us to perform for them. We decided to head our seven-year-old selves over to where Mr. Ellis was sitting.

Mr. Ellis always called us children flowers, and from a distance, the children who bouqueted tightly around him as he sat on a wooden stool looked like multi-colored flowers on small stem-like legs. They were draped around his neck, scattered at his feet, hanging on to his arms, dressed in their bright yellows and white, pinks and blues, orange and purple, striped and polka dotted shorts and tiny skirts. Their sunflower eyes focused on Mr. Ellis, turning upwards as if he were the sun at noon in the middle of July. Every child under the age of nine had found the way to Mr. Ellis. Their squealish laughter pierced the sky, rivaling for space with the laughter of the grown ups several feet away. When me and Rose reached Mr. Ellis, he had cousin Tanya on his lap tickling her. When he saw me and Rose join the circle of children, he stopped and smiled.

"Look at these two pretty flowers," he said. Looking at me and Rose standing before him, me in pink and white candy-stripped shorts and Rose in her yellow sundress, he said, "Come give Mr. Ellis a hug."

Like the tickling and lap sitting, I didn't like a lot of people outside of my family hugging me either, not even the folks at church. My mama always had to make me give folks a hug. She said people would think I was uppity or funny-acting if I didn't

The Thing About Love Is...

let them hug me, and that it embarrassed her when I didn't. I wasn't trying to act funny or be uppity. I just thought hugs were special and that you shouldn't give 'em to everybody, even if they asked for one. The same way you don't let any and everybody lay hands on you or prophesy over you in church. With a hug, it felt like you could reach right inside of someone and touch their spirit or they could touch yours, like their spirit could flow right out of their bodies into yours and bond with your soul. Soul-touching hugs from the right person can lift you up out of any pit, comfort you and make you feel safe and warm, bring gladness to fill dark inner corners of sadness, say "I'm glad to see" or "I've missed you." Most of all they are a silent reminder, when words will not come, that you are loved. No, I didn't give my hugs out too freely, not even to Mr. Ellis, as nice as he seemed to be. I had let Mr. Ellis hug me one time before. His hug was too tight, groping and desperate, like it was trying to suck something out of my spirit that I didn't want to give. So I wasn't hugging Mr. Ellis today. Besides his breath was always too hot and smelt sour, just like the homebrew. He had been drinking a lot of homebrew from the way he smelled.

Mr. Ellis played games with us and passed out nickels. As the sun started to set and darkness rolled in like a great dark carpet, soon me and Rose and Tanya were the only kids left playing with Mr. Ellis. Everyone else had left one by one. We had his complete attention.

In the distance strains of the song "Hoochie Coochie Man" could be heard in the background. The grown-ups had moved from doing the twist to dancing a slower-paced slow drag. The storytellers now told stories filled with sentimental memories instead of the fast-paced comical tales they had turned earlier in the day. The older girls were huddled off in corners talking about boyfriends and clothes, while the boys jumped from trees and

The Thing About Love Is...

chased the dogs that rambled throughout the yard. While all of this was going on, me, Rose and Tanya had Mr. Ellis all to ourselves.

"I'll tell you a secret," he said in a low slurred whispery voice. "How would you like Mr. Ellis to give you each a nice shiny quarter?" He dug his hand deep into his dark brown baggy pants. Quarters so shiny that they shone like stars in the palm of his dark hand appeared in the September dusk. Our faces lit up. No one ever gave us a quarter unless it was a special holiday or our birthday. As we reached out our hands to grab the quarters, Mr. Ellis closed his hand and drew it back.

"Now if I give you these quarters, you cain't tell nobody," he said. "Your mamas might not like it." And he was right because all of us had been told not to take money from strangers, but Mr. Ellis wasn't no stranger so we told him it would be alright if he gave them to us.

"Alrighty," he whispered with a smile, "but if I give you the quarters, you got to do something for me."

Already I was deciding what dance I was going to do and what song I was going to sing so I could outdo my cousins. I figured if I did really well Mr. Ellis might give me an extra quarter. I made up my mind I would sing "Won't You Come Home, Bill Bailey" and do my imitation of Pearl Bailey. Surely that must be worth an extra quarter to Mr. Ellis.

"If I give you the quarter," he hesitated, then whispered, "you have to pull your panties down."

Pull our panties down! Pull our panties down! None of the grown-ups had ever asked us to pull our panties down. I didn't like Mr. Ellis asking me that, but I didn't say nothing. I just looked at him. All of a sudden Mr. Ellis started looking and sounding real drunk, and I didn't like it. Red glassy eyes stared from out of his head. His words tumbled out of his mouth,

The Thing About Love Is...

falling over themselves like spilled building blocks.

"I'll do it," Tanya said before anyone had a chance to stop her, "but you'll have to give me a quarter and a nickel."

"Alright, I'll give you a quarter and a nickel," Mr. Ellis said.

He reached into his pocket smiling and pulled out more shiny coins. No one seemed to notice him with his tiny flowers in the silhouetted darkness as Tanya raised her polka-dotted dress and placed her thumbs inside the elastic waist of her bright pink-and-white-flowered panties and slowly started to pull them down. All the while she kept her eyes shut tight. But Mr. Ellis was looking. His eyes were wide open. His red glassy eyes had turned to bloody scratching fingers, eyes that seemed to jump out of his head, eyes that had already grabbed at Tanya's panties and pulled them down, eyes that already knew what little seven-year-old girls looked like under their panties. These eyes rolled around in his head as small pockets of white foam curled at the corners of his mouth as he watched Tanya. Mr. Ellis rubbed his hands along the length of his thighs, rubbing them back and forth as if trying to massage away some deep burning ache. And even though he licked his bottom lip with his red snake-like tongue, his mouth still looked cracked and broken. His smiled nailed into place. Looking at Mr. Ellis made me feel sick and queasy inside, the same sick that I felt when I was tossed up in the air and wasn't sure if the person below me was going to catch me, or sick like when the swing on the playground goes too high and I felt like I was flying, but remembered in mid-air that I had no wings. Just as Tanya had pulled her panties down far enough to expose her small brown navel and smooth flat stomach, I shouted out.

"I'm going to tell my granddaddy!"

Tanya's dress fell back down to cover her panties again, and Mr. Ellis started looking real sober right then.

"Did you hear me, Mr. Ellis? You can keep your old quarters

The Thing About Love Is...

'cause I'm going to tell my granddaddy."

I grabbed Rose by the hand, turned and ran off, barely escaping Mr. Ellis' out-stretched hand that was grasping for the back of my blouse. Tanya ran in behind us, crying, probably scared I was going to tell on her too. She knew just like I did that showing your panties wasn't right let alone showing the stuff that your panties was covering up. Mr. Ellis left the barbeque real quick. He didn't even bother to say goodbye to anybody.

I didn't tell. For some reason I was afraid to, but I made him think I did. I went over to my granddaddy, put my arms around his neck and whispered in his ear. I asked him could I have some ice cream. We didn't mention Mr. Ellis at all, not even among ourselves. Later that evening, me, Rose and Tanya went and made ourselves some honest money. The grown folks had drank enough homebrew by now and were ready for us to sing and dance for them for nickels. And that's just what we did. I looked for Mr. Ellis in the crowd as I sang. Even though I didn't see him, I swear, his eyes were there right in the middle of the crowd.

You Can Take This Shit to Your Mama

Sean Leenaerts

Folks will say they'd seen it coming.

Some will say he's just a boy, some will say he's trouble, and some will say he's never really been right in the head. But they'll all agree it was just a matter of time before the boy got around to killing someone. It's the kind of shit that happens when Life hands you a magician's deck and every card's the joker.

Start with his old man. A big man with a bigger mouth that's always talking bigger than he is. Everyone still remembers how he'd spent two weeks telling anyone who'd listen that he'd had a ringside seat to watch Mike Tyson, just out of jail, beat on some sorry-assed motherfucker. Said he sat two seats up from Mr. Don King and that he'd bought the man a beer. But everyone knows the boy's old man didn't see Don King, that he was just talking shit. Still, he'd spent his money big-time and came home broke all the same.

That's how it's always been.

The boy's old man would get a wad of cash, somehow, and go away for a while, only to come back when the money was spent. Everyone called him Houdini because he could make himself and money disappear. Only he kept coming back and the money

The Thing About Love Is...

didn't. No one knows how or where he got his cash, though everyone had their ideas. But all they really knew for sure is that the boy and his mama had never seen a cent of it. In any case, the boy's old man has been gone for a long time — longer than usual — and everyone believes that he probably went and finally got himself killed.

The boys mama, that's another story.

The people in the neighborhood will say that she does the best she can. She used to work a cash register at Woolworth's up on State, but it didn't pay enough to support a boy and pay the bills and still have a little left over to buy herself something nice. The benefits were low, and she got little in the way of a "thank you," "fuck you" or "go to hell" for busting her ass eight hours a day, six days a week. So one night some time ago, when her man was pulling one of his disappearing acts, she stopped in a bar after work for a drink and met a man who said he was in liquor sales. Now everyone will tell you that the boy's mama is a fine-looking woman, even though her nose is crooked from being broken once. That crooked nose sort of puts her looks at an angle, which makes her seem like she's from someplace far away.

The man seemed nice enough, so she talked with him, enjoying the way his eyes kept flicking over her like candlelight in the breeze. The next morning she woke up in bed alone, but with the smell of him still in the room and a hundred dollars on the table. She'd been drinking with him late into the night and had done some talking about her boy and the way her man had treated her. The money, she felt sure, was nothing more than sympathy. But it must have put the idea in her head all the same.

So now the boy's mama works the streetlamp-lighted hours and comes home when they start to dim. She tells the boy she's working the night shift at the phone company, and she never brings her business home. But the boy, he knows. He knows because her

The Thing About Love Is...

footsteps are so heavy when she walks through the door at dawn. They're the footsteps of a woman who's not been sitting at a switchboard through the night. And there's the smell — that musty-sweet smell of sex. It reaches out to the boy even beneath the covers when he sleeps. That smell drives him crazy, and inside he burns with shame and anger. Of course, people talk. And when some punk tells him "Your mama's a whore," he fights, wanting to drive their nose bones into their brains, not because of what they say but because he knows it's true.

As for the boy, he gets himself into trouble like most boys do, fighting and just plain acting wild. But there's an edgy meanness to him. Like the time the police brought him in for breaking windows. He was only seven then, and he walked along the street one night throwing rocks through liquor store windows just to hear the alarms go off. He didn't even try to run when the patrol car pulled up alongside of him. The boy just turned and reached for the handle of the back door. Three months later, he was back for dropping concrete blocks on cars from a freeway overpass.

The boy can't say why he does it — not that he'd want to tell anyone if they asked. Maybe if they tried to drag it out of him, he might say it's only for fun or that he's got something to prove. And maybe they'd believe that. But they'd only be fooling themselves, just like he's fooling them. Because the truth is the boy doesn't really know why, and he doesn't ask too many questions of himself. It's the kind of shit that just happens on its own.

Maybe it's because the boy doesn't sleep too well. The boy and his mama live across a narrow street from an all-night liquor store with a big neon sign above the door. That sign is almost bigger than the store itself, and it flickers something awful. There's a loose connection or something. Maybe not enough gas in the tubes. In any case, it's like a Chinese water torture to the boy. It shines right into the living room and casts its glow on the couch

The Thing About Love Is...

where he sleeps, stuttering in blue and red and white like some rundown disco light.

So it happened that last night the boy woke up, wet and twisted in the flickering neon-lit sheets, and he felt someone squeezing his hand. He held that hand awhile, not caring about whose it was or where it came from, just wanting to feel the warmth of it. It was only when he looked at the sign outside the window that realized the hand he was holding was own.

Everyone in the neighborhood believes the boy has no direction. But when he woke up last night, for once he knew where he was going. Knowing like a virus knows.

The boy dressed deliberately and in the dark, picking his clothes with the care of the color-blind. And he plucked at his throat because it was sore. He wondered aloud, just to hear a familiar voice in the darkness of the small apartment, if he'd been yelling in his sleep.

When the boy was dressed, he went to his mama's dresser and sifted through the twisted mounds of underwear until he found the gun. It was loaded because it was always ready. His mama's solo, and there are plenty of pimps around who want to make sure if a woman's not working for them she's not working at all. Also, she never knew when a john was going to get a funny idea in his head. So the boy's mama carries a snub-nose .38 in her bag and keeps a loaded .357 in her dresser. The big revolver was the last thing the boy's old man ever gave her. And like most everything else she'd gotten from him, it hadn't been given freely.

He'd handed it to her in an argument one night, back when she'd first started to hit the streets. He'd told her no way was any woman of his going to be a whore-cunt bitch. And she'd answered him with the kind of laugh from one who's used to disappointment, telling him he could take that kind of shit back to his mama in a voice as sharp and cold as the edge of a switch-

The Thing About Love Is...

blade knife. The boy's old man knew enough to know he should back off.

The boy's mama had said to him that as far as she and the boy were concerned, he was dead — hell, he never hung around long enough for folks to remember the details of his face — and that he had no say in how she was going to run her life.

"You start bringin' in some money instead of that hard and heavy cheesedick of yours, and then maybe I'll get off the streets," she'd told him, keeping her voice low in the hope that her boy in the next room wouldn't hear. "Until then, you are dead, and I don't listen to no dead man."

The boy's old man had stared through the floorboards, working his jaw like he'd been chewing on something too nasty for him to swallow. But instead of coming back with something mean or reaching out to strike her, he'd shrugged and reached into his coat, handing her the gun and saying she might as well finish the job, then.

The boy's mama had held the gun pointed at the floor, checked the chambers and found them loaded. She hadn't asked him where he'd gotten it or why he carried it, and she hadn't shown any fear when he'd pulled it out. The boy, watching through the keyhole in the bedroom door, had felt the blood running in his veins as he imagined the barrel being raised and seeing the bullet pass through his old man's body. He'd willed it to happen with all his heart. But his mama had just shaken her head, calling the man a fool, and had held the gun back out to him. He'd turned away and had walked to a part of the room where the boy couldn't see him, telling her to keep it.

"Gat like that'll just get me in trouble, anyway," he'd said.

The boy had watched his mama put the gun in a dresser drawer and, out of view, had heard the loose-change clinking of a belt coming undone.

The Thing About Love Is...

"Oh, so now you want to do the nasty," the boy had heard his mama say with a sigh. Then the keyhole had gone black.

Through the night the boy had stayed at the door, listening to his old man take his mama, silent but for the grunts and signs and sounds the bedsprings made. Then later, the snoring of his old man's sleeping. And the boy had nursed his anger, letting it fill him up inside, wanting to take the gun and kill his old man where he slept. He'd imagined the cold, dead weight of it in his hands, and he'd counted the bullets over and over in his mind until he'd fallen asleep. He'd awakened to the sound of chuckling and the sight of his old man's big feet stepping over him. And never had the boy felt so much hate.

Never, until last night. Only this time, he told himself, no one was stepping over him.

So before his mama's mirror, the boy tucked the gun into the waistband of his pants, like he'd seen some older boys in the neighborhood do, and he buttoned up his coat. When he left the apartment and stepped into the hall, the door slammed shut like a guillotine behind him.

The boy's hate went with him to the liquor store across the street. His hate was for no one in particular. Instead, he hated the life that Life had given him. He hated the cause of his hate, and he felt he'd find it in the liquor store, beneath the flickering neon lights.

The old man who runs the store watched the boy come in, wondering what it was that made him walk so softly and so late. Sure, he felt bad about the boy, about how his father was never around, about how his mother ... well, she was as good a lady as she could be, and he supposed she tried her best. He wasn't one to go passing judgements. It was just too bad, was all.

But he also knew the boy.

He knew that the darker hours were the boy's worst ones, and

The Thing About Love Is...

he pulled open the drawer beneath the register just a crack to take a reassuring glance down at the flash of chrome reflecting the fluorescent lights above. He told himself he was just making sure it was there. He told himself it was just a boy. Just a boy of ten.

"You know you ain't allowed in here without your mama, boy," the old man said, keeping the words in front of him so he wouldn't betray the fear in his throat. Jesus, that boy looks pure mean, the old man thought.

The boy looked back at the old man with eyes as dark and cold as yesterday's coffee. "I ain't no boy," he answered in a voice without anger or pitch. The old man just looked away and let it go at that.

The first thing the boy laid eyes on when he walked into the store was a cognac display. He'd been heading straight for it when the old man called to him, and he kept going to it after the old man had fallen silent. It wasn't a large display, and the ordered rows of dull, black bottles with their plain white labels weren't much to look at. But it was the ad mounted over the display that caught the boy's attention.

The ad showed a man and woman reclined at opposite ends of a sofa. The man wore the remnants of formal dress, his bow tie hanging black and limp around his neck, his wing-tip collar open, his jacket thrown casually over the sofa's back. A snifter of cognac was cradled in a languid hand that almost touched the floor. The woman, in a wisp of a black dress sprinkled with gold sequins, sat at the other end and held a snifter tilted to her lips. Her shoes were off and one black-stockinged foot was pressed against the man's thigh. Their eyes bored into each other with an intensity that tightened the small of the boy's back. And beneath the picture were the words, "Experience the Desire."

That image of the man and woman was familiar to the boy. It haunted his sleepless dreams and mocked his dreamless days. The

The Thing About Love Is...

clothes were cheaper, the furniture more worn, and they drank cheap scotch or bourbon from a bottle instead of French cognac from a fancy glass. But the looks they gave each other were the same. The woman's mock seduction and the man's pelvic lust were as real to the boy as living beings. His mama and a man. Any man. The kind of man who didn't own a bow tie.

The boy turned from the display, feeling sick and dizzy. He walked the aisles of bottles, up one and down the other, reading the labels in a blur. He imagined that the glass bottles resting on the metal shelves were the million windows of a city, and in each window he saw two people, a woman and a man in bed. And each woman was his mama, her breasts sagging from the rough touch of too many hands and the slack flesh of her belly jiggling with each fevered thrust of each different man. They didn't make love, his mama and the men. They fucked. Like the older boys playing ball on the playground said they did. Fucked like animals do—grunting, heaving, sweating, and finally crying out when the man was spent. Always, it was the man who ended up spent and sweating.

Afterwards, they'd drink. The men would tilt the bottle and drink as if gaining strength with every drop. When they passed the bottle to the boy's mama, she'd take a small sip, then pass the bottle back. She never let herself get drunk, saving it for the next john and another bottle. She only drank enough to wash the taste of the last man from her mouth.

The boy watched it all through the bottles, in ambers, whites, and deep, dark reds. And somewhere far away, in the twisted city of his mind, he heard a cash register's high-pitched ring.

At the front of the store, the old man was ringing up a sale. The boy heard the voices of a man and woman, and from the forced hacking of their laughter he knew that they were higher than the stars. He heard the old man speak to them in a tone that

The Thing About Love Is...

suggested he had better things to do with his voice.

"Well, you folks jus' gonna' stand there funnin' all night, or is you goin' to buy som'pin else?" the boy heard the old man say.

"Now jus' you skeep your b-britches on, old man," the man's words rolled. "I's s-still compentplatin' m-m-my c-course of axshion."

"Yeah — wha' he say?" the woman said.

And again there was laughter.

The boy walked slowly up the aisle, listening to the laughter and feeling dark inside. He'd heard that laughter so many times before, in his daylight waking hours and in his troubled sleep, carried on the night's cold wind from a city's million darkened rooms. In it was the nervous laughter of his mama, telling him what a night she'd had through lips clenched around a cigarette. In it was the heavy chuckling of his old man and the sound of heavy shoes. In it was the laughter of those who could not or would not understand, of the playground punks and the cops who'd been surprised that time he'd willingly stepped into the patrol car's backseat. In it was the heavy-handed laughter of one who hates, that laughter in the cold shadow of his heart. And he felt his shivering muscles grip his bones and every nerve turn raw.

He was going to kill the laughter before it finally killed him.

The boy saw them all in profile. The man was buying a White Owl cigar, and the old man had turned his back to him to get it. The man had skin the color of caramel, and his hair was slicked back in shiny black curls. From the side, his features were sharp and pronounced, with high cheekbones and a straight nose. Though his jaw was slack with drunken laughter, his eyes flashed with a knife-edged arrogance. He wore a grey striped suit of shiny fabric, pointed-toe black shoes, and a black leather trenchcoat. One hand held the neck of a bottle in a brown paper sack in a loose grip while the other hand fumbled around in the pocket of

The Thing About Love Is...

his trenchcoat.

The woman, she was pretty — the boy could tell that in spite of her heavy make-up. She had hair that hung down in thick black braids that brushed smooth, dark cheeks glittering with tiny flecks of gold beneath the harsh fluorescent lights. She stood shifting her weight from one stilettoed heel to the other, one hand resting on her purple-sequined purse, the other on the counter. Her long nails, polished in deep red, staccatoed on the countertop. The silver-sequined dress and the white fake fur she wore were of the same cropped length, both just brushing her at mid-thigh. Her long and slender legs glittered gold like her cheeks.

"Hurry up, old man. Don' wanta waste this fine feeling in h-here all nights," the man said.

The old man turned and put the cigar down next to the register, keeping his hand on it. The man pulled his free hand from his pocket and laid the change on the counter. And the boy, walking down the aisle, watched them all grow larger. He could smell them, separately, like places passed on a windy day: the man's heavy musk and sour liquor breath, the woman's too-sweet perfume and faint scent of cloves, the old man's stale smoke and faintly urine smell. He didn't take his eyes off any of them, and they never heard him coming until he stood right next to them.

"Yo, you lettin' boys buy in here?" the boy heard the man say as he drifted out of focus and the woman's sequins filled his vision.

The woman turned and almost bumped into him. Her lips parted in a grin. For an instant the boy saw her tongue flash pink and wet between the gap in her front teeth. She was still grinning like that when the boy leveled the gun at her and pulled the trigger.

It wasn't anything like the boy expected. To him, it sounded like a balloon being popped — loud and startling. No thunder-

The Thing About Love Is...

ing voice-of-God-like cannon roar the guns in movies make. No one flying in a slow-motion arc five feet in the air, blood gushing, when the bullet hits. Pull the trigger and people just disappear. The woman dropped so quickly that for a moment the boy thought he might have missed her. Behind the spot where she'd stood was the sound of something breaking.

"Sssssshhiiiit!"

The boy heard a fumbling sound to his right and turned to find the old man pulling out a chromed revolver from under the counter. Another balloon popped.

The old man's head snapped back with an uppercut's kind of violence. The chromed revolver shot out of his hand like a wet bar of soap and, backpedaling with outstretched arms flailing for the falling gun, the old man smashed into the shelf of liquor bottles behind him. Pint bottles of Johnny Walker Red and Black and Cutty Sark and Early Times came crashing down around him. The boy popped a balloon again, and the old man clutched at his chest, disappearing from view in a shower of falling bottles.

The man was frozen to the floor like his feet were nailed down. He'd never moved except to drop the bottle and wet his pants. The man looked at the boy with a wish for the door and the cold night's kiss on his cheek.

"Boy — I —"

The boy just sighted down the barrel and said, "I ain't your boy." And he popped the last balloon.

The back of the woman's coat looked like an angry dog had gotten to it. It was ripped and wet and crimson. The boy turned the woman over with his foot. She was dead. His shot had hit her in the chest, right between the breasts. The hole was the size of a dime, but the bullet had torn its way through her and had come out between her shoulder blades like a fist through a door. The boy stared at the round edges of the small hole and thought it

The Thing About Love Is...

was a lot like his life — how he'd come into it small and unnoticed, and he'd had to fight and tear his way through it until he finally broke free.

Life would no longer laugh at him, he thought. Not as long as he could tear the laughter out.

The woman was still grinning, and the boy reached down and closed her lips. Her lipstick smudged his fingertips. It was oily, and he felt the darkness once again inside him. He wiped his fingers viciously on his jeans, grinding the bright red into the material until it was no longer there.

Yes, she'd been a pretty-woman.

But the boy didn't like the make-up. It was always trying to hide something. There was always some flaw women were trying to cover up, some revealing part of themselves that they didn't want to show. It wasn't honest. People were always trying to hide something from the boy.

The boy didn't want to run. He wanted to be honest. He wanted to come clean to someone, anyone, with the truth of what he'd done. He wouldn't try to hide what never could be hidden — the filthy lies that murmured on the night's wind like a derelict's hoarse mumbling to himself. Like the voices of his mama and his old man through the bedroom door at night, talking their truths while they thought a child slept.

But when the boy thought he heard voices outside the store, felt sure he heard a tentative "Who's there?", he suddenly turned without a second glance at the woman on the floor and ran. He came tearing out the back of the liquor store, slamming the cold steel door against a cold graffitied wall. He sprinted down the dim-lit alley, keeping close to shadowed walls, feeling his empty heart rattle in his empty chest, and hearing the tentative "Who's there?" in his ears.

The boy ran all night through the nighttime streets, through

The Thing About Love Is...

the harsh white glow of the streetlamps and the shadows that split them up. He ran and the shadows grew longer, and he didn't stop running until the shadows were all that remained.

Thought Delayed

Jo-Ann Ledger

having peeled back skin
and stepped inside
two in messy motion
realize
the tenuous hold
each has on the other,
as every panted breath
acknowledges
that freedom's no longer the issue

Taking Off My Clothes
Robert N. Georgalas

The pull of memory is never as strong as when we feel some portion of our lives drawing to a close. Why I should think that tomorrow's procedure signals such an event is unclear. After all, it's not as if I'm about to lose my job, or divorce my wife, or emigrate to another country. And, as Doctor Simons has repeatedly assured me, the odds of anything going awry are on par with those of discovering truffles on Venus. Still, the thought of surgical invasion is enough to give anyone pause. Particularly when the illness was so unforeseen. All my adult life I have taken pride in caring for my body, exercising daily and limiting the intake of nitrates and fats. In fact, year after year, my physical exams underscored the efficacy of that regimen. Which is why I was so shaken when the aberration first appeared. Don't misunderstand. I'm well aware that control is an illusion. Fool ourselves as we might, none of us is more than the pawn of chance. And a month ago, chance moved me to a square vulnerable to attack.

Not knowing me, you're likely to conclude that this belief is the root of my fitful sleep. But whether lying in a hospital or resting in a five star hotel, I often experience insomnia in a strange bed. It's a condition that has dogged me since adolescence, a plight precipitated by a visit to my mother's younger sister during the summer before I entered college.

At odds with his in-laws since first meeting them, my father

The Thing About Love Is...

opted to forego an extended reunion. That left me to chauffeur my mother to Scranton, Pennsylvania. Having seen Aunt Kristin and Uncle Robert once when I was six, the two were strangers to me. And since I knew that they were childless, I looked upon the visit with trepidation, envisioning a week of soul numbing boredom. Within an hour of our arrival, though, I was captive to their genuine warmth and as we sat on their front porch, sipping iced tea and listening to my uncle tell jokes, I felt more at ease than I often did in my own home. Indeed, to my glee, I detected that my uncle's interest in baseball was as rabid as mine, and while Kristin and my mother rehashed family history in the kitchen, he and I played Home Run Derby in the park across the street.

Our stay proceeded pleasantly for three days. Then, on a Thursday morning, instead of being awakened by the piquant aroma of perking coffee and sizzling bacon, I was roused by a shout, followed by the scrape of work boots rushing up the stairs. Thinking I had dreamt the noise, I lay in my bed, my eyes adjusting to the tendrils of sunlight that poked through the blinds. A moment later, my complacency was shattered by a cry of, "Oh, Jesus." Startled, I flung back the covers, opened the door and rushed toward the voices emanating from my mother's room. Inside, my aunt knelt beside the bed, her temple pressed against the mattress, her hand draped over my mother's wrist. Standing above her, my uncle placed his palm on my mother's forehead, then bent his ear to her lips. "What is it?" I said. At the sound of me, my aunt lifted her head and my uncle turned to block my advance. An instant before he reached me, I marked the tears that spidered his wife's face.

"What is it?" I stuttered. "What's...?" My uncle's fingers dug into my shoulders, the force of his grip anchoring me to a spot near the doorway. Before he could utter a syllable, a bizarre

The Thing About Love Is...

thought exploded in my brain and the breath vanished from my lungs as if I'd just been punched in the solar plexus. Squirming in his grasp, I craned my neck to see passed him towards the bed, but he held me fast to his chest. "Your mother," he said. "She...." Awash with adrenaline, I wrestled free. Despite my aunt's quiet sobs, I knew that my mother was alive. But the chill of her cheek and the blue of her lips proved incontrovertible. Later that day, the neighborhood physician, an aged gnome in a rumpled brown suit and wire-rimmed glasses, explained to me that my mother had suffered a severe myocardial infarction as she slept.

Needless to say, the shock and grief that coursed through my blood that morning have long since dissipated, but each time I enter an unfamiliar bedroom, I remember my mother. And as I lie here this evening anticipating tomorrow's surgery, my attention wanders from the mute images on the television to an incident that unfolded thirty-three years ago on the afternoon of my twelfth birthday.

Roofed by a marble gray sky, my mother and I stood on an el platform in the Bronx, awaiting the number six local. Though uninspired by our destination, I was ecstatic that my father had granted me dispensation from school. The previous night, as he and I had waited at Enrico's for the large sausage pizza my mother had ordered, he ruffled my hair and said, "Marcus, you're a man of leisure tomorrow." My face burned in a neon smile. A parentally sanctioned absence would free me from the humiliation I suffered each Friday in my instrumental music class. ("That's a saxophone, Mr. Herman, not a drain pipe. Had you removed it from its case this week, you may have discovered that.") Delighted by my good fortune, I slapped my father on the shoulder. "Hey," he shrugged, "you're only a kid once."

Twenty minutes later, the torch of joy he had ignited was snuffed by my mother's announcement. Cutting the string of the

The Thing About Love Is...

oil-stained pizza box, she revealed that her gift was a subway ride to Manhattan to see the latest Disney film. Aghast, I ripped my paper plate and began to protest. "Aw, ma. I don't want to sit through some cartoon. If we have to go to a movie, let's see James Bond." She separated a cheesy triangle from the box and plopped it onto my father's dish. "Vat do you know from movies?" she said. "Dis iz a vunderful picture." Desperate for an ally, I glanced at my father. Rather than spring to my aid, he busied himself with a mouthful of blackened crust. I tried twice more, arguing on the basis of age and interest, but my mother's dismissive waves rendered my protests moot. "Enough," she finally said.

Defeated, I plodded through the meal in a fog of disappointment. My father's blessings had led me to imagine an afternoon of bowling and billiards with a group of friends eager to play truant. Those hopes now splintered, a pall of gloom settled over me. My mother ignored my silence until I was about to take out the garbage. Then, with an overly dramatic nudge, she elbowed my father. "Jack, you tolt him about Hong Fat's, didn't you?" My father stared at her dumbly. Sensing the tingle in my neck, she continued to play Hardy to my father's flummoxed Laurel. Once I learned that the three of us would meet for dinner in Chinatown, my mouth creased in a grin. No matter how dull the following afternoon, the promise of a feast at Hong Fat's was sure to steel my spine.

As the wind swept the el platform, I vaulted forward in time, doing my best to reconstruct the throbbing and exotic streets that surrounded our evening rendezvous. In my mind's ear, I heard the sing-song of the Cantonese crowds as they wended by carts filled with vegetables, or strode past shop windows curtained by hanging ducks. How strange that such a world existed only a dozen or so miles from where we stood.

"Marcus." My mother's voice plucked me from the daydream.

The Thing About Love Is...

"Button your koat," she said. "I don't vant you ketching kolt." Conscious of the two leather jacketed teens who had been measuring us since we set foot on the platform, I hesitated to obey. "I'm fine," I said. In response, my mother squatted beside me, stuffing the wooden toggles of my coat into their respective eyelets. I tsked loudly, then backed away to preserve my dignity. Pinching the final button home, I watched the taller teen brush his friend's boot with the tip of his shoe. The two of them gazed toward my mother and me. The dim bulbs that glowed in the wire cages above them highlighted the bewilderment furrowed into their brows. And the weight of their stares convinced me that they were puzzling the connection between myself and the stolid woman who raised my collar about my neck.

Loath as I was to admit it, I understood their curiosity. My mother's wrinkled hands and powder-white hair made me appear more like her grandchild than her son. Over the years, I had become indifferent to the vast gap in our ages and it no longer bothered me that my friends' mothers were so much younger and slimmer and more contemporary. What did force me to cringe was the sharpness of her accent. And when the beanpole guffawed at my mother's observation that it was "November und already ve haf vinter," I wanted to shake her and tell her that it was high time her tongue learned to obey her ears.

Instead, I walked to the edge of the platform in search of the train. A smudge of headlight discolored the horizon. "A vet vinter," my mother said behind me. "It's in de almanac." The smirks of the two teens seared through my coat. Anxious to escape them, I willed the train forward.

When the doors finally slid open my mother yanked me by the arm, bulled passed the straphangers and pushed me toward the small two-seater bench adjacent to the conductor's cabin. Fearful that someone else would lay claim to the seats, she ordered me to

The Thing About Love Is...

hurry. I plopped on the plastic. Within seconds, my mother perched beside me, wiggling her bottom and pleading for me to give her "zum room." Certain that the volume of her request had drawn the attention of the other passengers, I edged closer to the wall. Jesus, I wondered. What must they think? Of the galoshes on her feet when there is no snow? Of the ripped shopping bag dangling from her elbow? Of the plastic pink butterfly pinned to her lapel?

My body bunched and expanded as she searched for her comfort zone. Then, corralling the shopping bag between her knees, she said, "Marcus, if I fall asleep, you vake me by 86th Street. Ve change for de express dere."

I nodded, my eyes skating over her face. To strangers, the strawberry tint of her skin must have seemed a result of the brisk November air. But the fact was that her complexion remained the same despite the season. And once, crouched beneath the stairwell in the lobby of our building, I had heard my neighbors debate the source of her permanent blush. "Gotta be the bottle," Mr. Rourke said. "No," Miss Cantoni answered. "It's her temper. She's very excitable." "Hell," chimed Mr. Degan, "you're both wrong. She was burned in a fire in Munich when she was a kid."

The train abandoned the daylight and plunged below the city. By the time it squealed to a stop at 149th Street, the jerk and roll had lulled my mother to sleep. To distract myself from the kerchiefed head that hovered over my shoulder, I studied the car's occupants, assigning them professions based on their appearance. Ex-con become magazine salesman. Catholic school girl turned junkie. Bank teller on his way to embezzle a car payment. I continued the game until the next station. Then my mother began to snore and a string of drool dribbled past her chin. The attractive Puerto Rican woman standing above me screwed her face in disgust. Embarrassed, I pressed closer to the wall, but my mother's

The Thing About Love Is...

head stalked me as if magnetized. Finally, I bumped it upwards with my shoulder. The Puerto Rican girl met my eyes in sympathy. "Some people," she said. "Yeah," I agreed. "Some people."

Three stops later, I succumbed to the idea worming through my skull. And when half the car evacuated at 86th Street, I rose gingerly from my seat, exited the train and abandoned my mother to the garden of unconsciousness. Once above ground, I was giddy with elation. "Free," I muttered to myself. "Single and free." Fueled by laughter, I hurried down the block. Now the day would be mine. I looked at my watch. 1:30. Scouring my pockets as I walked, I located the ten that my father had stuffed in a birthday card. Then, spying a diner on the corner, I decided to splurge. Seated atop my counter stool, flanked by business people in tailored suits and stylish dresses, I ordered a cheeseburger and a cherry coke. And as the clamor of the diners swelled and receded, I felt guiltless. After all, eating here was far more dignified than slouching in a dark theater, waiting for my mother to unwrap the liverwurst sandwiches she had packed in her shopping bag.

True, I had left her. But so what? Nothing terrible would happen. She would wake by 59th Street, panic for a moment, then determine that I had played a joke on her. No harm. Besides, I intended to confess to my father shortly and since he was the first person she called in a crisis, I was satisfied that her fears would soon be erased. After that, she would go her way and I mine till we met again at Hong Fat's.

To a large extent, events held close to the scenario I had sketched. But as the clock inched toward six and I entered the twilight shadows of Canal Street, my apprehension mushroomed. I knew my mother's capacity for anger and despite my father's presence, it was not beyond her to lash out at me in a public place. Surprisingly, nothing like that occurred when the three of us regrouped. Instead, we ate our meal without mention of my

The Thing About Love Is...

prank and when dessert came my mother treated me to a second helping of almond cookies.

That night, as I undressed for bed, my mother knocked on my door. Resigned to the beating I knew would follow, I let her in. "I'm sure you dink you vere a komedian today," she said. I retreated towards my desk, slumped in the wooden chair and averted my eyes. Oddly, I was glad that she was about to confront me, for the truth was that my exhilaration had faded long before I had left the diner. And as I plunked my coins into a pay phone to dial my father, my head filled with images of her being beaten or robbed. "I'm sorry," I said. "I don't know what came over me." She crossed the room and took my chin in her hand. "I vant you to know zumthing," she said. Despite the softness of her grasp, my body tensed. "Vat?" she said. "You dink I'm going to hit you?" I gulped and slouched deeper in my chair. My mother released my chin. "Funny," she said, "dot it's me you shoult fear." I dragged my eyes from the floor and watched her remove the tiny statue of Jesus from my night table. "Ma, I...." As if to silence me, she shook her head and stuffed the Jesus into the pocket of her housecoat. Then, hand on the doorknob, she looked at me and said, "Remember, ve carry our zins both inzide und out." Confused, I began to stammer, but before anything comprehensible could emerge, the door swung shut.

In his office last Tuesday, Doctor Simons explained the operation to me. First, I would be given an IV sedation, then a colonoscope would be inserted into my rectum to locate the trouble spot. Next, the polyp would be snared and incised. After that, the bleeding lesion would be cauterized. Finally, the tissue would be sent to the pathology lab. There would be some minor pain when I awoke, but it would subside within a few hours and, given my medical history, he was encouraged that the biopsy would prove negative.

The Thing About Love Is...

Somewhere down the hall a cart overturns and the cacophony of metal bouncing on waxed linoleum fills the otherwise silent hall. The suddenness of it makes me start from the pillow and a film of sweat forms on my palms. Stupid, I say. It's nothing. Some orderly disrupting the distribution of pills. I wipe my hands on the sheets, but despite my repeated rubbing the sweat fails to evaporate.

Granted, moments of anxiety tend to trigger unpleasant thoughts. And if my wife had access to my earlier ruminations, she would contend that they were normal, since she believes that I wrap myself in nostalgia even when besieged by a cold. She's quite wrong, of course. Just as she is when she swears that, to this day, I will undress at night only in the dark.

No. The distant past has as little hold of me as gravity does of light. In fact, from the time of my mother's death, I have done nothing but look forward, divorcing myself from the streets and the superstitions of my youth. However, I am perplexed as to why this particular home movie has unreeled itself. All I know is that I can hear my mother's words as clearly as I can the nurse in the hall. And the force of their echo conjures a moment a few months prior to Scranton.

Having allowed the wash to accumulate for longer than usual, my mother enlisted my aid for a trip to the laundermat. Carts loaded with sheets and curtains and underwear, we traveled the five blocks in silence. A street away from our destination, we passed our neighbor, Mr. Degan. "Chores, chores," he said in greeting. My mother shrugged in acknowledgment and we walked on. From the corner of my eye, though, I saw him do what he always did after meeting her: shake his head in pity. Remembering the theory he had advanced about my mother's disfigurement, I determined to share something with her that my Biology teacher had told me. There was a condition called Acne

The Thing About Love Is...

Rosacea which might be responsible for the cast of her skin. Indeed, according to him, there was a treatment that could greatly reduce the intensity of her reddish blush.

"You dink I don't know dis?" she said.

"Then why don't you go to the doctor?"

"Because it's not about doktors."

I stopped walking. "What?" I said.

My mother continued on. Without preamble, she began to tell me a story of her childhood in Germany. When she was a girl, she said, a friend of hers received a gold ring from her parents. The ring was topped by a small ruby and when the girl displayed it to my mother at school, my mother was awestruck by its beauty. The child of indigent parents, she knew that she could never possess such an object. So, when her friend removed the ring to wash her hands before lunch, my mother palmed it. And as the girl dried herself on a towel, my mother turned her back and tucked the ring into the elastic band of her underwear. Frantic at the ring's disappearance, her friend scoured the bathroom on all fours. My mother pretended to aid in this search, but, as the lunch period ended, it was clear the ring would not be found.

That evening, her friend returned home and confessed the loss tearily to her parents. Her father responded with a flurry of slaps and a threat to interrogate every pupil in the school. Good to his word, he instigated an investigation and soon suspicion fell upon my mother. Though terrified, she held tight to the web of lies she had created, going as far as to engage the support of the principal, who vouched for her on the basis of her grades. "I don't know vhy I did dis," she said. "It vent against everything in my nature und my upbringing und I knew I coult never zhow de ring to anyone. Yet, despite my friend's pain, I vould not return it. Instead, I hid it in de ztuffing of my favorite doll, removing it each night to vatch it glisten in de moon." Within a month of

The Thing About Love Is...

the robbery, she said, her face began to darken, and one day, as she studied herself in the bathroom mirror, she knew that she had been slapped by God.

Obviously, my mother's medieval beliefs were laughable, the result of countless hours in churches that preached a vengeful deity. Still, as I turn and fidget, attempting to ferret out the origins of my own misfortune, I'm not as convinced as Doctor Simons that the fibrous pebble in my colon is the manifestation of age. Christ, I'm sure, is blameless, for it's a waste of his energies to afflict a non-believer like me. Yet, it is true that the gyrations of the mind affect the workings of the body. The only trouble with that is that very little weighs on my conscience. If anything, the transgressions I've committed in my life are minor: lust in my heart; a failed attempt to sabotage a colleague's career; a rash of falsified numbers on an income tax form. These are the minutiae of existence, the errant whiskers plucked from life's hoary beard. As to the skirmishes with my wife over her spending, and the conflagration with my son re: the woman he chose to wed, there's not much to say. Such dramas are little more than outbursts of anger and frustration, brushfires extinguished by an apologetic word.

No. The more I ponder the question, the more I realize that the scratches on my conscience are less the residue of operatic impieties than the vestiges of iniquities so minor they were dismissed quicker than they happened: the snide remark, the squint of condescension, the easy nullification of another's pain.

"Everything all right, Mr. Herman?"

I shut off the television and say "fine." The nurse feels my pulse and sticks a thermometer under my tongue. She is a pleasant woman with a chirpy personality, and as she scribbles a note on the chart that hangs from the foot of my bed, she wishes me luck with my operation. I thank her and watch her walk to the door.

The Thing About Love Is...

Before she leaves, she removes a scrap of paper from the pocket of her uniform, wads it into a ball, then tosses it into the wastebasket.

As it poofs against the plastic liner, a dust mite is unleashed from the pillowcase of memory. Three weeks before my visit to Doctor Simons, I stopped in a bar to have a drink with a friend who was visiting from out of town. An emergency call from my office forced me to cut the meeting short. Expressing my apologies, I retrieved my coat from the check room and exited to the street. As I neared the corner, it began to drizzle. At first, I simply draped my coat over my shoulders, but when the drizzle graduated to rain, I put it on and retreated under an awning. The street was jammed with cars and trucks and buses, but the downpour seemed to have dissolved all the taxis. To ease the wait, I reached into the pocket of my coat for a cigarette, but in place of the pack I always kept there, I discovered a folded piece of paper. Curious, I opened it, but the paper was thin and tore in the process. "Michael," the top half said, "I don't want it to end like this. I'll be at 555-7623 till seven. If I don't hear from you...." I did not bother to read the rest. Instead, I opened the coat. A glance at the label confirmed my suspicion. The hat-check girl had taken the wrong garment from the rack. Irritated, I crumpled the note, threw it to the sidewalk and trotted back to the restaurant to make the exchange.

From the nurse's station diagonally opposite my door comes the sound of heated voices. A resident is berating a nurse for failing to administer someone's 11 p.m. injection. "It's nothing," the nurse says. "We'll do it now." "Now?" responds the doctor. "And if I hadn't come?"

There is no humor in the argument. I know that. And yet, I have no control over the laugh that bursts past my lips. It's not a happy sound, you understand. Not the mirthful agitation of air

The Thing About Love Is...

that follows an especially exaggerated pratfall or a trenchant witticism. By contrast, it is a sharp, almost painful squeak. The giggle of someone who has watched another's plea for happiness float away on a stream of coffee brown rainwater. And as it dissolves in the sterile air, I look to the plaster ceiling and whisper for forgiveness.

Harold Cowley's Summer Laundry

William Meiners

"Mother and Father," read Harold Cowley's last bar napkin. It's black-inked in awful chicken scratch. The great big man writes real tiny. "I am sorry that you have to read this, and I hate leaving you this way. But it seems I have pursued loneliness my whole life, and at last, caught it. Captured and engulfed myself. The running, the poetry, the painting, the drifting. Scribbled and scratched for an audience of none. I have never been happy where I have been. Even as I write this, I pour spirits into my body, failing to find any. Like I'm hollow. It has merely become another routine in my host of unprofitable habits. I enjoyed having you as parents and regret not being a better son. Love, Harold."

I've been doing Harold's laundry all summer. It all started because I married and divorced an idea man, Raymond, who uprooted me from the South and dumped me in Chicago. He don't tell nobody where he gets all his ideas neither. It was my idea for the combination laundromat/bar. I always thought folks would enjoy a nice meal and a cocktail while doing their laundry.

Course, if you know me, you know of my love for clean laundry. As a little girl, even in the most humid of Carolina summers, I'd be there to wrap up in the fresh, warm blanket that come out of Mother's dryer. In the winter, I love walking behind a house

The Thing About Love Is...

that's spouting off Downy-steam from a working dryer. Makes me think that it must be a nice place to live. Beyond the beautiful smells and feelings that go along with laundry is the pure act of cleansing. There's both baptism and confession in them wash and rinse cycles. And a rebirth in the drying.

But in his own way, my old Raymond, my ex, the self-proclaimed "idear man," did in a small way thank me for what he stole. He gave me a job on the laundry side. We never had children so he don't pay no support. I always suspected his sperm count was low from tight jockey shorts. He was of the opinion that my eggs was scrambled.

But I work hard for him and keep a clean place clean. I can't say the same for the nasty little place next door. My original vision, though I weren't consulted, saw a place with good desserts, maybe some fruity drinks. Raymond put an Old Style sign out front and hired a couple of tarts with boob and butt cleavage. It's a joint for older men. They drink gin fizzes and other poisons in the dark. Some of the poorer old boys drink ice-cubed beers all day.

The dark bar, with hunched old men sipping slow death, is a direct contrast to the bright lights of the laundry side. The washing folks are up-and-comers in sweat suits scurrying around with baskets. There is a door that connects one place to the other, but other than a light-blinded lost drunk on a wrong turn from the john, only my old Raymond exits and enters both these far sides of paradise.

Over here is order. Sixty white washers lined up in six perfect rows in the middle. Large dryers, built into the walls, encase the room. In the rear, a short hall leads to a tinted glass door.

I tell stories poorly. I should probably start at the beginning of the summer, when I saw something sweet in Harold Cowley's down-turned face that June day he dropped off his first fifty pounds of laundry. Not many folks take advantage of my own-titled "Drop & Done," but I love everyone of them that does. The first ten pounds are free, thirty pounds minimum, and this summer we're up to 75 cents a pound. It is true: You can tell a lot by what a man wears. But you can tell a whole heck of a lot more by washing what he wears.

Harold Cowley didn't say much — just dropped off a stuffed Navy duffel bag with a mumbled promise to return in one day for everything clean and folded. He didn't bring hangers, but said he didn't need them. He hid a bald head under a hat, which is what Raymond done before he got his piece. He was what Raymond described as swarthy, but I'd just say he had a dark complexion. His face had been bad to him as a younger man, and it looked like he slept on a tennis racquet. He had a bit of a belly, and the rest of his story would be revealed through his clothes. I couldn't wait to dig into that man's laundry.

Item A, I could tell Harold Cowley was a drinker. I found twenty-two dollars of pocket-crunched ones, fives, and tens, not to mention about thirty-three cents in change. Having lived with Raymond, I know a truly thirsty man will drink till he can't pour another one down his neck. At home the pants come off, if they come off at all, with everything left to settle in the pockets. And the drunk man squeezes those dollars, sure as he's foolishly trying to squeeze something worthwhile into his mind by getting blind on liquor. There were also napkins, before the fatal one, and an occasional harlot's phone number.

Secondly, Harold Cowley didn't need no hangers 'cause all his clothes were shorts, and t-shirts — a real colorful bunch of blues and peach, orange and red. In the dryer it looked like they's children doing somersaults. He had cute little socks we called footies — but his didn't have the balls on the back — and several collared short-sleeve jobs, some with a horse riding golfer on them,

The Thing About Love Is...

that can be folded and kept quite nicely in a drawer for a hangerless man. I suspect, from the cigarette smell, that he wore them shirts while keeping up the corner of some bar.

I was happy to report that Harold Cowley was a boxer man, as I am convinced of the awful, sperm-killing clench placed on the testicles of the jockey wearer. I'm Pro-Life. He did, however, have a few pairs of Fruit of the Looms in frighteningly poor disarray. Of course, I could safely assume that he was alone. Even Raymond's laundry, which I still do, comes with an occasional bra and panties in it. I don't think Raymond's wearing them. Though he's starting to get the tits for it.

Now I believe in the strict confidentiality of the laundress and her clients. And I truly believe I was sparing the feelings of Harold Cowley by not pointing out all the money he was having laundered. He nearly had enough leftover drinking money to pay for his fifty pounds. But I didn't want to make the man feel stupid. I started a jar for him at home. I didn't spend one dime of that money on candy apples, or licorice, or lemon drops or any other treats. I wasn't even sure what I was saving up for, but I put HAROLD COWLEY's name in big old capitals on masking tape on a jar.

He picked his laundry up on Wednesday evenings, with the sun still shining. I liked the orderly routine, in terms of time, in this unordered, seemingly sad man. It made me look forward to every Wednesday morning, as Harold Cowley dropped his laundry off on Tuesday. I could have done it on Tuesdays, but I didn't want to deprive him of any of the fresh smells.

Though I believe he was severely depressed, I sensed something of hope when he picked up his laundry. They should put it in all the textbooks because having your laundry done, for one, just makes you feel good. Harold Cowley didn't do his own laundry because he either didn't like the task, or perhaps found it too dif-

The Thing About Love Is...

ficult. And I'm not no bragger, but I think he envied me a little in how I could turn that dirty pile of his into something restored and well... healed.

I never had more than three words with Harold Cowley all summer. He was your basic drop-off and pick-up man. His skin grew increasingly brown as the summer heated, and judging from some green socks and tennis shoes — which I allowed only in his case — and various paint stains on shorts and muscle man t-shirts, I figured him to be an odd-jobs man. It made me sad to think of a man working in the hot sun with a hangover. Raymond can at least cool in the Old Style bar with a Bloody Mary. There was always money and credit card receipts — with far too generous tips — pocketed, so I'm sure there was many a evening that Mr. Cowley could not recall. But from the stench and stains of his clothes, he did seem like a fella who always made it to work.

I think it was his shyness that intrigued me. He always seemed a little bit embarrassed when he picked up the garbage bag (four small bags, readied for each drawer of a standard dresser) that had all his folded underwear and socks in it. I admit no Fruit of the Looms had probably seen holier days. But I do like a shy man. When you break through, they really know how to treat you. Raymond is about as shy as a twenty-dollar lap dance. His type just knows how to lie and leave you.

Well here's me, Crazy Woman. The first thing I buy with Harold Cowley's mad money is some brand new Fruit of the Looms. The man had a ton of boxers, but every laundry batch had a few pairs of the elastic-losing jockeys. I took the new briefs out of the package, even washed them to give them the fabric softener scent, and tucked them away for his pick-up.

And you know that man never said a word to me about it. There weren't no gleam even to read in his Buster Brown eyes

The Thing About Love Is...

neither. 'Sides I'd have to lift his chin off his chest to see it. But I didn't say he didn't thank me. I come to find out Harold Cowley was a jogger. Soon after I'd given him that new underwear, he starts to run by my post every evening. I wouldn't have took him for a runner. I mean he had a real beer man's belly. But sure enough, I seen his skinny legs chasing after that arched belly. He weren't never gonna catch it. Belly looked too far gone. It was cute, though, how he started running by. Shy little show off.

"Look at me in my new running underwear," he seemed to be saying. Of course he kept them under them nylon gym shorts. I do think a man is wise to wear jockeys, or even a jockey strap, while jogging. Temporary sperm strangulation is better than the free swinging boxer when you got the whole package in motion.

He jogged in his baseball hat, and I wished he wouldn't. That black band of sweat ain't easy to get out, and he never thinks to drop his hat off for cleaning. Course it's my place to scour, not to scold.

Now I haven't prayed for a man since I first started to fear that Raymond was losing interest in me and my chocolate ways. Something told me early on to pray for Harold Cowley. His laundry reeked of displeasure. Though I don't suspect he drank in an Old Style bar, he felt the need to drink himself into a forgetful stupor night after night.

Well, the summer wore on. Harold Cowley was as dark as midnight by late August. My old Raymond had sexually harassed three waitresses away from his dark little world. Of course I fell in love with *Bridges of Madison County*, again. And even got a bit bothered and hot seeing Clint Westward in the movie — which weren't half as good as the book.

And then there's that time where you want it all to end. You never thought you would want summer to end. But even kids, you know, start wishing they was back at school. Old folks all around Chicago started dying — four or five hundred. They blamed it on the heat. Maybe they were just ready to die.

Finally we did get a bit of a cooling spell. Labor Day just around the corner, and there was a nice breeze at night to help you get to sleep. And just when you think every day of your life is going to grind on the same, God blesses us with the first changes of the season.

Course Harold Cowley's life seemed regular as bran — jogging, drinking, dropping off dirties. Now, personally, I've never lost a sock. I know how to do my own laundry, and I've done plenty of others'. But Harold, who I fear keeps a messy house, was constantly dropping off them footies without a mate. I started a sock drawer for him at home. I put his singles in, and matched them with the next week's load, and bought him some pairs at Target.

Harold Cowley's money jar was looking better than my vacation fund envelope, which I'm ashamed to admit has sticky fingerprints. I didn't want to blow all Harold's dough on socks and underwear. I stood by. I could sense that he would soon have a need for something bigger.

Last Wednesday was when I come across his napkin note. I kept the napkin and prayed. I prayed for about seven o'clock or thereabouts, when Harold usually picked up his laundry. Seven o'clock come but he don't. I mean, I figured he was a bit soused, feeling blue, probably wrote the note just to feel better. Sometimes you gotta get yourself way down in the dumps. In a weird way it don't even feel that bad. You know how you sometimes feel better after you throw up? And why would he leave the note for me? I bet like the rest of his pocket innards, he don't even remember putting it on paper.

By Friday, I'm a fright. Never blows in Wednesday. I can hardly eat Thursday. First thing Friday, I took his laundry home. I put

The Thing About Love Is...

all of Harold Cowley's laundry in a spare dresser in my little house. I folded it all and placed it away like a dutiful wife. I find it hard to believe that a wearer of such festive summer clothes could take such a dim view of life.

I had a few glasses of wine for courage, and called his phone number, which I obtained from the local information operator. I hung up when I heard a hello. I thanked the Lord and felt like my prayers had been answered. Then, dummy me, I remembered I had the man's entire summer wardrobe in my drawers.

A few more glasses of courage, I decided to call and tell him that I took his laundry home because Raymond was going to sell it. I would scold the man for being so forgetful as to not pick up his laundry on the appointed Wednesday, and perhaps, in undertone, suggest a more temperate lifestyle.

When I phoned again I heard the monotone hello and was already into my rehearsed spiel, when I heard a beep. Fortunately I stopped because I would have been blathering on his answering machine. I hung up again to come up with a third plan.

By this time I was convinced that the man was alive. I envisioned him stirring in his dreams when his voice clicked on the machine. It didn't occur to me to think otherwise because of that tremendous moment of relief I felt hearing his voice, though it weren't live. Too, I'm a positive thinker. My plan, conceived in part on Boone's Farm, was to invite Harold Cowley to dinner. I'd show him what a clean home I can offer. I know I can help a man like that turn the corner. I'd show him his big jar of money and ask him to imagine all the other things he could spend it on. I'd fix him healthy fat-free dinners, enabling his jogging to do some good. Heck maybe I'd start a fitness routine. I'd read his work or look at his paintings and praise them even if they weren't no good. I'd wash his hat out in the bathroom sink and put lotion on his brown arms and legs.

The Thing About Love Is...

I thought Harold Cowley would like it here, especially this time of year. There's a cool breeze at night, and it's real easy to sleep. As I drifted off I hoped I would dream of the man.

I can't never recall my dreams too much. Last night I kept waking. There was something pulling me from my usual rock state. Something from a dream maybe. This morning, besides a headache from the wine, I got this hollow lonely feeling. I ain't had it since I was married to Raymond. For years I just keep busy and stay pretty happy with that. But I can't work today. I'm calling in ill.

I wonder if it's the same feeling that Harold Cowley wakes up with. I wonder if it led to his death. A man who couldn't see nothing positive. A man who don't believe in prayer.

I kept pouring chocolate chips into the waffles I was making. Inside my buzzing head is a picture of Harold Cowley's face. It's so brown — so sad — kind of pockmarked, like some poor boy who didn't think the girls could see beyond that.

Scatter-brained and nervous like I never am — where I can't focus on nothing — I put all that chocolate waffle batter in the waffle iron, went to my living room and said a morning prayer just to try and calm down. I didn't remember it until I smelled it burning.

The Thing About Love Is...

Gypsy Threads
for Diana
Deborah E. Ryel

Our gypsy lineage survives in your wild hair
which you can never iron out, and in your
bold sense of color, the startling swatches
in your needlepoint (no kits like these in any
stores), and in your clothes, the skirt you wore
at the beach — it looked right, just right. You
in black, vestiges of our peasant stock, elbows
propped on a table, or that photo of you, wrapped
in a blanket at some windy shore. Your
silences and your sharp tongue are suited
to nomadic life, curled up with your two boys,
old world names aflame in their dark eyes.

You have found a house now in another country.
On your street a museum, your neighbors, Chinese.
Exotic surfaces become you — like your
singular beauty, erratic as sparks. You
strike against the edges of our small-town life.
Your flint (and ours too) this lawless impulse.

Once we would have lived together in a camp,
our bright painted wagons drawn up by the fire

The Thing About Love Is…

where our husbands danced after supper, their
wine bottles carried aloft on their songs
and their sweaty smiles. Grandmother could have
told our fortunes then, how we would be scattered
and lose the thread, to find it again in your
miniature tapestries, the ones we have hung in all
our rooms, fragments of tents we could have pitched
for our sons and the long skirts our daughters wore
when their fathers swung them to the strains
of our harsh music, and our blue fires roared.

Waltzing in the Garden of Forgiveness

Susan Strong-Dowd

ACT ONE
Scene 1

The Curtain Rises: The stage is bare, black. As the audience is seated, music of the late 1930s plays. At the curtain, the house goes black, the music fades out and the sound of a steam engine pulling into a station and stopping comes up. Entering from all wings and the back and sides of the audience are BROWN SHIRTS *speaking in German.* THEY *shine flashlights into the eyes of the audience and move around the entire space of the theater, searching until they "find" the* WOMAN *they're looking for. She is dressed in a long winter coat.*

FIRST BROWN SHIRT Come with us, please.

WOMAN Me? You want me?

(The WOMAN *stands, all the flashlights shine in her face. She moves over the people in the audience to stand in the aisle.* FIRST BROWN SHIRT *extends his hand and leads her down stage center. The* OTHER BROWN SHIRTS *keep their lights*

The Thing About Love Is...

shining on her. A lighting jell makes the shape of a railroad car window up stage right. Three figures: LIESEL (*age 13*) AARON (*her father*) ROSE (*her mother*) *enter from upstage right and appear within the lit area. They carry old leather suitcases and huddle together watching. Their suitcases contain all props they will need for the play.*)

FIRST BROWN SHIRT Come now, where is it?

WOMAN What? The lights. I can't see.

FIRST BROWN SHIRT Just tell us and you can be on your way.

WOMAN I don't understand.

FIRST BROWN SHIRT (*Moves in close to her.*) We have reliable information you're stealing from the Führer, from the Fatherland. Is this true?

WOMAN Reliable information?

FIRST BROWN SHIRT Come now. In here perhaps?

(*Upstage* AARON *removes his hat and turns it in his hands.*)

WOMAN (*Tries to pull away*) No. I have no idea.

FIRST BROWN SHIRT Lying *schmutzige Jude.* In here.

(THE BROWN SHIRTS *hold her arms out to her sides. her coat hangs open. She tries to struggle against them. They rip the*

The Thing About Love Is...

lining of her coat, exposing bills sewn into the hem. Up stage AARON *fiddles more with his hat.*)

ROSE Don't look, Liesel. Don't look.

(FIRST BROWN SHIRT *holds his pistol to* WOMAN'S *head.*)

WOMAN Please, no.

ROSE Aaron, what?

AARON Help me, Rose. What shall I do? Help me.

WOMAN My children. Please. I have small children.

LIESEL What's happening?

ROSE Aaron, do something, please.

(FIRST BROWN SHIRT *shoots the* WOMAN *in the temple. She falls in a heap on the floor. The* BROWN SHIRTS *tear at her coat, pocket the money.*)

FIRST BROWN SHIRT *Juden Schwein.*

LIESEL Mommy?

ROSE No, Liesel. Don't look.

(*The* BROWN SHIRTS *drag her off. The train steam is heard.* AARON *looks longingly at his hat and then throws it out into*

The Thing About Love Is...

the audience. As soon as the BROWN SHIRTS *are fully off stage, the steam sounds a final gasp. A* DARK FIGURE *enters upstage left dressed all in black and carrying a suitcase.)*

DARK FIGURE It was then I came into Liesel's life. It will take time for her to activate me and even longer to acknowledge me.

(DARK FIGURE *stands upstage in shadows with his back to the audience.)*

LIESEL (*To audience*) Daddy had sewn all our money into the band of his hat.

(THEY *pick up their suitcases and walk down stage.*)

ROSE All the money we had.

AARON I did the only thing I could do. The only thing.

ROSE Thanks God.

(*Down center stage,* THEY *pile their suitcases on top of one another and begin taking objects out of the top one: table cloth, candles, glasses, etc.* THEY *set up housekeeping as* THEY *tell their tale.*)

LIESEL It was in this way we came to America. Our first home was a tenement in New York City.

ROSE And our first friends were the janitor, his wife and—

LIESEL daughter, Sylvia. She took me to the movies. That was how I learned English. I tagged along behind her everywhere. We went down to the big hotels where the stars stayed and got their autographs. Look Mommy, look, Edward G. Robinson.

AARON Good people. They were good people.

ROSE But then my sister, Regina, sent word. There was more work with family in Chicago.

AARON Family is important.

LIESEL Family is to be honored and cherished. I didn't want to leave my new friend, Sylvia. I was just beginning to feel this was home. I hid my feelings from Mommy and Daddy as best I could, and we began to pack.

ROSE We didn't know it yet, but Aaron's nine siblings and their children would perish in concentration camps.

LIESEL And my Auntie Ann and Uncle Poldi and their three daughters, including my cousin Friedkin, who everyone said could have been my twin, would all perish.

AARON The only ones to survive would be Rose, her two sisters, Regina and Molly, and their families. So we moved again.

(Again, each of them has a suitcase to carry.)

AARON Chicago.

ROSE Chicago.

The Thing About Love Is...

LIESEL Chicago.

ALL THREE Chicago.

ROSE It sounds like home.

LIESEL Thank God for Sylvia. By now my English was great. I got to enroll into Marshall High School on the West Side.

AARON There was plenty of work on Roosevelt Road and on Maxwell Street.

LIESEL Everything they did was for me. Daddy. Mommy.

ROSE And I had my two sisters. We set up house near by.

(THEY *set up their suitcases to form a "house" center stage.*)

LIESEL It didn't take me long to grow up. To become an American. To be interested in boys and by the end of my junior year, one particular boy, the smartest boy I'd ever met, Arnie.

(ARNIE *enters stage left carrying a suitcase and takes her hand.*)

ROSE University of Chicago. She fell in love with his brain.

LIESEL Arnie. Brown eyes and a head of curly dark hair. Arnie.

AARON What are you going to do? They were young; they fell in love.

LIESEL The smartest boy I ever met.

The Thing About Love Is...

ARNIE As soon as she graduated, I asked for her hand in marriage, Liesel, my Liesel.

AARON My Liesel. You. Our Liesel and Arnie, the doctor's son.

ROSE Oy, my Liesel. Let me see. We were happy for them. I was happy.

AARON Be a good Jewish boy. You take care of our Liesel.

ARNIE I love her, Mr. Sager.

ROSE Now we can die in peace, Aaron. Now we can go to God and know our sweet little Liesel will be cared for.

LIESEL Mommy, don't talk like that.

ROSE Be good to her, Arnie.

AARON *Mazeltov.*

LIESEL Arnie.

ARNIE Liesel. (*Pause*) We moved into our own house.

(THEY *take their suitcases down stage center "defining" their new "house."* THEY *embrace.*)

LIESEL Then almost nine months to the day, our daughter was born.

(LIESEL *retrieves a baby from the suitcase. She presents the baby*

The Thing About Love Is...

to AARON, ROSE, ARNIE *and the audience.*)

AARON and ROSE Our first grandchild.

LIESEL Cheryl.

(LIESEL *uses the suitcase like a cradle.*)

Shhh. She's sleeping.

ARNIE Look how beautiful.

(*Enter* CHERYL *in youthful attire.*)

CHERYL And like all little girls, no matter how adorable, I grew.

(AARON *and* ROSE *age noticeably. They take their places up stage left watching.* CHERYL *practices at a ballet bar. An attractive* WOMAN *comes out of the audience and walks through the set.*)

LIESEL The minute I had the baby or maybe even while I was pregnant...

ARNIE My eyes started to roam and some of my other body parts followed.

(ARNIE *follows the woman off stage.*)

LIESEL Like all marriages, after a while we had our share of problems. We decided to try psychotherapy. I stuck with it.

The Thing About Love Is...

(ARNIE *re-enters on opposite side of stage and escorts the attractive* WOMAN *to her seat.*)

ARNIE What was the point? We are who we are and that isn't going to change no matter how much we talk. Therapy. A waste of time.

LIESEL Please, Arnie.

ARNIE Ten years she spent at it. Ten fucking years. Think of the money. I was sympathetic, her history and all. All those relatives killed in the camps. She needed it, not me.

(ARNIE *chooses another* WOMAN *from the audience.* LIESEL *cries.*)

CHERYL I was still growing, but I saw everything.

LIESEL I stuck with therapy even if Arnie didn't. I put myself into Cheryl and—

(LIESEL *uses her suitcase like an easel.*)

LIESEL painting and occasionally...

(*A handsome* MAN *comes out of the audience and gently caresses* LIESEL.)

Run along, Cheryl. Mommy has a meeting with this nice man.

(CHERYL *exits up stage right, but watches noticeably from the wings.*)

The Thing About Love Is...

I could justify my indiscretions. My men were destined to be famous, and he went for anything in a skirt, anything that moved, secretary bimbos. (*Pause*) I thought about leaving many times. (*To* AARON, ROSE *and audience*) He thinks we're made out of money. He spends the rent money on, on everything but the rent. Then I have to face the creditors, not him. He'd never do it.

AARON Liesel, Liesel. You have a husband, Liesel. In your old age he'll be with you.

LIESEL Is that why I have to borrow from you, Daddy?

AARON Everybody has some hard times. Why is there family? So, I can help.

ROSE Thank God for Arnie and your little Cheryl.

LIESEL And who pays Cheryl's tuition? You're supposed to be relaxing, resting in *your* old age, Daddy, not supporting my family now.

AARON Ah, what is money? When Mommy and I are gone, there will be someone to take care. Arnie will take care.

LIESEL (*To audience*) So why did I stay with him? you ask. Oy, I talked about this in therapy so much. For them. I stayed for them. I decided to make a go of it for Mommy and Daddy — so they could die in peace knowing I was married and cared for — and for Cheryl, my little Cheryl. A child needs her father.

CHERYL I left. Went to college, got an education and

(CHERYL *pulls her* YOUNG MAN *out of the audience.* YOUNG MAN, *too, carries a suitcase.* AARON *and* ROSE *come out of their "house" and greet* CHERYL.)

brought home a poet to marry. Look Nani Rose.

(CHERYL *flashes her engagement ring.*)

Isn't he handsome, Mommy?

ROSE Oy, how beautiful.

(CHERYL *pulls a bouquet out of her suitcase.* CHERYL *and her* YOUNG MAN *stand arm in arm, then there is animated hand shaking and kissing as if they'd married.* CHERYL *and her* HUSBAND *exit through the rear of the theater.* ARNIE, LIESEL, ROSE *and* AARON *wave good-bye.*)

AARON *Mazeltov.* Now we can rest. Now our little Cheryl is well cared for.

(AARON *and* ROSE *walk up stage to their "house."* ARNIE *and* LIESEL *stand motionless. There is an awkward silence.*)

LIESEL What now? (*Long pause*) What do we do now?

ARNIE I'm going to the bathroom.

(ARNIE *exits stage left.*)

LIESEL OK, well, good. I'll do the dishes.

The Thing About Love Is...

(LIESEL *begins doing the dishes in an imaginary sink, down stage right facing the audience.*)

Let's do something. (*Pause, long silence*) So, what do ya want to do later? (*Again, a long pause*) Want to go to the movies? (*Pause*) When you're finished, could you feed the animals? (*Pause, silence*) Can you hear me? (*Pause, silence*) Why don't you answer me? (*Pause, silence*) OK, I'll feed them. (*Pause, silence. LIESEL begins to feed the cat and dog.*) Here you go, *mein Leibkin* Jeremy. Oh, and some for you too, Elmer. You *meshuga* dog. (*Pause*) What in the hell are you doing in there anyway? (*Pause, silence*) Why is it always like this? Whenever we have time to talk, time to do anything together, you disappear and clam up. (*Pause, silence*) And not just when we have time alone together either. After every meal, I'm left to entertain everyone. You run away... (*Pause, silence. SHE walks to the "bathroom door."*) to the bathroom. (SHE *tries the door.*) OK, What'd ya lock the door for? (SHE *tries the door again, bangs.*) You've already locked me out, Arnie. It isn't necessary. (*Pause*) Look, Arnie. I'm reaching out to you. Don't do this to me, to us. We can still have a good life. Please. We've got to talk. Please. (*Long pause, silence.*) OK, suit yourself. Stay in there forever. (SHE *walks back to the sink — under her breath.*) Asshole.

(ARNIE *enters dressed in his tennis whites, carrying a small bag.*)

ARNIE I'm leaving.

LIESEL What? You're going to play tennis, now?

ARNIE No, I'm leaving.

The Thing About Love Is...

(LIESEL *moves toward* ARNIE *picks up raspberry jam left on the "table." The* DARK FIGURE *begins turning toward the audience so slowly throughout the rest of this scene, that it is almost imperceptible to the audience until* DARK FIGURE *is full front.*)

LIESEL What do you... (*Pause*) What did you say?

ARNIE I'm leaving.

LIESEL (*SHE smears jam on HIM.*) You. You coward. You waited until Cheryl was gone?

ARNIE What in the hell? Stop it! You're fuckin' crazy.

LIESEL Yeah I'm crazy. You *bastard*. You God damn bastard.

ARNIE Get away.

LIESEL I'll get away, but you won't you son-of-a-bitch.

(LIESEL *grabs small lamp off "table," smashes the top and goes after* ARNIE.)

ARNIE That's my favorite. You are mad.

LIESEL Your favorite.

ARNIE Get away from me with that.

(ARNIE *tries to escape her gouging, stabbing with the lamp. HE trips over his own feet.*)

The Thing About Love Is...

LIESEL Who is it, Arnie? Who is it this time, Arnie?

ARNIE You know who it is.

LIESEL Who? Not that mindless little secretary of yours.

ARNIE Put that down, Liesel.

LIESEL You are a motherfucker if ever there was one. You *God* damn motherfucker. I should kill you. I should cut off your balls.

ARNIE Please, Liesel, please. Put it down.

LIESEL Your timing is something else. You must want to kill me, you pig. I should kill you, you. (*Pause. SHE starts to cry.*) Get out. Get out of here. Go to your little bimbo. You deserve each other. Why didn't I leave you years ago? (ARNIE *scrambles to his feet, reaches for his bag.*) Oh, no, you don't.

ARNIE My bag.

LIESEL Leave it. Get out, now.

ARNIE But...

LIESEL Now, I said out. Now.

>(ARNIE *exits.* LIESEL *cries.* SHE *picks up his bag, removes items piece by piece and rips them up. The* DARK FIGURE *walks over, stands behind* LIESEL, *reaches into her blouse and pulls out a heart.* HE *takes a stone from his pocket, shows it to the audience much like a magician doing a trick, puts it into her*

heart, then puts the heart back into her blouse and stands behind her.)

LIESEL All I can think about is that cocksucker. I can't just sit here. I have to do something. (SHE dries tears.) And what do I know? A person's got to do what they know. (SHE takes a white coat out of her suitcase.) I need to help someone else.

DARK FIGURE This is good for her.

LIESEL I need to get out of myself and the *murderous feeling I have toward that pig of a husband.*

DARK FIGURE Ooo, now this is good for me. I just love it when you talk like this.

(All the way through this scene DARK FIGURE *takes articles of clothing out of his suitcase and "dresses-up" in a tuxedo.)*

LIESEL So I came here.

(LIESEL *directs the lights come up on stage and in the house.* FOUR PSYCH PATIENTS, *ages 16 to 18, enter in institutional green scrubs.* THEY *carry suitcases.)*

The psych ward at Children's Memorial. Plenty of work to do. They wanted me. They needed me.

DARK FIGURE If she keeps this up, I'm never going to get anywhere.

LIESEL Not like that *asshole* of a husband.

The Thing About Love Is...

DARK FIGURE Better. Much better.

LIESEL Bet you didn't know there were teenagers here. Lots of kids. It is difficult. How can I reach them? (SHE *follows the* PSYCH PATIENTS *around, tries to make contact, but* THEY *reject it.*) What happened in your tender young lives? (LIESEL *sits next to one* PSYCH PATIENT. SHE *puts her arm around* PSYCH PATIENT, *and it is rejected.*) To make you so mistrusting, so hard? What did I know to help them? All I knew was how *to pick a bastard for a mate.*

DARK FIGURE (*Singing, dancing and dressing*) Steppin' out with my baby.

LIESEL Painting. I know how to paint. I can show you. (SHE *opens her suitcase, removes the easel, paints and brushes, begins painting.*) If finding my life's work helped me, then it will work for you, too. (*The* PSYCH PATIENTS *show mild interest.*) A way to express yourselves.

DARK FIGURE No. This isn't what I need.

(THEY *move in closer to* LIESEL. *As soon as she looks at or acknowledges them in anyway,* THEY *scatter.*)

LIESEL Now try this. (SHE *folds a brush into the hand of one of the* PSYCH PATIENTS *even though the* PATIENT *resists.* LIESEL *helps* HER *make a few marks on the page.*) Look. You have talent. Let's see what you have. (THEY *back away.*)

DARK FIGURE Hello, I'm still here. Time to do something for me.

The Thing About Love Is...

LIESEL It went on like this for weeks. Little by little, day by day, more and more. Finally they all found things in their bags, parts of themselves they didn't know were there. (*The* FOUR PSYCH PATIENTS *sing, dance, paint and play a tin whistle.*) Aren't they great?

DARK FIGURE Oh, yeah, just peachy. Cut with the earth mother stuff and lets get back to castrating Arnie.

LIESEL Come sit by me. Let's talk. Come tell me about yourselves.

> (THEY *continue their activities, ignoring* HER. LIESEL *takes orange slices out of her suitcase and hands a section to each of them. At first* THEY *are reticent, but then* THEY *eat.*)

ONE OF THE PSYCH PATIENTS Thank you.

LIESEL (*To audience*) Did you hear that? She spoke to me.

DARK FIGURE Oh, yeah. Big whoop.

ANOTHER PSYCH PATIENT More.

LIESEL Food. It cures many ills. (LIESEL *hands out more fruits.* THEY *eat gleefully.*) Everything in the natural order.

DARK FIGURE What about me? Feed me. Some of that good old, home-cooked rage would be nice.

> (THEY *laugh.* LIESEL *dangles grapes in front of the* PSYCH PATIENT *who paints.* PATIENT *is visibly shaken* — SHE

The Thing About Love Is...

drops her paints and begins rocking. LIESEL *holds* HER *and rocks with HER.*)

LIESEL Sometimes, by accident, you knock something loose inside them. What is it? What's wrong? Katrina? What's wrong?

KATE Kate.

LIESEL Kate?

KATE Call me Kate.

LIESEL OK, Kate.

DARK FIGURE Boring.

KATE I remember the grapes.

LIESEL Yes, there's plenty.

KATE I asked for grapes.

LIESEL (SHE *offers more.*) See.

KATE (SHE *bats the grapes from* LIESEL'S *hand.*) The grapes. I *hate* him.

DARK FIGURE Well, it's about time. Finally someone is doing things my way.

LIESEL Who? Who do you hate?

The Thing About Love Is...

(*The other* PSYCH PATIENTS *stop dancing, playing and singing.* THEY *retreat to their bags.*)

KATE He told me to wait in the bedroom. We were watching Scoobydoo. He said he was going out for grapes.

LIESEL Yes.

KATE I can't.

LIESEL I didn't push it. She didn't tell me anymore that day. I made sure we got back to it though. (*Pause. The house lights come up. The other* PSYCH PATIENTS *exit and re-enter serving cake to everyone.*) It was food. Food triggered it. The whole thing. We were celebrating her birthday.

KATE It was magical. No one ever celebrated my birthday before.

LIESEL I made sure there were grapes.

KATE With a real cake.

PSYCH PATIENT #1 From Fine House of Chocolates...

PSYCH PATIENT #2 Or Schmeissing's...

PSYCH PATIENT #3 Or Rolf's or Swedish Bakery.

LIESEL Nothing but the best for my kids. Come on, everybody.

(THEY *all sing to* KATE.)

KATE But then she took out the grapes and...

(PSYCH PATIENTS *freeze.*)

LIESEL It worked before, right? She started that rocking thing again, so I just held her and listened.

KATE (*Rocking*) There was a knock at the front door. He answered it and then he went out for grapes. I stayed there in the bedroom and watched TV just like he told me. I heard him leave. I heard the front door close. All of a sudden there was a strange man at the door. He was big with spaces between his teeth and he had very big hands with hair, dark hair all over them, even on the fingers. He closed the door behind him. I told him my dad wasn't home. I told him to stay away from me, but he didn't. He came closer, he said my dad had given him permission. That I should be quiet and when I screamed, he slapped me across the face and knocked me clean off the bed. He picked me up and threw me back up on it and ripped my clothes. He rubbed those terrible hands all over me even up inside of me and then he took his pants off. He smelled like sweat and cigarettes and beer. He. He tried to kiss me. He tried to stick his big thick tongue in my mouth, but I wouldn't let him. He hit me and told me he'd paid for me and I better give it up, "Give it up you little slut," he said. He pulled my hair back and pinned me to the bed and I let him. I let him.

(KATE *rocks and cries.* LIESEL *holds* HER, *strokes her hair and rocks with* HER. *The* PSYCH PATIENTS *move in close around* LIESEL *and* KATE.)

LIESEL I'm here, Kate. Cry it out.

The Thing About Love Is...

KATE But there weren't any grapes. (*Pause*) There never were. He didn't go out for grapes.

LIESEL What? What do you mean, Kate?

KATE After the man left, I waited a long time, way past dark. I went out of the bedroom, even though he told me not to. There in the front room were Mom and Dad. They were all nodded out with their works lying right next to them on the floor.

LIESEL Works?

KATE Their needles, and cooking spoons and all that stuff for getting high. (*Crying*) They didn't even try to hide it. I was a little kid. I was only 9. (*Sobbing*) They sold me. They sold me to that man for a fucking fix. (*The* PSYCH PATIENTS *each open their bags and remove artifacts — a photo, a letter, a stuffed animal, etc. and give them to* LIESEL.) They loved their dope more than me.

DARK FIGURE All this is giving me a headache. Let's get back on track.

LIESEL Oh, Katie, my sweet Katie. I wish I could have told her she was wrong, that she'd gotten it all wrong, but I couldn't. They betrayed her trust... (*Pause*) just like...

DARK FIGURE Yes? Keep going.

LIESEL that *fucking husband of mine.*

DARK FIGURE (*Animated*) *Yes.*

(The DARK FIGURE *is nearly fully "dressed" in tux attire.* LIESEL *hand-feeds* KATE. SHE *gives more food to the* PSYCH PATIENTS. *With each bite,* THEY *stand taller, take their hospital attire off and put it in their bags.* THEY *"perform" their art.* LIESEL *hands out food to the* AUDIENCE.)

LIESEL No one can take your life's work from you. It's part of who you are.

KATE I can't give you an exact moment; it took time, but it was Liesel's great gift to me and to the others. (*Pause*) Food. She fed us. I had my painting and I grew in intellect. We grew in strength and confidence. She loved us and we grew in spirit and we changed.

(A festive atmosphere takes over: The PSYCH PATIENTS *eat, sing, dance, whistle, juggle.* KATE *paints.* LIESEL *brings dish after dish out of her suitcase.)*

DARK FIGURE Spare me the details.

LIESEL We grew together. I threw myself into loving them. I felt whole for the first time since Cheryl got married and left home.

DARK FIGURE Don't believe it for a second and what about my growth? I wasn't growing at all.

LIESEL Kate was like a daughter to me. I succeeded with these young people like I'd never done with Arnie. The sense of failure left me.

The Thing About Love Is...

KATE Liesel was like a mother. It was magic, not instant, but magic. We gave up the world of the hospital for the outside and Liesel was with us all the way. We were all ready to leave Children's and go make lives for ourselves.

(*The* DARK FIGURE *freezes on his suitcase.* LIESEL *moves her suitcase to define her home.* KATE *takes her suitcase and looks for a space to define as her own.* THEY *all exchange hugs. The* OTHER PSYCH PATIENTS *exit.*)

LIESEL I helped them find places.

KATE A place of my own.

(AARON *and* ROSE *enter with their bags, define their space.* ROSE *begins setting the Shabbos table.*)

LIESEL Right between my house...

AARON and ROSE And ours.

(THEY *all gather around the "table" and eat and pray and tell stories.*)

KATE We were very close. Every Friday evening, Liesel took me to Rose and Aaron's.

AARON (*To* KATE) Call me Papa Aaron.

ROSE (*To* KATE) I'm Nani Rose.

KATE For Shabbos. I have a family, a real family.

The Thing About Love Is...

AARON Thanks God.

ROSE She was good to us and good for our Liesel, too. We could see.

AARON *Adenoy Elohaynu.*

ROSE Kate even came with us to Temple for Rosh Hashanah and Yom Kippur.

KATE I liked it. I prayed in temple, then broke the fast with them. Eating had never been so good. And every year, seder, either here or at Liesel's.

AARON When I got too old to drive anymore, Kate drove us wherever we needed.

ROSE Sometimes she drove us for little trips out in the countryside. Small vacations. Thanks God for Kate. More brisket?

KATE (*Laughing*) Nani, remember the time we went to Galena, and I drove up on this really narrow road on a steep hill and you got so scared you just wanted me to stop the car and get out. I know you were really frightened, but what were we going to do after we left the car?

LIESEL It was frightening.

KATE I still have that beautiful blue vase you bought me on that trip, Nani. I think of you every time I use it.

(*The sound of a small yapping dog.*)

The Thing About Love Is...

AARON No one's leaving out this *meshuga* dog, Elmer.

LIESEL Oy, Elmer, the nut case. You funny little dog. Remember when he had an obsession for that stuffed animal I had, Doggie Woggie. Elmer humped the dog so much he scared us half to death he bled from all the humping and every time we tried to take it away from him, he got so angry, so vicious. Didn't you, little boy.

KATE Now there's a couple of things here I could respond to — first of all the animals — Liesel and Rose and Aaron fed all the animals in the city of Chicago and all those passing through too! I was always picking up bird seed for the birds or peanuts for the squirrels so they could feed their animals.

AARON Which the neighbors complained only fed the rats.

KATE Liesel carried things to an extreme — her love of animals. She might have even looked a little nuts to some people, but to me she was extraordinarily loving. One very cold morning soon after I'd moved out of the psych ward, she called me crying in empathy for the pigeon's cold feet. She was so sensitive.

AARON A blessing and a curse.

ROSE Don't forget the first fish Liesel ever caught back in Germany. She made her daddy take it back and put it in the river. She didn't want to kill it.

KATE See what I mean about appearing a little cuckoo? Anyway, the other thing I was going to say was about being vicious and angry. I'm sure you've noticed Liesel's uncontrollable rage toward

The Thing About Love Is...

Arnie.

DARK FIGURE Oh, yeah, now we're talking. She's telling you like you didn't get that part?

AARON Son-of-a-bitch. Rose and I counted on him.

ROSE He broke our hearts, all of us.

KATE I never knew the guy, never met him, but every time I was with Liesel or even talked to her on the phone, she would always bring him up with pure venom in her voice. By her, he was the devil incarnate.

LIESEL What was I supposed to do?

ROSE But, Liesel, it was a long time ago now.

(*The dog barks.*)

LIESEL Elmer knows. Don't you, boy? Arnie was a *God damn pig,* wasn't he? It wasn't just me he hurt. Look how he hurt Mommy and Daddy, and that's something I'll never forgive.

DARK FIGURE Better start worrying about yourself.

ROSE and AARON Liesel, don't.

LIESEL OK, I'll give you another thing. I love to cook, right? I love to feed people. You can see this. It was natural. Something Arnie never appreciated.

DARK FIGURE See, what did I tell you? Just a matter of time.

LIESEL One time I made a lentil soup with big chunks of sausage in it and served it with French bread and the *bastard* looked in the pot and said, "Is that all there is?" and went out for a hot dog.

DARK FIGURE Right on cue.

KATE Oh, my gosh. Where'd the time go? I've got to get going. Let me help with the dishes, Nani.

AARON We'll all help.

> (AARON, ROSE *and* KATE *clear the table and exit. The* DARK FIGURE *pulls on a swastika arm band, and stands at attention in his tuxedo, straightens his tie, using the audience as a mirror.* HE *looks very dashing, attractive.* HE *walks down stage toward* LIESEL, *takes* LIESEL'S *hand and kisses it.*)

DARK FIGURE Now, vee vill dance.

LIESEL (*Taken with his attention.*) I know you from somewhere, don't I?

DARK FIGURE Zis is true. I've been vis you all along, but I vas hibernating, und now you have avakened me. It is time to dance.

LIESEL Dance? (*They dance.*) What is your name?

DARK FIGURE I go by many names, but for you I'm Breast Cancer.

The Thing About Love Is...

LIESEL (THEY *waltz around the stage.*) Odd. (*Pause*) I'm tired. Can we stop now?

(HE *pulls* HER *close.* SHE *is uncomfortable.*)

DARK FIGURE No.

LIESEL How long must we do this?

DARK FIGURE We're going to dance for the next five years just like this and then...

LIESEL Five years. You must be out of your mind. I'm not going to... How can I get you to stop this? Let me sit down.

DARK FIGURE How?

LIESEL Yes, how? This is ridiculous.

DARK FIGURE You aren't going to like it, Liesel. (*Pause*) First of all, you'll have to forgive Arnie.

LIESEL Forgive Arnie? Why in hell does Arnie need forgiving?

DARK FIGURE It's not something Arnie needs; it's something you need.

LIESEL And just how am I supposed to do that? He's not worthy of forgiving. Arnie is a *pig* and everyone knows it.

DARK FIGURE (HE *tightens his grip.*) Suit yourself. Oh, and while you're at it, find a way for Kate and Cheryl to be friends,

The Thing About Love Is...

too.

LIESEL Kate and Cheryl? They hardly know each other.

DARK FIGURE Exactly.

LIESEL I don't understand.

DARK FIGURE Oh, you will. You'll see. You've got five years to figure it out.

(THEY *continue to dance. The lights fade to black out.*)

ACT ONE
Scene 2

(*When the lights come up,* LIESEL *and* DARK FIGURE *are center stage.* ROSE *and* KATE *are down stage center.* DARK FIGURE *is always close to* LIESEL. HE *touches* HER, *holds* HER *hand, puts his arm around* HER, *etc. Shows intimacy with* HER.)

LIESEL I had the most terrible dream. If I were a big drinker, I'd think I'd gotten drunk. I feel hungover and my feet are killing me.

ROSE Thanks God I knew nothing about her illness. Dream, Liesel? I don't think it's a dream. I'm sick, Liesel.

DARK FIGURE Hey, let's not confuse the issue.

The Thing About Love Is...

(LIESEL *holds* ROSE *and feeds* HER.)

ROSE (*Pause*) I'm dying, Liesel.

LIESEL (*Yelling*) Daddy, Daddy. (*To* KATE) Kate, would you get Papa and tell him Nani is sick and then call Cheryl. Tell her she should come to Chicago. Tell her her grandmother is dying.

(KATE *exits, then enters with very aged* AARON.)

AARON Oy, Rose. Don't leave me, Rose.

KATE (*Yells*) Cheryl, come home, your grandmother is dying and if you don't come now, you'll miss her.

AARON For more than 60 years. Oh, my sweet Rose.

(CHERYL *enters.* THEY *all hug* ROSE *good-bye.* ROSE *begins her exit.*)

ROSE Good-bye, everyone. Take good care of each other.

KATE, CHERYL, LIESEL and AARON We will.

LIESEL I love you, Mommy.

(ROSE *waves to* EVERYONE *and exits through the back of the theater with her bag.*)

CHERYL Right after the funeral, I went back to New York.

(CHERYL *exits.*)

AARON Then Liesel was diagnosed. Cancer. Oy.

DARK FIGURE (*Cavorting around* LIESEL *suggestively.*) I was official.

AARON It broke my heart through and through.

KATE In the beginning, we were all hopeful. She had the surgery — a lumpectomy — and the radiation, and even though she didn't want it, eventually she had the chemotherapy.

(LIESEL *holds* AARON *and feeds him.*)

LIESEL Then Daddy got sick. We were surrounded by sickness and death.

DARK FIGURE OK, yes, so?

LIESEL Daddy. Kate, would you call Cheryl and tell her if she wants to see her grandfather, she needs to come now.

AARON I couldn't go on.

KATE (*Yelling*) Cheryl, come now if you want to see your grandfather before he dies.

(CHERYL *enters.*)

CHERYL Why are you calling me? Why doesn't my mother call?

KATE She wants you to come without asking herself, I suppose.

The Thing About Love Is...

AARON (*Pause*) Kate, come here.

KATE Yes, Papa, what is it?

AARON Promise me you'll take care of Liesel.

LIESEL Daddy.

CHERYL Papa? Stop that. He's my Papa, not yours. Why did he ask her for that? Why didn't he ask me?

(DARK FIGURE *rubs up against* CHERYL.)

KATE I promise, Papa. I'll watch over her.

(LIESEL *pushes* DARK FIGURE.)

LIESEL You wouldn't.

AARON It's time for me to go, Liesel.

LIESEL I love you, Daddy.

(AARON *picks up his suitcase and exits through the back of the theater.*)

CHERYL I'll look out for her, Papa.

(AARON *turns and waves.*)

CHERYL After Papa was buried, there was really not much reason for me to stay.

KATE Except your mother would have loved it.

   (DARK FIGURE *circles* KATE.)

CHERYL So I went back to New York.

   (CHERYL *exits*.)

KATE Self-involved little baby. What is wrong with her? Can't she see?

LIESEL Kate.

KATE I'm sorry, Liesel. I can't stand the way she hurts you so much.

LIESEL What do you mean?

   (DARK FIGURE *touches, examines* KATE.)

KATE I can't stand the way you protect that little baby. I hate her.

LIESEL You stay away from her.

KATE Liesel, how could you think... I wouldn't touch her. I love you too much to do anything to her.

LIESEL No, not you. Never mind. Go ahead.

DARK FIGURE There's only one way to keep me out of it.

The Thing About Love Is...

KATE She shouldn't run away all the time. If you were my mother, I'd be right here with you. I'd take care of you.

LIESEL You can't carry the burden of my pain for me.

KATE Isn't that what you do with your hatred of Arnie?

LIESEL What do you mean?

KATE You always said Arnie was a pig because of what he did to Nani and Papa. You always said what he did to you was nothing compared to what he did to them. So it was their pain you were carrying around. He hurt the people you loved most.

DARK FIGURE Listen to her.

LIESEL Oh, shut up.

KATE I'm not going to, Liesel.

LIESEL I didn't mean...

KATE Cheryl is hurting the person I love most in the world. You've been like a mother to me, but she's the one you want. Why won't she just come and stay here with you?

LIESEL Maybe it's because I am her mother. (*Pause*) Tell me Kate did you forgive your parents?

KATE Forgive? Well I suppose that's what you'd call it. Yes.

LIESEL For all those terrible things? How? How did you do that

The Thing About Love Is...

after what they did?

KATE You taught me how.

LIESEL Me?

KATE It took time, that's the main thing you taught me. And I wanted to. My hatred of them was holding me back. I was spending all my energy hating them. You showed me that with your love.

DARK FIGURE Time. You don't have a lot of that.

KATE I saw they were only people, just like me.

LIESEL How did you come to that?

KATE When I visited with my dad once, and he told me his dad used to force him to watch his parents have sex.

LIESEL Oh? my God.

KATE His dad told him he was trying to teach him the facts of life. Instead it screwed him up for life.

(KATE *takes out some cookies.* SHE *and* LIESEL *eat.*)

LIESEL That was how you forgave him. Did you forgive your mother?

KATE That was harder. I had to walk right up to her and say, "You hurt me so much, why did you do that?" And then I had to really listen to her answer.

LIESEL What did she say?

KATE Well, first of all, she cried real tears. I could see she was really sorry for all the terrible things that had happened. It wasn't that her reasons were so great. I mean, how could a mother allow her daughter to be... I mean she understood better than anyone. Basically she said she thought it was better to stay with my dad than leave him. And then it was like if you can't beat them join them, so she joined him. She was doing the best she could.

(DARK FIGURE *hugs* LIESEL *tightly.*)

KATE We all thought Liesel was going to be OK, but then the cancer moved from her breast to her bones. Even though we didn't say it, we all knew it was only a matter of time. Her bones started breaking for the silliest reasons.

LIESEL I woke up one morning and took the covers off. Broken arm.

(PSYCH PATIENTS *enter and mill around the entire theater.*)

KATE Someone was always calling Cheryl to let her know.

PSYCH PATIENT (*Yells*) Cheryl, come home. Your mother broke her arm.

LIESEL I was falling apart.

PSYCH PATIENT (*Yells*) Cheryl, come home. Your mother's

The Thing About Love Is...

ribs are broken.

(CHERYL *enters.*)

CHERYL I was flying back to Chicago every time you turned around.

KATE And turning around every time you flew in. (CHERYL *exits.*) There was nothing we could do to stop it. We knew she would die and we could do nothing more than watch it happen.

(KATE *exits into the audience and watches* LIESEL *and the* DARK FIGURE.)

DARK FIGURE (*Singing*) My day will come, and I'll have everything.

LIESEL Leave those girls alone.

DARK FIGURE You've made progress, but you're not there yet, honey.

LIESEL And I'm sick of you pawing all over me all the time; I'm tired of it.

(SHE *pushes* HIM.)

DARK FIGURE Ooo, getting pretty feisty, aren't we.

LIESEL I mean it.

DARK FIGURE It's not that easy, Liesel.

The Thing About Love Is...

(HE *grabs* HER *and holds* HER *tightly.* THEY *struggle.*)

LIESEL Let go of me. You're hurting me.

> (DARK FIGURE *pulls out a mask of* ARNIE *and holds it up to his face.* THEY *continue to fight.* ARNIE'S *voice is heard when* DARK FIGURE *speaks.*)

LIESEL You're hurting me. You hurt me so much.

ARNIE I'm sorry, Liesel. I only wanted...

LIESEL It was always about what you wanted.

ARNIE The marriage was no good. Even you knew that. I'll even admit I was no good.

LIESEL I was thinking about more than myself. What about Aaron and Rose? Think of what you did to them.

ARNIE And what about you?

LIESEL I was supposed to take care of them, and I did my best, but then you, you... All they needed, all they wanted was to think I was well cared for.

ARNIE And if we'd continued the charade, would you have been well cared for?

LIESEL At least they would have thought so.

ARNIE And what about you, Liesel? What about you?

The Thing About Love Is...

LIESEL (*Crying*) I knew it was over.

ARNIE But you didn't have the courage to end it.

LIESEL No, I had the courage to try and make it work.

ARNIE We were living a lie, Liesel.

LIESEL You hurt me so much. Why did you do that, Arnie, why?

ARNIE Oh, Liesel, I am so sorry. I didn't mean to hurt you.

LIESEL And what about Cheryl?

ARNIE She'll be all right.

LIESEL How can you say that? Have you seen her lately?

ARNIE Yes, every time she comes to see you, she sees me, too.

LIESEL And when I'm gone, who will she have? What kind of a family?

ARNIE I'll be here, and don't forget, she has her poet.

LIESEL Her poet has never been there for *her*. Why do you think she always comes here alone and hurries back so quickly?

ARNIE Liesel, please, Liesel.

LIESEL Oh Arnie, I never wanted it to be like this. I never

The Thing About Love Is...

wanted to hate you the way I have, but I couldn't help myself.

ARNIE (HE *strokes her hair.*) Liesel.

LIESEL I'm sorry, Arnie.

ARNIE If I forgive you, will you forgive me?

   (THEY *laugh.*)

LIESEL Only if you promise to look after Cheryl.

ARNIE I promise. (*Pause*) Cheryl was the best thing we ever did. I love her, Liesel.

   (DARK FIGURE *holds* LIESEL *and slips the mask away.*)

KATE It was early in December, toward the end of the fifth year she'd been struggling with the disease, when she said...

LIESEL I'm going to die soon.

KATE Three days later, she broke her hip.

   (*The* PSYCH PATIENTS *roll a gurney onto the stage.* DARK FIGURE *helps* LIESEL *up on the gurney, pushes it center stage and props* HER *up.*)

LIESEL Climbing the stairs and my hip broke.

KATE She knew this would be her last trip to the hospital, but did she know she'd never go home again?

The Thing About Love Is...

DARK FIGURE You've done so well, but there is still some work before you go and time is running out, Liesel.

PSYCH PATIENTS (*Yelling, delivered like an echoing chant*) Cheryl, come home. Come home. Come home. (*Pause*) If you want to see your mother alive. If you want to see your mother alive. See your mother alive again. Come home. Now. Now. Now.

KATE It was hard watching her deteriorate. More and more Liesel was talking some strange off-the-wall stuff, things that didn't make sense, like she was losing her mind.

(The PSYCH PATIENTS *exit.*)

LIESEL Let's go home now, Kate. I want to feed the birds.

KATE It's OK, Liesel. I'll feed them.

LIESEL And the squirrels. And Daddy's birds.

KATE I'll feed them, too.

(CHERYL *enters.*)

CHERYL Mommy. (*Pause*) Please, Kate.

LIESEL And Cheryl, will you feed Cheryl, too?

(DARK FIGURE *circles* KATE *and* CHERYL, *looking* THEM *up and down.*)

KATE I think Liesel wants to go home.

The Thing About Love Is...

CHERYL I'll be the judge of that.

LIESEL I want to die in peace. I want to finish my business before I go.

CHERYL Mommy.

DARK FIGURE You're almost there, Liesel.

LIESEL Not with you circling around like a shark.

CHERYL What's that supposed to mean?

KATE They needed some time to themselves. I think I'll go get a cup of coffee.

   (KATE *exits.*)

CHERYL Good.

DARK FIGURE Alone together.

CHERYL Maybe I should go call for your lunch.

LIESEL Don't go, Cheryl. Don't. I want us to talk. (*Pause*) I want to talk about you and me and your father.

CHERYL Daddy?

LIESEL Yes.

CHERYL What about him?

The Thing About Love Is...

LIESEL I want to know if you ever forgave him... if you ever forgave him and me for what we did?

CHERYL Forgave?

LIESEL Yes, I know you see him.

CHERYL Yes.

LIESEL Did you forgive him?

CHERYL I don't understand what you want from me, Mommy. I see Daddy because he is my father. I didn't tell you because I thought you'd think I was disloyal. I thought you'd think...

LIESEL You thought I wouldn't love you if you had a relationship with your father?

CHERYL Yes.

LIESEL Oh, Cheryl. (THEY *embrace.*) I'm sorry. I did that to you. I did that with my constant anger. Forgive me, Cheryl. I'm sorry. (*Pause*) I will always love you, always. You're mine, my daughter.

CHERYL You don't act like it sometimes.

LIESEL Yes...?

CHERYL You'd think Kate was your daughter.

LIESEL I love Kate. She's been very good to me.

The Thing About Love Is...

CHERYL But...

LIESEL But you're the only one who can call me Mommy. You're my only daughter, my only child and I love you with all my heart.

CHERYL Oh, Mommy. (THEY *embrace*.)

LIESEL There's one other thing. (*Pause*) I want your forgiveness, Cheryl.

CHERYL Why? What for?

LIESEL I... I want your forgiveness for being so, so indiscreet when you were a kid. It was bad enough that your father... I shouldn't have.

CHERYL Indiscreet?

LIESEL I should have been more attentive to you and to your needs when you were a kid, but with the difficulties your father and I were having. I know you saw things you shouldn't have, I know I brought men around...

CHERYL Don't. Mommy, it's OK. Please, don't. I...

(KATE *enters carrying a tray of coffee.*)

KATE Coffee? (*Pause*) I'm not disturbing, am I?

LIESEL No. No.

The Thing About Love Is...

CHERYL Come on in.

KATE I thought you might like a cup of coffee.

CHERYL Oh, I almost forgot, I brought some pastries. We can have coffee and...

(CHERYL *takes pastries from her bag and the* THREE *eat.*)

KATE A few days later, Cheryl and I were together with her again.

CHERYL She'd been practically unintelligible all day. She was having difficulty breathing, when she said...

LIESEL Kate.

KATE Clear as a bell. Yes, Liesel, what is it? I had to put my ear up next to her mouth.

LIESEL Kate, am nwa po di javel ca, promise?

KATE The only thing I could understand was Kate and promise. I didn't have a clue what she was trying to say. What is it, Liesel?

LIESEL Kate, am nwa po di javel ca, promise?

KATE I wanted to put her mind at ease. She was struggling so hard and still I couldn't understand her.

LIESEL Kate, am nwa po di javel ca, promise?

The Thing About Love Is...

KATE So I said, "I promise, Liesel. I promise," even though I didn't know what I was promising.

CHERYL They did that several times, my mother asking Kate to promise to do something I didn't understand and Kate promising, so I asked, "What did you promise, Kate?"

(DARK FIGURE *grabs* KATE's *head and whispers in her ear.*)

KATE And then the strangest thing. Something just came over me; I don't know why. I had an uncontrollable urge to say, "I promised your mother you and I would keep in touch. I promised her we'd try to be friends."

CHERYL Mommy died the next morning.

KATE At six o'clock.

CHERYL No one was with her.

DARK FIGURE But she was at peace.

(KATE *and* CHERYL *pull the sheet over* LIESEL. *The* PSYCH PATIENTS *enter and, along with* KATE *and* CHERYL, *act as pall bearers and wheel the gurney through the audience and out the back of the theater.*)

DARK FIGURE OK, OK so I cheated. I helped it along a little. What can I say? She was so close. (*Pause*) Besides, I've always wanted to play the good guy, and I finally had my chance. (*Pause*) Not bad for a Nazi named Breast Cancer, huh? (*Yells*) Come on, boys. (*The* BROWN SHIRTS *enter from the back and sides.*) Who knows? Maybe under the right circumstances, everything could be forgiven.

(THEY *do an about face. The lights fade to black.* THEY *exit.*)

CURTAIN

Taking Small Steps
for Arthur
Deborah E. Ryel

We are taking small steps home from school,
your hand in mine, like the warm bird we rescued
from the cat this morning or its small
fluttering heart. One eye fixes us even now,
so we must stop at all the sewer grates
and divine for water. You drop in a twig
or a pebble, whatever is handy,
and then peer down through narrow slits
to study the widening circles afloat
like the moon in greater darkness.

There are no straight lines for us to follow.
The narrow curb is broken, and rusty water
runs along the gutter where we find ourselves poised,
you with one shoe lifted. "Can I put it in?"
you ask. "It won't really get wet."

Two in one, your hand uncharacteristically
a part of mine as it rides toward home.
Now we are counting the look-alike houses
sheathed in their odor of wet leaves.
They listen to the chirping notes of your story,

The Thing About Love Is...

told over and over in rhythm with our small steps
through the hushed neighborhood. We pass the cat
in the shrubbery, whose eyes alone observe us,
and small birds leap up from the locust tree.

The Value of Pain

Tom Montgomery-Fate

Every peak is a crater. This is the law of volcanoes....
—Adrienne Rich

The brown silhouette of *El Fuego* is so foreign to Nora that she doesn't notice when the coffee arrives. She gapes at the stark ashen cone expectantly, as if it will erupt while she isn't looking, while she is patiently trying to translate Robert's determined attempts at Spanish. It did erupt two years earlier, but now there is only the illusion of vitality — an occasional molten discharge and the deep irregular rumbles which cause the tourists to roll over in their beds at night.

Corazon, a vendor Nora had met on the plaza that morning, claimed that you could actually see the red orange lava bubbling inside the crater from the other side of the lake, if you were in the right place and patient enough. *"Si. Vale la pena!"* she had urged. Not knowing the phrase, Nora tried to translate it literally: "The pain has value." Her Berlitz grammar text disagreed: "Worth the effort." Nora believed Corazon completely, but she knew Robert wouldn't want to go. They'd have to hire a jeep with four-wheel drive. Too expensive. Not practical. Maybe dangerous.

Corazon had also warned Nora. She had clasped Nora's small hands completely inside her own and insisted that she not go near *Fuego* alone. Her concern both surprised and pleased Nora.

The Thing About Love Is...

There were typically one or two eruptions per year. These were spectacular but brief, most of the lava and rock falling back in or near the crater, or running to the lake. Corazon feared a severe eruption due to the length of the dormancy. But Nora doesn't want to miss it. She wants it to happen before she leaves.

Robert makes eye contact with the waiter: *"Perdon* me. *El baño.* Where is it, *por favor?"* His Spanglish both amuses and embarrasses Nora. The waiter graciously points to a bathroom in the rear of the cafe. Robert leaves. Nora looks back out the window at *El Fuego*. The dark form of a bird circles the crater. As she traces its graceful pattern around the rocky apex, she wonders if it is close enough to feel the heat of the burning heart of energy deep within the stone facade.

A drunk Miami lawyer at the bar the previous night had seemed embarrassed by his date. He downed a gin and tonic and then abruptly answered a question no one had asked. "Men *always* feel hornier around volcanoes," he said. Then a pause and the punchline: "We want to get our rocks off too!" He nearly gagged on his laughter. The dark-eyed adolescent on his arm had looked confused. She didn't speak English. Robert had quickly snatched up their beers and headed back to their table. Nora appreciated his disgust. They had seen a dozen men like the lawyer on the Atlantic Coast the week before: overweight, middle-aged white men who strutted on the beach like sunburnt penguins. Slight, young, brown women trudged behind them through the sand.

Robert returns and is disappointed that the food hasn't arrived.

"He forgot to give the cook our order. Look. It's still on the counter. I can read it from here."

"No, that's not it. Just wait. He knows what he's doing," Nora says.

"Oh, yeah. Waiting's part of the culture. Right?"

The Thing About Love Is...

"Yeah, right," Nora smiles, surprised at Robert's resignation. She fiddles with her silver bracelet and looks back out the window at the volcano. She wants to tell him.

Robert had enjoyed their late-morning shopping spree at the *Mercado Nacional*. He feels better now because they have something concrete to show for their trip. He spills their wicker basket of souvenirs out on the table: brightly painted gourd maracas from Guanacaste, a shiny pink conch from Limon, bamboo pan pipes from Ciudad Quesada, and three black coral bracelets from Puerto Viejo.

Nora bought a black coral necklace at the same market several days earlier, but Robert had discouraged her. He thought it was a fake. Luckily, Jan Warren had been shopping at the same booth. Jan was a Peace Corps volunteer Nora had met on Tamarindo Beach the weekend they arrived. It had been nearly two weeks since that chance encounter.

Jan vouched enthusiastically for the authenticity of the coral, and after an appropriate "May I?" helped Nora put the necklace on. Her hands cupped Nora's bare shoulders for several seconds after she fastened the clasp. They rested there, warm and comfortable. Then she moved Nora, by the shoulders, in front of a small mirror in the next booth.

"There. How's that?" Jan had asked, smiling.

After buying the necklace, on the way to lunch that afternoon, she had watched herself in the display windows that lined the street. The long polished bar of coral was striking against her pale skin. She wondered if she looked different, if others noticed.

Nora wants to tell him. The waiter brings ham sandwiches. Robert eats quickly. He pours the last of his silver pot of hot milk into the remainder of his coffee, drains it in a single gulp, and looks up at Nora expectantly. He clears his throat loudly. He can't help himself Nora knows this. She ignores him. He asks the question that they had both come to dread.

"Well, are we about ready?"

"You are, I'm not."

"OK, I'm sorry. I was just thinking we might like to do something," he says.

"Robert, we *are* doing something."

Just then the volcano rumbles. The windows rattle and the floor trembles for several seconds. The gringos buzz. When the tremor stops they all rush upstairs to the open veranda on the second floor. Nora and Robert push in front in time to see a great belch of ash rise in a powdery grey plume from the brown cone. They join in the communal gasp as the ominous cloud slowly begins to drift toward the city.

"My God! Look at it." Nora says.

"Shit," Robert says.

The rumbling stops. Nora is euphoric. Robert is sweating. They finally return to their table downstairs.

"Can you imagine what it would be like if it really blew? I mean if the lava came shooting out like in the movies. God, it'd be incredible," Nora says.

"Yeah, but I think I'd rather watch from a distance — like on TV," Robert replies.

They order beer. Robert no longer wants to leave. Like the others in the cafe, he and Nora take long, thoughtful sips from their cold green bottles, and wonder if the mini-eruption portends a major one. Robert orders another round, and another an hour later. The excitement finally wanes. Nora knows this is the perfect time. She is carefully forming the sentences when Robert digs out the photos from Tamarindo beach. They had just arrived that day. He spreads a few out on the glass table top. Nora immediately spots the shot of Jan and herself sitting on a rock watching the pelicans feed at sunset. Their backs are to the camera. They are

The Thing About Love Is...

illuminated by exotic bands of orange and red light. A few minutes after the picture was taken, most of the color had seeped below the horizon, and someone turned the moon on. That was when Robert had gone back to the hotel, to avoid the mosquitoes and fruitbats and drink beer.

They had remained on the beach for nearly an hour, watching the ungainly pelicans lumber about on the rocks and dive for fish in the brilliant moonlight. The pelicans often struggled for the first few seconds before achieving flight, but once aloft they were easy in the air, coasting inches above the cresting whitecaps. Or they would loop in long ovals, scanning for fish. The unmistakably awkward shadows plunging boldly into the abyss had delighted Nora. She never grew tired of watching them.

She had been afraid to swim in the dark, though. She stumbled as she followed Jan, wading out into the gentle rhythm of the water. Their tee shirts lifted and swirled in the current as they walked. Jan took hers off, wadded it up, and threw it in to shore. A black bikini strap divided her short, sturdy back into two shiny, brown quadrants. Even in the moonlight she looked tan. Nora left her tee shirt on.

They kept walking. The pebbles and sand below were unpredictable, shifting with the tide. Nora thought she stepped on a crab. Jan checked. Nothing. They walked out another twenty yards, then thirty. The water was still shallow, just above their waists, but it had become even more rocky.

"Be careful here," Jan had warned. She took Nora's hand. They slowly took a few more sliding steps together, their feet rolling over small rocks. Then the grade dropped severely.

"This is it," Jan said.

"What? What is it?" Sensing danger, Nora panicked. Suddenly she was sliding again, falling off a cliff in slow motion. The bottom fell out. She began thrashing her arms and gasping for

The Thing About Love Is...

breath.

"It's OK. It's OK." Jan said, coming up alongside her. "Just keep treading."

Nora trusted her voice. She kept treading.

"We just slid off the ledge," Jan said finally. "It's two hundred feet deep here."

"What?" Nora gasped again. "Is it safe?"

"Yeah. There's a huge shelf here. It's a popular spot for scuba diving. There's a shipwreck out about another 100 yards."

Together they treaded out until they were parallel with the large rock where the pelicans were diving. Bobbing in the shimmering black green water, suspended by their beating arms and the miracle of laughter, Nora grew less and less concerned about the depth of the world below them, the world she couldn't know. She was keenly aware of her body, of her breathing, of the play of cool water and warm air on her skin.

After treading for several minutes, they became tired and swam into shore, collapsing on the beach, lying in the surf, feeling the rush of the small waves, the light, sucking pull of the undertow. Nora sat up to pull off her heavy tee shirt. When it got stuck, Jan sat up and crawled up behind her. She slowly rolled the shirt up to Nora's armpits, then, grabbing the soggy roll, pulled it over her head. They sat cross-legged next to each other in the surf, watching the pelicans. The moon continued to brighten. Nora looked down at her legs. The black volcanic sand stuck to her wet, salty skin, forming many odd, beautiful shapes.

"Look," Jan said, standing and then leaning down to fish something out of the water.

"A floating rock. Have you ever seen one? It's called pumice."

Nora took the rock from Jan's hand, walked out a few steps and dropped it in the sea.

Floating on the surface, it washed back to her. She laughed and

The Thing About Love Is...

threw it in again and again, each time encouraged by the seeming defiance of nature.

Later that night, more certain of her decision, she whirled back to the hotel under a yellow moon like a reckless top, clumsily spinning around palm trees, defiantly jumping over driftwood, wildly pirouetting along a sandy stage to the music of the water. She had been so tightly wound for so long, that as she moved her arms, her legs, her fingers, her muscles, her bones, her tendons, her nerves, her heart, erupted with energy, with relief.

She had tried to tell him for days. But what could she say? "Robert, things just aren't working for me." Or "Robert, I need some space, some creative space." Or "Robert, I'm not going home with you.

"Robert there's something wrong with me ... with us," is what she hears herself say.

"What do you mean?" he asks.

"I mean something happened, and I let it happen. I wanted it to happen. I know it's my fault..."

"What are you trying to say?"

"I'm sorry. There is so much I love about you. But I need to be alone now. There are things I need to do..."

As they walk back to the hotel, she tries to explain to him that it doesn't feel like a phase, or something temporary, as he suspects. She begins to cry. They leave the cafe. On the street she grabs his arm, leans close, and says familiar words — "We can get through this." This doesn't calm him. His pace slows, and Nora notices that his hands have begun to tremble. Inside, layers of shared memory are splitting open.

When they arrive at the hotel, Robert stops and turns to face her. His voice is shaking. "Are you sure you know what you're doing?" he says. "Can't we see a therapist or something?"

Three days later, when Nora simply says, "I'm staying," Robert doesn't ask how long. She knows he needs a reality check, to get on the plane, to start his car, to mow the lawn, to play a round of golf, to go to work, to turn on the computer, to tell his secretary to do something. "We'll sort it out when you get back then," he says in a tone somewhere between practicality and despair. "I'm sorry," Nora says. She has said it a dozen times. She can't simply unlove Robert. He is good to her, and faithful. She would return to Oak Grove within the month. They would have to work this out with Martin, their teenaged son. Robert would lie to his friends at first. Then maybe he would discover what he'd known for a long time somewhere deep beneath the stable strata of routine, somewhere so deep that he had lost access.

"Call me," he says as he kisses Nora on the cheek and climbs into the airport taxi. "I'll do my best with Martin..." His dark, exhausted eyes, full of questions Nora can't answer, peer through the dirty window as the taxi rolls off into the rush of traffic.

The next day Nora and Jan take a long walk through the plaza. They drink *limonadas* on a bench in the dappled shade of the *sangre* trees. In the evening they have dinner at the Hotel Grande. The waiter seats them near a window which looks out on a stone courtyard. They order grilled red snapper and white chablis. They listen to the piano music and a bubbling marble fountain in the center of the dining room. The wine arrives.

"What do you think I should do?" Nora says abruptly.

"About what?"

"I'm a forty-something first-grade teacher from suburban Chicago, and I've just abandoned my husband and son. Tell me I'm not completely nuts."

Jan smiles and pours Nora a glass of wine. "You haven't abandoned anyone. Call Martin tomorrow to ease your conscience. Then set your return flight. In the meantime, stay with me. Save your money and gather your energy."

The Thing About Love Is...

The waiter brings plates of food and arranges them on the table. They finish a second bottle of wine, dessert, coffee, and walk back to Jan's one-room apartment. They undress in the sinister rotating shadows cast by the bent ceiling fan blades. Jan is drunk. The short, firm lines of her compact body are exaggerated in the revolving darkness. Her biceps roll up into tight little balls when she bends her arms. "Bombs away," she says, dropping naked and face down onto the futon. Her buttocks are hard and round. Her long, straight hair divides, and falls over her shoulders, exposing a small, red heart tattoo at the edge of her hairline which Nora has never noticed. She doesn't mention it. Jan pulls a sheet over her head.

"Good night," Nora says. She is thinking about Robert. Only a week earlier in their hotel suite, they had made love, but it felt like guilt. She turns on a lamp and sits in a white rattan chair in her bra and panties and rubs her neck with the ends of her fingers. After Jan falls asleep, Nora listens to her quiet, rhythmic breathing. She sits awake and dreams of pelicans. On the street outside dogs open and scatter bags of garbage in the rain. Buses barrel by, and diesel exhaust wafts through the open window. Nora imagines the grinding electric drone of the garage door and Robert pulling the Volvo out on to the fresh black top, humming between the even rows of brick homes, and bright green lawns, on his way to the office. She misses Martin and Robert, but not Oak Grove — not the investing club, the health club, the PTA, the endless small talk at church, nor the rest of their automatically piloted lives.

Cold and stiff-necked, Nora wakes in the chair at daybreak. The rain has stopped and the street is quiet. She leaves before Jan awakens, carries her bag to the hotel, and checks back in. After breakfast she books a return flight to Chicago, allowing two more days in San Jose. At noon she calls Jan and asks where she can

The Thing About Love Is...

rent a four wheel drive jeep. Jan is excited. She insists on going with her. "It's not safe alone," she claims. "And I can help with the Spanish." After a difficult, circuitous discussion, Nora thanks Jan, but says she needs to go alone.

When Nora tells Manuel, the rental agent, where she is going, he offers to throw in a free guide for the day. She turns him down. Concerned for her safety, Manuel persists. Nora quietly says, "No," to each of Manuel's pleas. Finally he gets the forms and she signs everything.

Manuel delivers the shiny, white jeep to Nora's hotel with a full tank of gas the next morning at seven. Nervous, yet relieved, she climbs in, turns the key, and pulls away in an accidental rush of gasoline.

She drives to the Plaza to find Corazon. She is in her plywood stall slicing green mangoes. They embrace. Corazon is worried. But after repeated warnings, she finally squats down, and with a thick lump of chalk, makes a crude drawing on the sidewalk.

Follow the highway to the first gravel road after the sugar refinery, turn left and continue until reaching El Leon, a small squatter community. There turn right on to a dirt road which will cross four small rivers. After the fourth river, near a large acacia tree, turn on to a logging trail, proceed past a waterfall, park, and then hike several kilometers up a steep adjacent mountain path to a spot which is a bit higher than the actual crater. If the rains come, return immediately. There is a lot of loose rock, even on the steepest grades. Wear good shoes and go slow. Take a rope. It is a dangerous climb and there are no good maps.

In The Tackle Shop
(after Diane Wakoski)
Deborah E. Ryel

This is where I have failed
without an anchor
the days I seem to drift
and drift until you are there
a weight on my line.
Then I don't feel like a bobber
a foolish plastic ball
      half white, half red
  a simple, man-made device.

It can be a bright summer day.
The air shimmers after rain.
The garden has been planted—
a harvest of beans
marigolds bloom — yet I could have
broken loose. Can. May.

If found by chance on the beach
tie me to another line. I would work, you know.

There are all kinds of weights in the tackle shop.
Enough line to circle the globe

The Thing About Love Is...

more, more than I can be responsible for
than we can dispose of
though who knows what we need
what we really
need.

Plastic line in the willows
in the sane, hooks in the mud
aluminum flies that flip in the wind
on a summer day when light is everywhere.

How can it be?
Life without shadows?
Without a familiar tug on the line?

Without an anchor
I have failed to be fast or
deep
or true.
Failed.
More so than life?

Look, my friend says,
You did what you came to do.
Choke cherries — how they do take over.
Too bitter for reproof.

No.
It's true.
This is not about love
possession/fidelity
domestic arrangements.

The Thing About Love Is…

We can always rig something up.
Anyone who wants to may cast into this pond.

What I think is I can pick my spot.
This hook can handle what they've got here.
This line will hold.
This waiting will pay off.
I know what I'm doing, I think
and how to tell the story—

a story about sun on the water
and no anchor
about having enough line
or weight, about you,
my love, the depths you inhabit
and this tie that beckons me to fathom them
if I could break the surface tension
if I could sink
      and live
and then learn
how to tell this story.

Not about love
about an anchor
which is love
which is love.

The Dead Sleep

Mark Wukas

My first corpse, and I could only stare. It was floating face down in the bathtub of a shabby Uptown three-flat, bound at the wrists and ankles with an electrical cord, heels pointing toward the ceiling. Her hair spread like a dirty mop in maroon water, and her dress billowed around her thighs. The shower curtain had been torn down, and children's bath toys lay scattered in a puddle on the floor. Detectives and evidence technicians stepped casually around the apartment, murmuring among themselves, dusting for fingerprints, examining locks and door handles. Their detached professionalism made the horror commonplace. I stood behind two television reporters and their camera crews, listening to them question police, trying to ask my own questions and not sound like I was covering my first murder.

After the TV reporters got their bites, I was able to corner one of the homicide detectives. Ramona Sanchez, 24, mother of three, appeared to have been raped and stabbed several times before being stuffed in the bathtub. No sign of forced entry. Her children had come home from school and found the body. They now were with a neighbor. Police were looking for her ex-husband.

"Take a good look, kid," the detective said. "Looks like she's sleepin', don't it? You're lucky this one's fresh. Never forget my first. Pulled him out of a car trunk at O'Hare. You should smell them after they've been setting around a couple of days and explode. Especially in summer. Can't even tell what sex they are."

After work I described the scene to a few fellow night-shift reporters over beers.

"You were lucky," said Michael Christopher, a Dartmouth grad who had moved to Chicago to take his first job in journalism. "I wish they'd send me to cover a murder. I've been doing this shit for two months and I haven't seen one yet. It's just phone calls to the hospital, the cops, maybe the family. Pretty boring."

"It was wild," I said, "but I expected more. It was like, here was death, you know, and it was no big deal — like something off TV. Do they always look like broken mannequins?"

"You didn't see her face, did you, Bill?" asked Sarah Schultz, a six-month veteran who had trained me on my first day on the job. I shook my head. "That might've made the difference."

I tried to picture the woman's face, but I couldn't. Ramona Sanchez meant nothing to me, like the epileptic mother who suffered a seizure while drawing her daughter's bath and drowned; or the baby who suffocated when her grandmother mistakenly folded her into a sofabed; or the missing 9-year-old girl police unofficially dismissed either as dead or working as a prostitute in New York; or the city college student who broke up with his fiancée and hanged himself because he was "despondent," the reason police gave for every suicide. Michael was right — police reporting was boring unless you were on the scene. Otherwise the dead were just faceless names on police reports and the medical examiner's list, requiring the familiar routine of a few phone calls followed by a four-paragraph story on the wires before we forgot them and waited for the next name of the newly deceased. As the summer wore on, the only interesting stories were the macabre or perversely funny, which we laughed at over drinks every night after work.

The Thing About Love Is...

I didn't see another corpse until the end of the summer.

In my first year out of college, I lived in a garden studio apartment wedged between a gentrifying North Side neighborhood and a Hispanic area where I covered gang shootings. My parents, who lived in a farm town in another state, worried that it was not a "safe area" for me to live in, but it was all I could afford on $175 a week. The neighborhood was a No Man's Land of empty lots, broken sidewalks and run-down buildings with front lawns of dirt and weeds. During the day, packs of kids ran screaming and laughing through the gangways; at night, teens with boomboxes sat listlessly on the front porch of the six-flat next door, and I could hear the elevated rumbling on its way between the airport and downtown.

My apartment was dark. Even on the brightest days, only a dingy light filtered through the burglar-barred windows; any breeze carried only gangway dirt. I slept on a mattress in one corner and had a desk opposite that also served as a dining room table. Brick-and-board bookshelves of college texts and paperbacks flanked the kitchenette. The room held all the clues of my late nights — clothes that smelled like cigarettes littered the floor and the backs of my two chairs; empty beer bottles stood at attention on my desk and on my nightstand next to my alarm clock; dishes choked my kitchen sink. This was no life for a classics major.

Whatever discomforts I suffered, life as a police reporter more than compensated. It was hard, exhilarating work, and although I cursed it more often than not, I was learning that everything I thought I knew about the city was wrong. It's one thing to read about crime in the city, quite another when you live in the midst of it, alive to the possibility of danger that not only hid in the shadows but walked the streets in daylight as well. Gang graffiti

The Thing About Love Is...

was scribbled on apartment-building walls and garages all through my neighborhood; what at first seemed about as decipherable as Linear A became as easy to read as a grammar-school primer, so that with each fresh set of symbols I could tell who had been in the neighborhood the night before and why. Hubcaps and car stereos disappeared, and glass from broken car windows sparkled on the curb like diamonds. I often saw police reports on muggings within a block or two of my apartment.

I drank at the Gorgon, an after-hours dance club two blocks from my apartment. I would stop for a couple of beers on my nights off, maybe play some pinball. The club was two high-ceilinged rooms separated by a narrow corridor. The bar was in front, with booths along the walls and a few tables and chairs spread randomly about; a pinball machine and a photo booth stood in one corner. In back, the dance floor was a black-walled vortex of thumping music and flashing lights where it was almost impossible to see or talk or do anything but gyrate wildly, elbow-to-elbow with other club patrons. It was in the Gorgon that June that I first met Mimi. I was elbowing my way to the bar to get a beer, when a woman dressed in Inquisition black slipped in front of me. There were beads of sweat on her brow and a faint odor of perspiration and perfume. She was not beautiful but exotically attractive — short-cropped hair, dark eyes and an angular, small-breasted build.

"What are they playing back there?" I asked.

"Why don't you come back and find out for yourself?" she retorted.

The next night I saw Mimi sitting in a booth with another woman; I said hello when she came to the bar. She remembered me.

"You didn't come back to dance last night."

"Trick knee," I said.

The Thing About Love Is...

"What kind of tricks?" Mimi asked.

"It unscrews."

Mimi suggested that I take a load off by joining her and her friend. I pushed an ashtray filled with lipstick-tipped cigarette butts toward them as I placed my bottle of beer on the table. She had studied design at the Art Institute and currently worked in Sears' advertising department, lived in the neighborhood because rent was cheap but was pissed at the gentrifying yuppies driving up rents. I guessed she was in her early thirties, about ten years older than me. In the following weeks, we kept crossing paths at the Gorgon; each time we met, we talked a little longer, she looked a little better, and I liked her a little more. Five weeks after first meeting, Mimi asked me to walk her home and invited me up for a drink. As she handed me a beer, I leaned toward her and kissed her. Within minutes we stumbled from her couch to her bedroom for alcohol-primed first-fuck fireworks. Afterwards, as we lay on her sweat-soaked sheets, Mimi surprised me by insisting that I leave — she had a strict policy of never waking up with someone she'd brought home.

"It's just one of those things that you're going to have to accept if we're going to keep seeing each other," Mimi said. I shrugged it off. So it wasn't going to be love — just one of those things — but the next day I could think of nothing except her fingernails digging into my scapulae. I called her and suggested a movie and drinks.

"I can't make it tonight," she said. "I'm booked, and I'm busy this weekend."

"So am I. I work." She accepted for a night the following week.

Mimi was on the phone when I arrived. I sat on her couch, patted it fondly and flipped through a fashion magazine. I didn't have to strain to hear her conversation. To me: "Bill, would you like a beer?" Into the phone: "Oh, he's just a neighbor." Then

The Thing About Love Is...

Mimi asked, "Why would you need to get in touch with me while I'm gone?" She refused to tell the caller where she would be staying and hung up with a "love you, too," and an insincere one at that. Mimi refilled her glass with wine and sat next to me; we had one drink, then another, then a third. As we edged closer, both a little drunk, I wondered whether we'd have a repeat of the other night. I was telling her about my plans to be a foreign correspondent, and she said she'd visit and we could take exotic vacations. I put my arm around her and said that those vacations were a long way away and that I'd settle for skinny-dipping some weekend in Wisconsin. Mimi embroidered the scene with lakeside walks during the day and candlelight dinners before our evening frolic. We found our way to her bedroom after the fourth drink. Mimi, smashed after four glasses of wine, continued her furious pace, keeping a glass and bottle within easy reach on her nightstand and taking deep gulps during our pauses. Kisses on her couch that held a sweet trace of wine tasted like a pulp of fresh fruit in her bed.

By 3 a.m., I was walking home exhausted and exhilarated. The night was humid, nearly stifling, with a bit of fog and a deep stillness. I was aware of everything on the block, from a bedroom light winking out to music and voices carrying through an open window. Two things happened with Mimi that night that, for me, set the boundaries of our relationship. First, the phone rang around 1:30, and she didn't answer. Her answering machine clicked on, but the volume was turned down so I couldn't hear the message. I didn't mind her ignoring the call — in fact, I was grateful — but Mimi became nervous. She smiled, took another sip of wine and kissed me with renewed intensity as if to make me forget about the interruption. Second, she called me Mike. Twice.

Mimi and I continued seeing each other, usually every week,

The Thing About Love Is...

either on my night off or, rarely, late on a weekend. We never talked on the phone except to arrange our next rendezvous. We seldom met at my place, and we never spent the whole night together, according to her rule, even if it meant walking home by dawn's early light. Our conversations were often lively, but we never delved too deeply into our personal lives for fear of exposing parts neither of us wanted the other to see. She never mentioned seeing other men and never called me Mike again. We remained happily ignorant of each other's other romances.

Terry Meyer, another regular at the Gorgon, worked as a pharmacist at the University of Illinois Medical Center.

Terry was long on ego — women he'd had, important friends, clubs he'd been to that required membership IDs — yet everything he said, every gesture, carried the bluster of the secretly insecure. He held a tenacious grip on his narrow view of the world and suffered nothing that would dislodge him. During the time I knew him, I watched him pursue women arduously, oozing charm, flashing cash, taking them to restaurants and shows that I never could afford. At first these women were put off by his violent rush, but, flattered by his persistence, eventually they lowered their guards for two weeks of heaven. That's about when Terry became bored, usually after he'd slept with them two or three times. Then he galloped to the next one who fired his imagination.

I asked him what these women said to him during their parting shots.

"They call me an asshole. Shit like that. Hey, maybe I'm a little arrogant, but that's just the way I am, so fuck 'em," Terry cackled, as if confessing his obnoxious behavior made it more acceptable.

Terry's grandfather and father were North Shore doctors, but,

The Thing About Love Is...

to his father's profound disappointment (as Terry told me one drunken evening), he didn't have the grades for medical school. Despite his father's connections, glowing letters of recommendation and returned favors, nothing secured him a coveted spot in a first-year class anywhere. He waited another year and applied to a less prestigious school but was rejected again. Terry was always bitter on this point, ranting that his rightful place in medical school was "probably given to some fucking shine." His family pressured him to stay in a medically related field, so he trained as a pharmacist. His father set him up in the pharmacy at the medical center where he taught. Terry had been working there seven or eight years.

Terry was never without controlled substances, which made him popular with many Gorgon regulars. I, too, benefitted from Terry's drug connections. He kept me in speed for long nights of sitting in police stations and waiting for people to be raped, robbed and murdered. I often saw him in the Gorgon setting up buys and hitting on women, but aside from the one night he told me why he didn't go to med school, our conversations never went beyond anecdotal bar banter. I never considered him more than a passing acquaintance, which is why I was surprised when he phoned one sweltering August night and invited me to his apartment "to talk" after I got off work.

The neighborhood bank blinked 84 degrees at 2:23 a.m. It had been a busy night. Heat smothered the city, and tempers ran as high as the temperatures. My biggest story was about a 6-year-old girl who was caught in gang crossfire while playing in front of her house near Humboldt Park. She bled to death in her father's arms before paramedics arrived. The desk thought it important enough to send me to the scene, but by the time I got there the ambulance had come and gone. Neighbors loitered near the victim's three-flat to show their sympathy but otherwise were unsure

The Thing About Love Is...

what to do; children danced around a dark stain on the sidewalk. I questioned them about the girl, the gangs. Adults wept at the senselessness, posturing gangbangers vowed revenge.

A heavy-metal anthem to youth and excess wailed on the stereo as I entered Terry's apartment. He stood barefoot in a t-shirt and dirty gym shorts, looking as if he hadn't slept in days. He shook my hand and handed me a beer; I gratefully pressed the slick, cold bottle to my forehead. Sports and rock 'n' roll magazines covered one side of the coffee table in front of his couch; in a clean corner, a pipe and a bag of marijuana sat next to the ashtray. I fell into an old leather chair and turned his table fan toward me. Terry sank to the floor in front of the couch and stretched his long legs under the coffee table. We waved our beers in salute and took long swallows. Terry began sprinkling dope on a leaf of rolling paper.

"Sorry about the A.C.," he said, nodding toward an air conditioner in the window. "It busted this afternoon. Can't get a repairman 'til the day after tomorrow."

"No problem."

"So how's it going?" he asked.

"All right. How 'bout you?"

"Ah, same old shit." Terry licked the paper and tightly rolled the ends of the joint; he lit up, took a deep drag and passed it to me. I took a drag and passed it back.

"You know Mimi Brickman, right? Skinny chick. Hangs at the Gorgon. Dresses in black all the time."

That description included more than half of the women in the Gorgon, but I nodded: "I think I know who you're talking about."

"Right," he smiled. "A little over a month ago, maybe six weeks, Mimi and me were sitting at the Gorgon just talking and ended up closing the place. I invited her back here for a joint, and we both got pretty fucked up. One thing led to another." He paused and added with a wink, "You know how it goes."

"Sure." I shifted in the chair and sipped my beer, quietly seething. It was one thing to assume that Mimi slept with other guys, but another thing to face one. Terry? I felt sick to my stomach that I'd shared the same loins with him and consoled myself that at least I'd had her first. Or so I hoped.

Terry said that the first night Mimi had asked no questions about when they would see each other again — she just dressed and left: "It was great, like she wanted it the same way I did. Didn't stay the night. Wouldn't let me walk her home. Wouldn't even take cab fare. But I liked her, you know, so I started calling her and in no time we were spending a couple of nights a week together, sometimes her place, usually mine. It went like this for the last month until three nights ago when Mimi started crying and said she loved me." He took a long drag on his jay and extended it to me. I raised my beer to let him know I was fine. He exhaled slowly, completely, and took another long drag.

"Last night, she told me she was pregnant," he said as he exhaled again.

"What?" My neck and arms tingled with surprise; my stomach tightened sharply. Mimi — *pregnant.* Terry's story was going too fast. Mimi told me she was on the pill and insisted that kids were not in her future.

"I can't fucking believe it," Terry said, taking another long drag on the joint, oblivious to my reaction.

Neither could I. Mimi and I last made love three weeks earlier, and I'd been avoiding her since. I called her apartment only when I knew she wouldn't be home and left messages on her answering machine that stated my good intentions about seeing her soon and apologizing for missing connections. Our liaisons had been growing more frustrating. We liked each other well enough — or

The Thing About Love Is...

so I thought — but I was getting bored with our quick chats, a couple of drinks and ninety minutes of sex before being sent on my way. We didn't have much to say to one another that last night. When we did get down to things, there was something mechanical about it all, and she drank more than usual. Did she know then?

"She said she was being careful," Terry said. "Now look at this mess she's got me into. And she doesn't want to get an abortion."

"She wants to keep it?" I asked, still numb at the news.

Terry shook his head. "Worse. I think she wants to move in, get married."

"You're not going to marry her?" I tried to picture Mimi in white.

"No way." Terry picked at the label on his bottle and laughed. "I brought up the subject of us living together once before. You know, that bullshit that comes after they first tell you they love you. Move in? Sure. Someday, sweetie. Now let's fuck."

"You in love with her?"

"No way." Terry took a drag and held his breath. "But I think she's cool, you know? Anyway, now she's fucking pregnant, and this is going to royally fuck up my life. She won't get an abortion — says she wants a baby. Says I don't have to marry her, but you know what'll happen if I don't."

"Sure," I said, but I had no clue. I leaned forward to pull my sweaty shirt from the back of the chair.

"I can't marry her," he said after a moment's reflection. "It'd fuck up everything. I want to have fun for a few more years before settling down."

"Sure you're the father?"

"Positive. She loves me."

Terry's arrogance made me bristle.

"So what's the problem? What do you need me for? Make her

get an abortion. Tell her it's better than fucking up two lives, maybe three. If she loves you, she ought to do it."

"Tried that. She won't buy it. Says it's murder."

"Murder? Shit, she doesn't know the meaning of the word. Murder is when three crackheads from the West Side shoot a deaf-mute to death after mistaking his sign language for gang hand signals. That's fucking murder."

"Hey, man, I know," Terry said.

"So what're you going to do?"

"Well, I know that you and Mimi used to, um, go out, right?" he asked, with slight emphasis on the past tense. It stung. "I figure my only way out of this is if there's some doubt who the father is. Of course, I know that's asking a lot." Terry passed me the joint.

"Is she threatening you with some paternity suit?" It didn't sound like Mimi.

"Not yet."

"What makes you think she will?"

"Just thinking ahead, man, trying to cover my ass. Look, you wouldn't have to do a thing. I just need to know I can count on you if she actually goes to court. All I need is to be able to tell her that you're willing to testify you've been fucking her and that the kid might not be mine. After all, it was the truth. This'll make her look real bad, so I figure I can talk her into the abortion. No harm done to anyone."

"You know, they have tests now that would blow that argument away."

Terry ignored me: "I'll offer to pay for it and everything. Won't cost her a dime."

I finished my beer with a long swallow and rose to leave. I was trembling with rage at Terry's cavalier attitude as well as his stupidity for concocting such an idiot scheme, but I was also furious at Mimi for her duplicity.

"I'll think about it," I said.

"Sure. Sure. Let me know when you decide. And Bill, you know I'd be pretty grateful for your help." As he shook my hand, he gave me a small envelope. I looked at him. "Just a little something," he said.

Outside I checked — ten amphetamines.

The next night at the Gorgon, I saw Mimi, black t-shirt and shorts, sitting cross-legged at the bar, empty barstools on either side. She was staring into her gin and tonic, stirring it slowly, and grinding a cigarette into the ashtray in front of her. I crept behind her and put my arms around her waist and kissed her neck; the scent of familiar perfume sparked memories of our late evenings.

"Hi there," Mimi purred until she turned and realized it was me. She pushed me away with one arm. "Well, Will-*yam*. Haven't seen *you* in a while."

"Couple of weeks. You know how my schedule is. I'd hoped to find you here."

"Spare me the bullshit. I know your schedule." Mimi turned away and fished in her purse for another cigarette.

"You're not always around either, you know," I said.

The bass from the music in the back room thumped like a war drum. I climbed on to a stool next to her and ordered a beer; we sat without speaking.

"Are you ignoring me?" I asked.

"What do you want, Bill?" she asked in a clipped voice.

"Are you gaining weight?"

Mimi pivoted sharply.

"Just asking," I said innocently. "Haven't seen you in a while. Looks good on you."

The Thing About Love Is...

"Fuck you," she snapped and turned back to her drink.

"What the hell's the matter with you? I just paid you a compliment."

"I have nothing to say to you. Go."

"Can I buy you a drink?"

"No. Go away."

"Sure?"

"Yes. Just leave me alone."

Mimi turned her back to me and kept her eye on the door via the bar mirror. I watched, too, and in a few minutes Terry entered. Mimi quickly stood to hug and kiss him as he walked to her. Seeing them embrace made me furious. I wanted to wedge my arms between them like a boxing referee and push them to opposite corners of the bar.

"Hey, there's Bill," Terry said with a nervous laugh as we shook hands. "Long time, no see, dude. How's it going?"

"Fine, dude," I said with equal camaraderie, wanting to slug him.

"I'm surprised you were able to get a night off from the cop shop."

"Can't work every night. You know how it is."

"Sure do."

I stood for a moment, savoring the tension. One word now about her being pregnant and the talk I'd had with Terry would blow the roof. I looked at Mimi, tucked under his arm, trying to ignore us yet hanging on every word. I put my half-empty bottle on the bar.

"Well, gotta go. See you guys later."

Mimi said nothing.

"I'll give you a call," Terry said with a wink as I walked past him to the door.

The Thing About Love Is...

That night, I found a pair of Mimi's earrings on the floor between my mattress and the wall. I remembered the night she wore them on one of her few nights at my place, different-sized cotter pins hanging from large hoops. I dangled them from my fingers and pictured Mimi sitting naked in my bed, smiling and tilting her head to each side as she took them off.

Terry never called. I didn't hear from Mimi either — nor did I expect to. For the next week I spent idle moments wondering whether she and Terry were together. I tortured myself with fantasies of them in bed, laughing at me behind my back. I spent my next night off in the Gorgon waiting for Mimi, but she never showed. I called the next night from a police station and suggested dinner.

"No can do, Bill."

"Why not?" I pressed. "I was good enough for dinner a few weeks ago."

"Look, I'm sorry about the other night, but we just can't see each other anymore. You were fun, but it's over. I'm with Terry now."

"Really?"

"Yes."

"Terry?"

"Yes."

"What happened to Mike?"

One night that week after work, Sarah and I went to an after-hours bar for a few early-morning beers. Sarah was an elfin five-foot-two with pale eyes yet she took no guff from recalcitrant cops; three years older than I, she had become a confidante, always ready with advice and willing to go for a late drink. That night in a Lincoln Avenue bar where bureau reporters often met,

The Thing About Love Is...

I told her about me and Mimi and Terry. By now, Terry's silence led me to believe that his plan was off, but I was so angry at Mimi that I remained more than willing to play my part.

"Why do you want to hurt her?" Sarah asked. "What's she done to you?"

"Come on, I used to date her."

"You used to sleep with her, you mean. And you let her go. What's the matter? Jealous? A little wounded ego here?"

"No. Of course not."

"Really? Then why are you being so stupid about all this?"

"I'm not being stupid. It's just that I'd want to talk and get everything straightened out. If she still wants to break it off, then fine. At least I'll have had my say."

"What is it you want to say to her?" Sarah asked.

Her question jolted me.

"I'm not sure really. I just want to talk, I guess."

"So? Call her. What's the problem?"

"Mimi won't talk to me. She won't return my calls." I pulled a crisp cottage fry from the basket sitting between us, tore it in half and dropped it back in without eating it.

"Maybe it's just Terry," I said. "He really pissed me off being so cocky about the whole thing. I know you and Mimi used to date. Shit. Fuck him. What do I care? If he can get her, he can have her."

"That was fast."

I turned sideways in our booth, leaned against the wall, and put my foot up on the bench. Sarah was not providing the sympathetic ear I'd wanted.

"Well, if you want my opinion, it sounds to me like she's trying to test him," she said after a long sip of beer. "I heard of a girl in college who told her boyfriend she was pregnant just to see what he'd do, and then told him she lost the kid or it was a false alarm or something like that. Maybe Mimi wants to see how serious Terry is about her to see what he'll do. She obviously knows you're not."

"I've got news for Mimi. Terry's not serious about her either."

"How do you know? Did it ever occur to you that just maybe she likes him better than you? That he might be better for her than you? That she might really love him? These things happen, you know."

"Maybe, but not this time. Meyer's a maggot. She's got to see that."

"Does that mean she's too good for him?"

"No contest."

"And you're so much better for her."

"Hey, I thought you were my friend," I said.

"And I am," Sarah said.

"Yeah, well, maybe she'll do him a favor and kill herself," I said. "Then I can do the story and call Terry with the good news."

"That's not funny," Sarah fired back, rapping the table twice.

"You're right. Sorry."

The bartender turned on the house lights. I popped the last cold cottage fry into my mouth and finished my beer. On the street, the 4 a.m. die-hards disrupted the pre-dawn quiet as they navigated noisily to their cars. The morning humidity felt like a sauna after the bar's air conditioning. Tavern lights blinked off as I walked Sarah to her car.

"Well," Sarah said, trying to lighten the end of our evening, "if Mimi does decide to kill herself, I hope she has better luck than this story I had tonight. This woman, about 30 or so, slashes both her wrists, swallows a bottle of iodine and drives her car straight into a brick wall in some alley on the near North Side. You'd think she'd be dead, right? Wrong. When her car hit the wall, the steering column came forward, hit her in the stomach

The Thing About Love Is...

and made her vomit the iodine."

I chuckled, anticipating how the story would end.

"Neighbors heard the crash and called an ambulance," she said. "Paramedics showed up, bandaged her wrists, and she walked out of the hospital two hours later."

"And we didn't do a story on that?"

Sarah shook her head. "Why? After all, she did live."

"Too bad. That one's a classic. But wasn't she at least admitted for psychiatric observation? Wasn't she despondent or something?"

"She was admitted, but no one would say for sure." Sarah reached up to give me a quick peck good night. "Just think, Bill. If we do something stupid when we die, there's going to be some bureau reporter making calls on us."

"And laughing," I said.

My social life came to an abrupt halt when the desk put me on the midnight to 8 a.m. shift at police headquarters on 11th Street. The overnight was a blur of phone calls to tired and ill-humored cops, nurses and other vampires who didn't want to answer my questions any more than I wanted to ask them. Despite the grind, I enjoyed the shift. It's a different city at night: You can see its secrets. Like a roach-infested kitchen, neighborhoods came alive at night with nocturnal creatures who seldom see the light of day. I saw them all on the first deputy's sheet, where every crime in the city is recorded, before I began to make my calls. On my nights off, I tried to keep the same hours and would drive around the city and look for the people about whom I had written: Couples arguing until one was left bleeding to death with a gunshot wound to the head; transvestites hustling on Broadway; muggers prowling the shadows of well-to-do neighborhoods; insurance-inspired arsonists lurking in alleys with

The Thing About Love Is...

cans of gasoline; gang members planning bloody revenge for some insult whether real or imagined. At the end of my shift as I walked into the day's sunshine amid the lemmings on their way to work, I could see in their foggy eyes that they had no idea what had transpired on their streets in the previous twelve hours. I knew, and I reveled in knowing.

When the streets were quiet, I left a wake-up call with a sympathetic rewrite at the office and tried to grab three hours of sleep on the press-room couch, but that was rare. Every night about 4 a.m. — as the after-hours bars were emptying — I drove to the coroner's office for the latest list of medical examiner cases. I copied the names, ages, addresses, hospitals and investigating police from a clothbound folio ledger and hustled back to the press room to start my calls. That was never easy, especially when the victim had been found in several pieces next to railroad tracks or some floater that'd spent the winter under the ice in the Chicago River. In my nightmares, I still see entries that read: "Name unknown. Age unknown. Address unknown. Unknown causes. Cook County Hospital. No police." And the desk saying, "Moore, we want it before you go home."

The isolation of the overnight created a special loneliness, reducing me to a zombie-like existence. I seldom socialized, and the business with Terry and Mimi receded as I gradually severed ties with reality. Sleep became the most important thing in my life, and I never had enough. I'd get home from work around 9 or 10 in the morning, eat breakfast at a local greasy spoon, read until noon or so and pull my phone before falling into a fitful tossing interrupted by neighborhood noise. After giving up on sleep for the day, I'd grab a sandwich and watch the news before going in. I never went out in the evening before work. I had no appetite, didn't exercise, and felt myself getting fat on junk food from the ninth-floor canteen at police headquarters. Desperate to

The Thing About Love Is...

stay awake all night, I had left a few messages with Terry telling him I needed some more speed, but it was more than a week before he called me at work and said there would be no problem with "the prescription." I stopped at his apartment the next night on my way to work.

"When do you sleep?" he asked.

"Always. Never. I don't know. I'll sleep when I'm dead."

Terry disappeared into his bedroom and returned with an envelope.

"How's your love life?" I asked as I paid for two dozen uppers.

"Bad. I'm going to have to use you now," he said.

"Why? What's up?"

"I ended things with Mimi last week. She wasn't happy about it, and now she's threatening to go to the hospital."

"I thought that's what you wanted."

"Not that. Not an abortion. She says she's going to blow this thing wide open if I don't marry her. She says she's going to tell the hospital that I'm ripping off the pharmacy. Letters to the administration, my boss. The works. Then I'm fucked. My old man will fucking die."

"What pharmacy? At the hospital? I thought your suppliers were outside."

"Don't tell me you never knew," Terry said. "How do you think I got such good quality? This stuff isn't street shit. I've got a connection in the pharmacy."

"But why?" I asked, wondering what would possess Mimi to make such wild, desperate threats — it was just not like her.

"I need the pocket money. After all, fun is not cheap."

"No. I mean her. Why would she do something like that?"

Terry shrugged. "I don't know, man, but if I'm going down, I'm taking her with me."

The Thing About Love Is...

I decided to tell Mimi that I was not part of Terry's plan and that if she wanted to keep the child, I'd back her up; but she ignored my calls, and it was a week before I finally caught her late on a Saturday night as I was getting ready for work.

"We have to talk," I said.

"Oh, yeah?" I heard her sniffle. "Why? What about?"

"About Terry."

Silence.

"Well, fuck you, too," Mimi said.

I called back, but she wouldn't answer.

I walked past Mimi's apartment later that night before going to work and saw the light of the television blinking on the wall of her darkened front room. I rang her bell; she buzzed me up. Mimi, wine glass in hand, answered the door; her nightgown hung on her like a jacket on a scarecrow. Patches of hair stuck out wildly, and her skin was so pale and translucent that I could see purple veins criss-crossing her hands and chest. I could tell from the dark rings around her eyes she'd been crying. When I saw her, I wanted to take her in my arms and hold her and protect her.

"Hi," she said weakly.

Without inviting me in, she left the door open and walked slowly back into the apartment. I stepped in and closed the door but remained standing. Mimi sat cross-armed and cross-legged on her sofa bed. She wouldn't look at me. The TV was on, volume off; a jazz album played softly on the stereo. She lit a cigarette.

We were silent for a minute, maybe two. Mimi took a drag, exhaled through her nose and said, "Say what you came to say and get out."

I sat on the opposite end of the couch and faced her; Mimi pulled her knees up under her chin and sat like a gargoyle, taut

The Thing About Love Is...

and blank-eyed. I could scarcely recognize the woman who once fit snugly under my arm.

"How are you?" I asked nervously.

"Fine," she said flatly.

"You don't look it."

"Been sick."

"Anyone taking care of you?"

Mimi shook her head and kept her eyes on the television.

"Do you need anything?" I asked.

"My sister's coming over tomorrow with her kids. We're going shopping."

"Your sister? You never told me you had a sister. Younger or older?"

"Younger," she said.

"She have any kids?"

"Don't you listen? She's got two. Get to the point, will you?" She fumbled with another cigarette and a book of matches; her hand trembled as she raised the flame.

"Look, about Terry," I said.

Mimi raised her hand to silence me. "Too late. It's over. You're too late." She waved out the match and dropped it in an overflowing ashtray on her coffee table.

"Over?"

"Everything. Terry's got nothing to worry about anymore." Mimi wiped her eyes and blew her nose; her body shuddered and then relaxed. "I went over to his apartment this week to tell him. You know, that bastard wouldn't even invite me in. He made me wait outside his door until he came out with a paper bag full of things that I'd left at his place. It was like he was taking out the garbage. Then he starts saying how it didn't make any difference whether I kept the baby or not because you and some of his other friends were going to say you'd been screwing me and make it look like I didn't know who the father really was. I can't believe he'd do something that fucking cold, as if he believed it'd work."

"Why'd you do it?"

"What kind of life could I give a baby on my salary?" She took a long drag on her cigarette.

"So you decided to get married."

"Get married? I never said a word to him about marriage. I didn't want to marry that asshole any more than I wanted to marry you. All I wanted to do was to scare him into a little child support. That's all."

"Is that why you threatened Terry about the pharmacy?"

Mimi turned and pointed at me, her forefinger extended like a fencer's foil. "No! Bill, I never. No. I just didn't want him getting caught ripping them off and then really screwing things up."

"Was it Terry's?" I don't know why I asked this question, except that she didn't sound as angry at Terry as I expected she might if he was the father.

"No."

I froze. "You sure?"

"I know."

"How?"

"What do you think I am? An idiot? I can count."

"You were with two guys. Maybe more. How the hell could you possibly know?"

Mimi paused and took a long drag on her cigarette. "Because I was pregnant before I started sleeping with Terry."

"What about your other guys?"

"There weren't any."

"Who was Mike?"

"My last boyfriend before you. How do you know about him?"

"Never mind. Was it mine?"

Mimi looked away, and in her averted glance I saw the truth.

"Jesus Christ. Why didn't you tell me?" I erupted — but I also was relieved it was gone.

"Because I wanted to keep the baby."

"But I was the father. Why go to Terry?" I remembered Terry's and my earlier conversations, and now I wanted to kill the smug bastard.

"I found out I was pregnant right after Terry and I started sleeping together, but we had been using condoms so I knew it had to be yours. I figured he could afford it. He's going to be a doctor."

"Oh, he's going to be a doctor," I echoed. "Is that what he told you? You mean you thought he could afford you and your kid, you fucking mercenary. Listen, Mimi. Terry is not going to medical school. Not now. Not soon. Not ever. He was never accepted. He's going to stay a pharmacist. And they don't make that much either."

"It doesn't matter, Bill," Mimi said tersely. "Look, you make a hundred and seventy-five bucks a week. I've seen your apartment. You can barely take care of yourself, let alone a wife and child. I couldn't have a baby with you. I wouldn't feel secure. You're still too young, too irresponsible."

"Too irresponsible? Are you kidding me? I may make jack shit now, and maybe I'll never make as much as Terry, but don't tell me I couldn't take care of you and a baby. There are other things besides money, you know."

"Hey, I don't need you or anybody to take care of me. I can take care of myself. I've been doing it since you were playing little league and thought girls were yukky. I was worried about my baby. I wanted to make sure I could take care of my baby."

I stabbed a finger at her: "Fuck you."

"No. Fuck *you*. Sure, I lied to Terry to make him think the kid was his so I could stick him for child support. But you want to

The Thing About Love Is...

know why I picked up with Terry in the first place? It's because you were never around. I liked you, Bill, but you were always working nights, weekends. Drinking with your friends after work. You stopped coming over except when you wanted to get laid. I got tired of being your fuck buddy."

"You didn't seem to mind. Besides, how can I get serious when you're with other guys?"

"I wasn't seeing other guys while we were together."

"How was I supposed to know?"

"You weren't listening."

"Bull-shit."

"It's true, Bill. And if you deny it, you're a goddam liar."

"Mimi."

"What? Just go away, will you?"

"Why didn't you tell me about the baby?"

"You're young. You've got a long way to go before you settle down. Besides, I wanted to have a baby." She let out a deprecatory laugh and flattened her cigarette into an ashtray. "So much for that idea." Mimi leaned back and stared at the ceiling. I moved closer to her on the couch and placed my hand carefully on the back of her neck. She moved toward me, into the crook of my arm.

"Look, there may be other chances," I whispered.

"No," she said. "No, Bill. There won't."

"Sure there will. Why can't you have kids? Women older than you have babies all the time."

"This was my second abortion. I got the first one when I was in college, and it went bad. The doctor was a real hack and messed up me pretty bad. I mean, I like still shiver at the sound of knives and forks clinking in kitchen sinks. Now my doctor says after that she's surprised I even got pregnant again. She told me that if I really wanted a kid, it was now or never." Mimi paused. "Guess

The Thing About Love Is...

it's never."

The moon hovered over the lake and Grant Park like a huge Chinese lantern. I dragged myself to work expecting a wild night, and I wasn't disappointed. On the South Side, eight teenagers kidnapped a 15-year-old girl and gang-raped her in a basement. Police were able to round up the suspects because one of them, identified by the victim, was stupid enough to have walked her home. In the west Loop, two muggers shot and critically wounded a lost conventioneer after he told them they'd dropped one of his dollar bills as they were trotting away.

I threw myself into these stories, working the phones, calling cops and neighbors. Sometime early in the shift — I can't remember when — Terry called me. I was neck-deep in the Loop shooting. I told him I'd call back in half an hour but didn't. I went over to the county morgue around a quarter after five that morning, later than usual because of all the work. The moon now hung high and bright in the west; the first violet of dawn were rising from the lake. A distant mournful siren echoed in the empty streets like a banshee's wail.

George, an assistant medical examiner who'd become a professional acquaintance, looked exhausted as he tossed me the ledger for the night's cases.

"Busy night?" I asked. He rolled his eyes and lifted his hands in supplication. "Yeah, I know. Me, too."

"You should see the one we just got in," he said. "Suicide. Just a fucking mess. Shot herself through the mouth with a high-caliber handgun. Blew the back of her head off."

"Really? How old was she?" I asked.

"Twenty-nine — with a bullet," George snapped. We erupted into laughter. He offered to take me down to the "icebox" and show me.

The Thing About Love Is...

I smiled. "Sounds great. Let's go." I'd never seen one on a slab before. I figured since I'd be writing about her eventually, I may as well put a face to a name.

"You sure? This one's really bad news."

"Let's see."

"You know," George said as we started down the stairs, "the funny thing about this one is that women don't usually choose violent suicides. They prefer pills, ODs. Sometimes razor blades. But never guns."

"Whose weapon?" I asked.

"Cops are still checking."

Refrigerated death filled the morgue's high-ceilinged halls, and the stale air became more pungent as I followed George through steel fire doors. After the heat and humidity of the press room, the cool air raised goose bumps on my neck and arms. Two tiers of square drawers with large silver handles lined the wall. George walked straight to one waist-high on the far end of the room and pulled it out; he waited until I stood next to the drawer and said, "If you have to puke, there's a sink over there." He was serious.

"Don't worry," I said. "I'm a big boy."

"Right." He gently pulled the sheet back to the body's waist.

The first thing I noticed was the skin, the dark white, almost grey, pallor of the arms and chest. Her dark nipples withered on her small breasts. Brains and dried blood matted the hair, and some lingering body fluid dampened the sheet below the head. Powder burns blackened her mouth and cheeks, but I could still see where tears ran through the purple mascara below her eyes. I took deep breaths and started thinking about all the suicides I'd covered. All the self-inflicted gunshot wounds. All the carbon monoxide poisonings. The hangings. Overdoses. All so sanitized on paper compared to the horrible reality. I looked at George and smiled with embarrassment. I glanced back at the corpse, its face. It could have been anyone, someone I passed on the street that afternoon, someone I knew. I felt dizzy.

"What's the name on this one?" I asked. George checked the toe tag and told me. I stepped back and heard George quickly slide the drawer into the wall and stand next to me with a glass of water.

"You okay? I warned you," he said and patted me on the shoulder.

"Yeah. I'm fine. Thought it was someone I knew." Back upstairs, I asked George for details of the scene from the police report; he pulled out a few Polaroids taken by the evidence technicians, and the pictures made the scene more garish and surreal. In one, the woman was lying sprawled on her bed, arms flung wide; the sheets below her head were soaked crimson. The Polaroid flash gave her glazed eyes a reddish glare in the close-up. I pictured her sitting back, putting the gun in her mouth and pulling the trigger. *Here we go. Fuck everything.* One twitch — and then oblivion.

"Why'd she do it?" I asked.

"Cops said she was despondent."

There was no dawn that morning. Angry clouds swept in before sunrise and covered the city like a trapdoor. I left work that morning to find my car had been towed. Exhausted, I walked five miles home, the last one in the rain. Passing shop windows on Milwaukee Avenue, I looked at my rain-distorted reflection and wondered what I would look like, what it'd feel like, if I put a .45 in my mouth and pulled the trigger.

My cramped apartment was stifling. I tossed my clothes across the bone-cold radiator. I hunted in the refrigerator for something to eat but found only a carton of spoiled milk and moldy

The Thing About Love Is...

oranges. I pulled my phone and fell into bed.

I started awake, frightened, unsure for a moment where I was. My nightstand light was still burning; a slice of afternoon sunlight cut through my blinds.

In my dream, a woman with mutilated features held a snugly wrapped infant to her chest, rocking it gently, singing a lullaby.

Contributors

Adria Bernardi's novel, *The Day Laid on the Altar*, which won the Katharine Bakeless Nason Fiction Prize by the Bread Loaf Writers' Conference and Middlebury College, will be published by Middlebury College/University Press of New England in August 2000. Her translations of the poetry of Italian screenwriter Tonino Guerra recently were published under the title *Abandoned Places*, by Guernica Editions of Toronto. She is the author of *Houses with Names: The Italian Immigrants of Highwood, Illinois* (University of Illinois Press, 1990). Her essay, "Hep-Lock," was awarded the 1999 Editors' Prize by *The Missouri Review*, and another essay, "The Errant Steps of Wooden Shoes," was included in the anthology, *Traveler's Tales: Italy*. She was the 1998 recipient of the A.E. Coppard Award for Short Fiction. She was the 1995 recipient of the James Fellowship for Novel awarded by the Heekin Group Foundation. Her fiction has appeared in the *Santa Monica Review, River Oak Review,* in the anthology, *The Voices We Carry,* and will be published in a forthcoming issue of *Voices in Italian Americana*. She lives in Worcester, Mass.

Michael Burke's stories, poems and essays have appeared in *TriQuarterly, American Way* (the American Airlines magazine), *Private Arts, Rambunctious Review, Sport Literate, Backspace, Strong Coffee, Bluff City* and *The Prairie Light Review*. His plays — *Wama-Wama Zing Bing* and *Let's Spend Money* — have been produced in Chicago by Strawdog Theatre and OverBored Productions. Burke is currently completing a collection of short stories. "I hope 'Big Love' accomplishes what I try to do with almost all of my stories: record the hope and struggle of ordinary life while reminding people what we have in common with one another — both good and bad."

Jotham Burrello is co-editor of *Sport Literate* magazine. He received his MFA from Columbia College in Chicago. "Finding Momma" began in a fiction workshop during his final year in school. Jotham is happy the story has finally found a home.

Cris Burks teaches fiction at Columbia College. Her poems have been published in *The Black Maria, Thunder Egg, Ambrosia, Emergence* and *Shooting Star Review*. Her short stories have been published in *Hair Trigger, Kaleidoscope, Short Fiction by Women* and *Emergence*. "Bizarro Ballad" is an excerpt from a novel-in-progress.

Robert N. Georgalas is a Chicago-based writer and teacher. Among the publications in which his fiction, poetry and essays have appeared are: *Hair Trigger, Rambunctious Review, Poetry Motel, F.O.C. Review, Arizona Literary Magazine, Aurora University Review, Urban Spaghetti, Willow Review* and *Prairie Light Review*. In addition, his story "Unscheduled Stops" was translated to the screen by Magic Fountain Films and his one act play "And Now?" was given a staged reading by The Chicago Dramatists Workshop. Georgalas' fiction often suggests that while love can be one of the most ennobling of emotions, it can also be one of the most destructive.

Jo-Ann Ledger was born in England, where her passion for writing truly took root upon publication, in the Chapter School for Girls 1983 Yearbook, of a poem about her dog. Since then she has moved to another country, new learning institutions, and broader topics. Currently a part-time student at the College of Du Page, she is majoring in English and serves as the editor for the college liberal arts magazine, *The Prairie Light Review*. During the day, she supports her reading and writing habits by entering freight bills at FAB Express.

Sean Leenaerts is a former Chicagoan now living in Minneapolis with his wife and hyperactive Labrador. "Though I live in Minnesota, Chicago continues to be the inspiration and setting for most of my stories. The quality of life is better here, but complacency makes the muse fat and listless. So I make my pilgrimages to 'the city of sin' as the good Lutherans here like to call Chicago. Like a smoky-voiced woman in a lonely bar, you know the city's no good for you, but it's a hell of a lot more fun." His writing has appeared in *Other Voices, Sport Literate, HairTrigger, Poetry Motel, OYEZ Review,* and *Damaged Goods*.

Freyda Libman was born in Chicago in 1947. She was educated at Northwestern University, where she earned a B.A. and M.A. in English, Phi Beta Kappa, and graduated *summa cum laude*. She is fascinated by the creative process as it crosses disciplines and merges with critical thinking. She has read widely in the literature of the Holocaust and teaches this class, among others, at the College of DuPage, where she is an associate professor of English. Her poetry explores her urban childhood, immigrant heritage, and the insistence of time on perception. She is the mother of two children and lives in Naperville, Ill.

Janice Tuck Lively holds a Master's degree in English from the

The Thing About Love Is...

University of Illinois at Chicago, where she currently is completing a Ph.D. in Creative Writing while teaching composition and creative writing. She is writing a novel, whose working title is *The Burning Bush*. "In my fiction, I strive to take ordinary people and portray the extraordinary aspects of their lives." Lively lives with her husband and two children in Chicago.

Nikki Lynch is a sophomore at the College of DuPage majoring in English literature and minoring in Film. "I have been writing poetry since I was eight. I would like to become a professor of English and someday write and direct a film. My mentors include my parents, Buddha, Professor Georgalas, Kerouac, and Kristen Garcia. My first love was a boy from Brooklyn, whom I will never forget and who will always be the most beautiful poem to me."

David McGrath has been teaching writing and literature for more than twenty years. During that time, his essays and stories have appeared in such publications as *The American Educator, Carolina Sportsman, Education Digest* and *Midwest Outdoors*. His essay, "Castle in Ruins" (in *Contemporary Education*), which addressed the failure of the Chicago Public Schools prior to its recent wholesale reform, was a finalist in the EdPress Competition for best feature article of 1993. Recent stories have been published in *Artful Dodge* and *Sport Literate* magazines. An associate professor of English at College of DuPage, he is currently at work on a novel.

William Meiners is the creator and coeditor of *Sport Literate* magazine, a creative nonfiction journal out of Chicago. His essays and stories have appeared in *Notre Dame Magazine, The Indianapolis Star, Hair Trigger,* and elsewhere. His short story

The Thing About Love Is...

"The Devil in Gloria's Pipes," received a Gold Circle Award from the Columbia University Scholastic Press Association, placing first in the category of traditional fiction. He currently writes and edits at Purdue University in West Lafayette, Ind.

Scott Mintzer grew up in Brooklyn, N.Y., and was educated at the University of Michigan and the University of Chicago Pritzker School of Medicine. He currently lives with his wife in Los Angeles, where he is a neurologist specializing in epilepsy at UCLA Medical Center. "Insurance" is his first published story.

Tom Montgomery-Fate is the author of *Beyond the White Noise* (Chalice Press, 1997), a collection of essays about living and teaching in the Philippines.

Richard V. Russo has earned degrees in English from the University of Illinois at Urbana-Champaign and Richmond College of the City University of New York. He has taught at Lehman College and Pace University in New York and has published fiction and poetry. Currently he is vice president and director of corporate development with a New York Stock Exchange member firm. He lives in New York, where he continues to write and moonlights as a jazz musician.

Deborah Ryel lives in Wheaton, Ill., with her family, 2 cats and a dog and teaches English at the College of DuPage. She has been writing poetry since grade school, primarily for family and friends and the occasional poetry reading event, and studied briefly under Ralph Mills at the University of Illinois, Chicago.

Susan Strong-Dowd, trained in Stanislavski and Story Theater, worked for many years with Second City founder Fritzie Sahlins.

Currently, she is the artistic director of the Naive Theater Company performing original works, folk tales and dramatized stories with student actors/writers for Chicago-area day-care centers, summer camps, libraries and convalescent homes. She teaches writing in the Fiction Writing Department of Columbia College and writing and theater for Columbia's Upward Bound Program. She believes in ensemble theater companies and the healing power of story.

Edward Underhill is a Chicago lawyer, who holds a keen interest in writing and writers. His short fiction has been published in several law-based periodicals, and he is currently focused on the craft of playwriting. His first one-act play, *Curse the Darkness,* was produced in 1997 by a local theatre company, and now he is completing his first three-act play, *On a Certain Morning.* Underhill can be contacted at <eunderhill@masudafunai.com>.

Mark Wukas based his story, "The Dead Sleep," on experiences during a stint as a police reporter for City News Bureau, when he spent six months sitting in Chicago police stations waiting for people to be raped, robbed and murdered. ("Business was good.") He currently is developing "The Dead Sleep" into a novel. He was cited in the "Notable Sports Writing of 1997" appendix of the 1998 edition of *The Best American Sports Writing* for his essay, "Running with Ghosts," which appeared in *Sport Literate* magazine.

To order copies of *The Thing About Love Is...*, send $15.95 per copy (Illinois residents add 8.25 percent sales tax) plus $3 shipping and handling to:

Polyphony Press
PMB 317
207 E. Ohio St.
Chicago, IL 60611